Mastering Oracle Database

From Basics to Expert Proficiency

Contents

Introduction

Oracle Database is a sophisticated and powerful relational database management system (RDBMS) that has been the backbone of numerous enterprise applications worldwide. Its robust architecture, comprehensive feature set, scalability, and reliability make it a preferred choice for organizations seeking to manage and analyze their critical data assets.

This book, 'Mastering Oracle Database: From Basics to Expert Proficiency', has been meticulously structured to provide a thorough understanding of Oracle Database, from fundamental concepts to advanced techniques. The aim is to equip readers with the knowledge and skills necessary to manage and utilize Oracle Database effectively, whether they are beginners or seasoned professionals looking to enhance their expertise.

Oracle Database has evolved significantly over the years, incorporating new features and technologies to meet the changing demands of the industry. This introduction chapter sets the stage by offering an overview of database systems, the history and evolution of Oracle Database, its key features and benefits, and the essential tools and interfaces that facilitate database management and development.

Database systems are essential for storing, retrieving, and managing data efficiently. They ensure data consistency, integrity, and security while providing mechanisms for data access and modification. Oracle Database, in particular, stands out due to its advanced capabilities, including data warehousing, online transaction processing, and mixed workload management.

Understanding the historical context of Oracle Database helps appreciate its development and the innovations it has introduced over the years. From its inception by Oracle Corporation in the late 1970s to the present day, Oracle Database has continuously evolved, integrating cutting-edge technologies and setting benchmarks in the database industry.

One of the most significant aspects of Oracle Database is its diverse editions and options. These editions cater to different organizational needs and budgets, ranging from the Oracle Database Express Edition (XE) for small applications to the Oracle Database Enterprise Edition with advanced features for large-scale, mission-critical applications.

Installing and configuring Oracle Database is a critical first step in deploying any database solution. This process involves setting up the necessary hardware and software environments, following best practices to ensure optimal performance and stability. This book provides a step-by-step guide to help readers navigate this essential process.

Once the database is installed, creating and configuring an Oracle Database involves defining its structure and parameters, ensuring it meets the application's specific requirements. This book covers the essential tasks involved in this stage, enabling readers to establish a functional and efficient database system.

A comprehensive understanding of Oracle Database architecture is crucial for effective database management. This architecture encompasses various components, including memory structures, process structures, and storage structures. Knowing how these components interact and work together is fundamental to optimizing database performance and reliability.

Oracle Database offers numerous tools and interfaces that simplify database management and development. SQL*Plus and Oracle SQL Developer are two primary tools that users employ to interact with the database, execute SQL commands, and develop database applications. Familiarity with these tools is essential for performing a wide range of database tasks.

Lastly, this chapter introduces readers to the basic Oracle Database terminology. Understanding these terms is vital for grasping the concepts discussed in subsequent chapters and for communicating effectively within the database community.

By the end of this book, readers will possess a solid foundation in Oracle Database, with the capability to perform complex database management and development tasks efficiently. This comprehensive guide serves as a valuable resource for anyone aspiring to master Oracle Database, ensuring they are well-prepared to tackle real-world challenges in the ever-evolving field of database technology.

Chapter 1

Introduction to Oracle Database

This chapter provides an essential introduction to Oracle Database, encompassing its historical development, key features, and benefits. It covers various Oracle Database editions, installation and configuration procedures, and offers an overview of its architecture and tools. The chapter aims to familiarize readers with fundamental concepts and terminology, setting the foundation for deeper exploration in subsequent chapters.

1.1 Overview of Database Systems

Database systems are integral components in the field of data management and are employed in various domains including commerce, telecommunications, and healthcare. Database systems allow for the efficient storage, retrieval, and manipulation of data. Understanding the core concepts associated with database systems is crucial for the effective use of Oracle Database.

Database systems can be categorized broadly into relational and non-relational databases. **Relational databases**, based on the relational model proposed by E. F. Codd in 1970, use structured query language (SQL) for defining and manipulating data. Data in relational databases is stored in tables, and relationships between tables are established through foreign keys. The tables are composed of rows and columns, where each row represents a record and each column represents a data field.

- **Tables:** The fundamental structure in a relational database is a table. It consists of columns and rows where each column has a specific datatype and constraints.
- **Rows:** Also known as tuples, rows represent individual records in a table.
- **Columns:** Each column, or attribute, in a table has a schema that defines the type of data it can hold, such as integers, strings, or dates.
- **Keys:** Keys are unique identifiers used to establish and identify relationships between tables. The primary key uniquely identifies a record in a table, while a foreign key is used to create a link between two tables.

The relational model emphasizes data integrity and supports ACID (Atomicity, Consistency, Isolation, Durability) properties which ensure reliable transaction processing. An example of creating a table in SQL is illustrated below:

```
CREATE TABLE employee (
    employee_id INT PRIMARY KEY,
    first_name VARCHAR(50),
    last_name VARCHAR(50),
    birth_date DATE,
    hire_date DATE
);
```

Conversely, **non-relational databases**, often referred to as NoSQL databases, are designed to handle a wide variety of data models including key-value, document, columnar, and graph formats. NoSQL databases are typically used for large-scale data storage and for applications requiring high flexibility, speed, and scalability. Common types of NoSQL databases include:

- **Key-Value Stores:** Databases that store data as a collection of key-value pairs. Examples include Redis and DynamoDB.
- **Document Stores:** Databases that store data in document format, typically JSON or BSON. Examples include MongoDB and CouchDB.

- **Columnar Stores:** Databases that store data by columns rather than rows. Examples include Apache Cassandra and HBase.
- **Graph Databases:** Databases that represent data in graph structures with nodes, edges, and properties. Examples include Neo4j and JanusGraph.

Database Management Systems (DBMS) are software systems that provide interfaces for users to define, create, maintain, and control access to the database. A DBMS ensures the data integrity, security, and concurrency control. Examples of DBMS include Oracle Database, MySQL, Microsoft SQL Server, and PostgreSQL for relational databases, and MongoDB, Cassandra, and Redis for non-relational databases.

To interact with databases, users typically employ **query languages**. SQL is the standard language for interacting with relational databases. A basic SQL query to retrieve data from the 'employee' table is shown below:

```
SELECT first_name, last_name
FROM employee;
```

The output of this query is:

```
first_name | last_name
-----------|------------
John       | Doe
Jane       | Smith
```

Database systems also support various data manipulation operations such as inserting, updating, deleting, and querying data. A comprehensive understanding of these operations is fundamental for effectively managing data.

The architecture of database systems typically includes several key components:

- **Storage Engine:** Manages the storage, retrieval, and update of data.
- **Query Processor:** Translates SQL queries into actions and optimizes query performance.
- **Transaction Manager:** Ensures transactions are processed reliably and adheres to ACID properties.
- **Buffer Manager:** Manages memory buffers to store data temporarily during read and write operations.

Understanding these components and their interactions is essential for database administrators and application developers who work with database systems.

These foundational concepts of database systems provide a critical framework for comprehending more advanced topics and functionalities as you progress through the exploration of Oracle Database.

1.2 History and Evolution of Oracle Database

The history of Oracle Database is closely intertwined with the evolution of database management systems (DBMS) as a whole, reflecting the advancements in computer science and technology over the past several decades. Oracle Corporation, founded in 1977 by Larry Ellison, Bob Miner, and Ed Oates, has been a significant player in the database market since its inception. This section details the significant milestones and technological innovations from the origins of Oracle Database to its present state, encapsulating the transformative journey of this influential DBMS.

Oracle Database began as a project named "Oracle" within Software Development Laboratories (SDL), which was the original name of Oracle Corporation. The inspiration for the database stemmed from Ellison's reading of an IBM research paper on System R, a pioneering relational database management system (RDBMS). The founders aimed to create a similar product that could efficiently manage large volumes of data with high reliability and robustness.

Oracle Version 2 (1979): The first commercial version of the Oracle Database was released in 1979. Named Oracle Version 2, this was a major milestone, being the world's first commercially available SQL-based RDBMS. The choice of starting with version 2 was a marketing decision to imply maturity and reliability. Though primitive by today's standards, Oracle Version 2 provided the foundational features necessary for an RDBMS, such as basic SQL query capabilities, data manipulation, and storage management.

Oracle Version 3 (1983): Enhancements were made in the subsequent release, known as Oracle Version 3. This release introduced the use of the C programming language, which improved portability and performance. Additionally, Version 3 supported transactions and provided basic concurrency control mechanisms, crucial for data integrity and consistency.

Oracle Version 4 (1984): Oracle Version 4 saw the introduction of read consistency, a vital feature that ensures users see consistent data during transactions. This helped mitigate the dirty read problem and was a step forward in maintaining data accuracy during concurrent access.

Oracle Version 5 (1985): The next major release, Oracle Version 5, supported the client-server architecture, which allowed the database to run on mainframes, minicomputers, and personal computers, facilitating broader usage across various systems. This version also introduced multi-version read consistency, enhancing data accuracy and reliability under concurrent transactions.

Oracle Version 6 (1988): Version 6 introduced several key features, including the PL/SQL language, which combined SQL with procedural programming. This allowed for more complex and powerful data manipulation and querying. The introduction of row-level locking improved concurrent user handling, and the hot backup feature enabled the database to be backed up without shutting down, increasing availability.

Oracle7 (1992): Oracle7 included many significant enhancements, such as stored procedures, triggers, and distributed databases, which enabled managing data across multiple databases. Other features included the introduction of bitmapped indexes, parallel query processing, shared server architecture, and support for a wider range of platforms.

Oracle8 (1997): Oracle8 was a major step towards the internet and e-commerce era. It introduced object-oriented features, supporting user-defined types, and object manipulation in the database. The release also included key enhancements like partitioning, advanced queuing, and improvements in scalability and performance.

Oracle8i (1999): The 'i' in Oracle8i stood for 'internet'. This version was optimized for internet-related applications and included a built-in Java Virtual Machine (JVM), allowing Java code to run within the database. This version also focused on XML support, enabling better handling of web data formats.

Oracle9i (2001): Oracle9i included more than 400 new features, with a focus on performance, availability, and scalability. Significant features included Real Application Clusters (RAC), which allowed multiple instances of Oracle to run on different servers but access the same database, providing high availability and fault tolerance. This version also improved web services integration and enhanced support for XML.

Oracle Database 10g (2003): Introduced as a grid computing solution, Oracle 10g aimed to provide higher efficiency and lower costs in data management through the use of grid infrastructure. This version included self-managing capabilities, such as the Automatic Storage Management (ASM) and improved diagnostic tools.

Oracle Database 11g (2007): Continuing the trend of automation and self-management, Oracle 11g introduced features like the Automated Storage Management, Automatic SQL Tuning, and enhanced data compression techniques. These innovations aimed to reduce administrative overhead and improve data processing efficiency.

Oracle Database 12c (2013): The 'c' in Oracle 12c stood for 'cloud', reflecting Oracle's focus on cloud computing. This version introduced a multi-tenant architecture, allowing multiple pluggable databases within a single container database, easing management and improving resource utilization. Oracle 12c also emphasized enhanced security features and improved performance for data analytics.

Oracle Database 18c and 19c (2018, 2019): These releases further refined the cloud capabilities introduced in 12c and stressed autonomous features, such as self-patching, self-tuning, and machine learning-based analytics. Oracle 19c, in particular, became the long-term support release, ensuring extended reliability and stability for enterprise users.

Each iteration of Oracle Database has brought about significant enhancements, reflecting the evolving needs of database management and technological advancements. From humble beginnings to its current status as a leading enterprise database solution, Oracle Database continues to set benchmarks in performance, scalability, and innovation. The continuous evolution of Oracle Database underscores its adaptability and enduring relevance in a rapidly changing technological landscape.

1.3 Key Features and Benefits of Oracle Database

Oracle Database, widely acknowledged for its robustness and comprehensive set of features, is designed to handle a vast array of data management tasks while ensuring high performance, reliability, and security. This section delves into the core features and the significant benefits provided by Oracle Database, elaborating on how these capabilities enhance the system's efficacy and use case versatility.

Scalability and Performance: Oracle Database is engineered for high performance with scalability that spans from departmental applications to large-scale enterprise systems. It supports Real Application Clusters (RAC), which allow multiple computers to run Oracle RDBMS software simultaneously while accessing a single database, providing fault tolerance, performance improvement, and scalability.

High Availability: Oracle ensures data is always accessible through its comprehensive high availability solutions. Notable features include Data Guard, which maintains standby databases to protect from data loss due to failures, and Oracle GoldenGate, which enables real-time data integration and replication across heterogeneous environments. These tools ensure data continuity and integrity.

Security: Oracle Database offers advanced security features to protect sensitive data. Security measures include Transparent Data Encryption (TDE) for encrypting data at rest, Data Redaction to hide sensitive data in real-time, and Virtual Private Database (VPD) for implementing fine-grained access control. Additionally, Oracle Label Security and Database Vault add layers of security policies and enforcement against unauthorized access.

Data Warehousing and Analytics: Oracle provides powerful tools for data warehousing and business intelligence. Oracle Exadata is optimized for running Oracle Database and supports large-scale data warehouses, enabling rapid data loading and querying. Oracle's analytic functions and in-database processing capabilities allow complex analyses to be performed directly within the database, maximizing performance and efficiency.

Comprehensive Data Management: Oracle Database offers complete data lifecycle management with features such as Automatic Storage Management (ASM) that simplifies storage and file management, and Oracle Data Pump, which provides high-speed movement of data and metadata between databases. Oracle's advanced indexing and partitioning strategies improve data retrieval times and overall database performance.

Development and Integration: Oracle supports a wide array of development tools and languages, facilitating the creation of database-centric applications. Oracle SQL*Plus and SQL Developer offer interfaces for database management and PL/SQL development. Additionally, Oracle provides APIs for Java, RESTful Web Services, and other programming languages, promoting seamless integration and interoperability with various applications and systems.

Cloud-Ready: Oracle Database's architecture is designed for cloud readiness, supporting both on-premises and cloud deployments. Oracle Autonomous Database, available on Oracle Cloud Infrastructure (OCI), leverages machine learning to automate database management tasks such as tuning, backup, and patching, significantly reducing administrative overhead and improving operational efficiency.

Consider the various high availability solutions provided by Oracle. When configuring Data Guard, primary and standby databases must be maintained in synchronization to prevent data loss during failures. Below is an example command using SQL*Plus to show the status of Data Guard configuration:

```
SELECT db_unique_name, database_role, protection_mode
FROM v$database;

DB_UNIQUE_NAME DATABASE_ROLE PROTECTION_MODE
--------------- --------------- ---------------
primary_db PRIMARY MAXIMUM AVAILABILITY
standby_db PHYSICAL STANDBY MAXIMUM AVAILABILITY
```

This output:

```
DB_UNIQUE_NAME    DATABASE_ROLE    PROTECTION_MODE
--------------- --------------- ---------------
primary_db        PRIMARY          MAXIMUM AVAILABILITY
standby_db        PHYSICAL STANDBY MAXIMUM AVAILABILITY
```

indicates active Data Guard configuration with a primary database configured for maximum availability, ensuring data integrity and availability during unexpected scenarios.

Considering data security, implementing Transparent Data Encryption (TDE) involves setting the encryption key and encrypting tablespaces. For example:

```
ADMINISTER KEY MANAGEMENT SET KEY IDENTIFIED BY "
    your_keystore_password"
WITH BACKUP;

ALTER TABLESPACE users ENCRYPTION
ONLINE USING 'AES256' ENCRYPT;
```

Oracle Data Pump enables efficient data export and import via the expdp and impdp utilities. For instance, exporting a full database schema can be achieved with:

```
expdp system/password schemas=HR directory=DATA_PUMP_DIR dumpfile=
    hr_schema.dmp logfile=hr_export.log
```

Importing the schema:

```
impdp system/password schemas=HR directory=DATA_PUMP_DIR dumpfile=
    hr_schema.dmp logfile=hr_import.log
```

Enhancing system performance through partitioning allows large tables to be divided into smaller, more manageable pieces called partitions. Creating a range-partitioned table can be demonstrated with:

```
CREATE TABLE sales
(
    sale_id NUMBER,
    sale_date DATE,
    amount NUMBER
)
PARTITION BY RANGE (sale_date)
(
    PARTITION p1 VALUES LESS THAN (TO_DATE('2022-01-01','YYYY-MM-DD')
        ),
    PARTITION p2 VALUES LESS THAN (TO_DATE('2023-01-01','YYYY-MM-DD')
        ),
    PARTITION p3 VALUES LESS THAN (MAXVALUE)
);
```

This structure optimizes query performance and management flexibility.

The extensive key features and benefits of Oracle Database, from its high availability solutions to robust security measures and comprehensive data management capabilities, demonstrate its versatility and powerful role in modern data management practices. Oracle Database stands out as a comprehensive solution designed to meet the diverse needs of enterprises and developers while ensuring data is managed efficiently, securely, and reliably.

1.4 Oracle Database Editions and Options

Oracle Database is available in several editions, each designed to meet the needs of different types of organizations and use cases. The editions mainly differ in terms of features, performance, and scale. Choosing the right edition depends on factors such as the size of the organization, the complexity of the database requirements, and budget constraints. This section elucidates the various Oracle Database editions available, their features, and the options they provide.

Oracle Database Standard Edition 2 (SE2)

Oracle Database Standard Edition 2 (SE2) is designed for small to medium-sized businesses. It provides core database functionality required by such organizations without the need for additional cost associated with more advanced features found in higher editions. SE2 supports the following capabilities:

- Basic relational database functionalities
- PL/SQL support
- Oracle Real Application Clusters (limited to two nodes)
- Advanced queuing and stored procedures
- Basic compression for data
- Basic database and user security

A key limitation to note is that SE2 can only be deployed on servers with a maximum of two sockets, and it also enforces a strict limit on the number of CPU threads that can be utilized.

Oracle Database Enterprise Edition (EE)

Oracle Database Enterprise Edition (EE) is a more advanced edition intended for large-scale enterprises requiring robust performance, scalability, and extensive features. This edition supports all Standard Edition 2 features and includes additional capabilities such as:

- Advanced security options including Oracle Label Security and Oracle Advanced Security
- Comprehensive data warehousing features like partitioning, parallel query, and Data Pump
- Higher availability with Oracle Real Application Clusters (RAC) support without node limitations
- Automated Storage Management (ASM)
- Advanced data compression, including OLTP and Hybrid Columnar Compression
- Enhanced performance with in-memory processing and index-organized tables

- Advanced backup and recovery options like Oracle Data Guard

Oracle Database Personal Edition

Oracle Database Personal Edition is tailored for single-user development environments. It includes all functionalities available in the Enterprise Edition but is restricted to single-user usage. This edition is ideal for application developers who need a fully functional Oracle Database to develop and test their applications but do not require multi-user capabilities. It is available on Windows operating systems and provides the following:

- Full Oracle Enterprise Edition capabilities on a single-user basis
- Integrated development environment
- Cost-effective solution for developers

Oracle Database Express Edition (XE)

Oracle Database Express Edition (XE) is a free, entry-level edition of Oracle Database. XE is suitable for small-scale applications, students, and educators who need a lightweight database for learning or prototyping purposes. Despite being free, XE includes several robust features:

- Support for up to 12 GB of user data
- Single instance database with limited resource usage (1 GB of RAM, 2 CPU threads, and 12 GB of user data)
- Basic relational database functionalities
- PL/SQL support
- Comprehensive development environment compatible with SQL Developer
- Web-based management interface for easy administration

The key constraints are the limited resources and the cap on the size of the database, making it unsuitable for larger, mission-critical applications.

Oracle Database Cloud

Oracle also offers Oracle Database Cloud services, which include multiple deployment models ranging from Infrastructure as a Service (IaaS) to Platform as a Service (PaaS). Key services include:

- Oracle Database Cloud Service (DBaaS)
- Autonomous Database Services that provide self-managing capabilities
- Functions supporting automatic scaling, patching, and backup
- Transparent data encryption, comprehensive auditing, and monitoring services
- High availability through Oracle's globally distributed cloud infrastructure

In choosing an Oracle Database edition, it is essential to consider the business requirements, including the need for high availability, advanced security features, and performance scalability. Each edition is aligned to provide the necessary features and capabilities to address specific organizational demands efficiently.

1.5 Installing Oracle Database: Step-by-Step Guide

Installing Oracle Database is a meticulous process that involves multiple steps to ensure a successful and efficient setup. This section provides a comprehensive guide, detailing each phase in the installation process for Oracle Database 19c on a Linux operating system. Proper completion of these steps is critical for the database to function optimally.

1. Pre-Installation Requirements

Before installing Oracle Database, it is imperative to verify and set up the necessary prerequisites:

- **Hardware Requirements**: Ensure your system meets the minimum hardware requirements. This includes validating CPU, memory, and storage capacity.
  - **CPU**: Minimum 2 core processor
  - **Memory**: Minimum 2 GB of RAM
  - **Storage**: At least 15 GB of available disk space

- **Software Requirements**: Verify the system software meets the prerequisites:
  - Proper Linux distribution (e.g., Oracle Linux, Red Hat Enterprise Linux)
  - Required packages and libraries such as binutils, gcc, glibc, etc.
  - Configured kernel parameters and limits

2. Downloading Oracle Database Software

Access the Oracle Technology Network (OTN) to download the Oracle Database installation files:

- Navigate to the oracle.com website.
- Select 'Downloads' and choose the appropriate Oracle Database version.
- Download the zip files for the database installer.

3. Preparing the Environment

Set up the installation environment:

- Extract the downloaded zip files to a directory, such as /u01/app/oracle.
- Set necessary environment variables in the shell profile file (e.g., .bashrc or .bash_profile).

```
export ORACLE_BASE=/u01/app/oracle
export ORACLE_HOME=$ORACLE_BASE/product/19.0.0/dbhome_1
export PATH=$PATH:$ORACLE_HOME/bin
```

4. Configuring Oracle User and Groups

Before beginning the installation, configure the Oracle user and appropriate groups for managing database software:

- Create the oracle user and primary group (typically oinstall) and secondary group (dba):

```
groupadd oinstall
groupadd dba
useradd -g oinstall -G dba oracle
passwd oracle
```

- Change ownership and permissions for the Oracle base directory:

```
mkdir -p /u01/app/oracle
chown -R oracle:oinstall /u01
chmod -R 775 /u01
```

5. Starting the Oracle Universal Installer (OUI)

As the oracle user, initiate the Oracle Universal Installer to guide you through the database installation process:

```
su - oracle
cd $ORACLE_HOME
./runInstaller
```

Follow the GUI steps to specify Oracle base, Oracle home, and installation options. These include:

- **Select Installation Type**: Choose 'Set Up Software Only' or 'Install and Configure a Database.'
- **Specify Oracle Home User**: For simplicity in a test environment, use the Oracle software owner.
- **Create Inventory**: Provide an inventory directory or use the default suggested path.
- **Oracle Configuration Manager Registration**: Option to configure or skip.
- **Prerequisite Checks**: Ensure all system prerequisites are met, and resolve any failed checks.

6. Executing Root Scripts

Once OUI completes, it prompts to run root scripts as the root user. Open a new terminal window and execute:

```
sudo /u01/app/oracle/product/19.0.0/dbhome_1/root.sh
```

7. Creating and Configuring the Database

Post software installation, proceed to create and configure an Oracle Database:

- Invoke the Database Configuration Assistant (DBCA) to create and configure the database. Run the DBCA:

```
cd $ORACLE_HOME/bin
./dbca
```

- Select 'Create a Database' and follow the DBCA prompts to:
  - Choose database type (e.g., Single Instance).
  - Provide Global Database Name (e.g., orcl).
  - Configure administrative passwords.
  - Specify database storage options, memory allocations, and other configurations.

8. Post-Installation Steps

Complete essential post-installation tasks:

- Verify Oracle Listener is up and running:

```
lsnrctl status
```

- Test database connection via sqlplus:

```
sqlplus / as sysdba
SQL> select * from dual;
```

```
D
-
X
```

- Validate that environment variables are correctly set in shell profile for persistence across sessions.
- Consider securing the database following Oracle's security guidelines.

This precise procedure ensures that the Oracle Database is correctly installed, configured, and operational, providing a robust foundation for further exploration and utilization of Oracle Database capabilities.

1.6 Creating and Configuring an Oracle Database

Creating and configuring an Oracle Database is a multifaceted process that requires meticulous attention to detail. Primarily, it involves establishing a functional database environment through a series of steps that ensure the system is optimally prepared to support various operations and applications.

Creating an Oracle Database

1. **Preparation and Planning:** Before creating an Oracle Database, it is vital to understand the specific requirements and resources of your environment. This planning phase must include an analysis of storage capacity, memory allocation, and network configuration.

2. **Installation of Oracle Database Software:** Assuming the Oracle software is already installed, the creation of the database can proceed. The database creation process can either be automated using Oracle's Database Configuration Assistant (DBCA) or manual through SQL commands.

3. **Using Database Configuration Assistant (DBCA):** DBCA is a graphical tool that streamlines the database creation process via a user-friendly interface. Below is a simplified DBCA process:

    1. Launch DBCA from the Oracle Home directory:

       ```
       $ORACLE_HOME/bin/dbca
       ```

    2. Follow the on-screen prompts to navigate through the database creation process, selecting options pertinent to your requirements, such as database name (SID) and storage settings.

    3. Specify Management and Sizing options. Here, you decide on the memory parameters and storage options.

    4. Configure network options and specify the database initialization parameters.

    5. Review the summary and click 'Finish' to create the database.

Manual Database Creation:

For those who prefer or need to create a database manually, a sequence of SQL commands must be meticulously executed in SQL*Plus, Oracle's command-line tool.

Sample SQL Script for Manual Creation:

```
-- Start the database creation process
CREATE DATABASE orcl
   USER SYS IDENTIFIED BY <password>
   USER SYSTEM IDENTIFIED BY <password>
   LOGFILE GROUP 1 ('/u01/app/oracle/oradata/orcl/redo01.log') SIZE 100M,
           GROUP 2 ('/u01/app/oracle/oradata/orcl/redo02.log') SIZE 100M
   MAXLOGFILES 5
   MAXLOGHISTORY 1
   MAXDATAFILES 100
   MAXINSTANCES 1
   CHARACTER SET AL32UTF8
   NATIONAL CHARACTER SET AL16UTF16
   DATAFILE '/u01/app/oracle/oradata/orcl/system01.dbf' SIZE 700M
   SYSAUX DATAFILE '/u01/app/oracle/oradata/orcl/sysaux01.dbf' SIZE 600M
   DEFAULT TABLESPACE users
      DATAFILE '/u01/app/oracle/oradata/orcl/users01.dbf' SIZE 500M
   DEFAULT TEMPORARY TABLESPACE temp
      TEMPFILE '/u01/app/oracle/oradata/orcl/temp01.dbf' SIZE 20M
   UNDO TABLESPACE undotbs1
      DATAFILE '/u01/app/oracle/oradata/orcl/undotbs01.dbf' SIZE 200M;
```

Configuring an Oracle Database

Once the database is created, several configuration steps must be undertaken to ensure optimal performance and security:

1. **Initialization Parameters:** Oracle uses a file named 'init.ora' (or 'spfile.ora' for server parameter files) to store initialization parameters. These parameters are crucial for defining database properties such as memory allocation, process limits, and character sets.

```
ALTER SYSTEM SET db_cache_size = 64M;
ALTER SYSTEM SET shared_pool_size = 128M;
ALTER SYSTEM SET log_buffer = 512K;
```

2. **Network Configuration:** Configuring the Oracle Net Services is essential for establishing database connectivity. The essential configuration files include:

- **listener.ora**: Configures the Oracle Net Listener, which listens for incoming network connections. - **tnsnames.ora**: Contains network service names to facilitate client connections to the database.

Example 'listener.ora' configuration:

```
SID_LIST_LISTENER =
  (SID_LIST =
    (SID_DESC =
      (SID_NAME = orcl)
      (ORACLE_HOME = /u01/app/oracle/product/19.0.0/dbhome_1)
    )
  )
```

```
LISTENER =
  (ADDRESS = (PROTOCOL = TCP)(HOST = myhost)(PORT = 1521))
```

Example 'tnsnames.ora' entry:

```
ORCL =
  (DESCRIPTION =
    (ADDRESS = (PROTOCOL = TCP)(HOST = myhost)(PORT = 1521))
    (CONNECT_DATA =
      (SERVER = DEDICATED)
      (SERVICE_NAME = orcl)
    )
  )
```

3. **User and Schema Management:** Secure access and efficient resource management are paramount. Creating users and assigning roles ensures a structured approach to database administration.

```
CREATE USER john IDENTIFIED BY johndoe;
GRANT CONNECT, RESOURCE TO john;
ALTER USER john QUOTA 100M ON users;
```

4. **Backup and Recovery Configuration:** Configuring Oracle Recovery Manager (RMAN) for backups is critical for data recovery and integrity.

```
RMAN> CONFIGURE RETENTION POLICY TO REDUNDANCY 2;
RMAN> CONFIGURE BACKUP OPTIMIZATION ON;
RMAN> BACKUP DATABASE PLUS ARCHIVELOG;
```

5. **Performance Tuning:** Performance tuning often involves adjusting memory allocation, disk I/O optimization, and SQL query tuning. Continuous monitoring using tools such as Automatic Workload Repository (AWR) and Active Session History (ASH) reports can provide insights.

Start AWR Report:

```
@?/rdbms/admin/awrrpt.sql
```

Configuring and creating an Oracle Database necessitates a methodical and structured approach to ensure system stability, performance, and security.

1.7 Oracle Database Architecture Overview

Oracle Database architecture comprises physical and logical structures optimized for efficient data processing and management. Understanding this architecture is critical for database administrators and developers to maintain, tune, and develop applications effectively. The architecture is segmented into three primary components: the **memory structures**, the **process structures**, and the **storage structures**. Each component works in tandem to support database operations.

Memory Structures

The memory structures involved in Oracle Database operations can be classified into three major components: the **System Global Area (SGA)**, the **Program Global Area (PGA)**, and the **Software Code Area**.

- **System Global Area (SGA)**: The SGA is a shared memory region that contains data and control information for one Oracle Database instance. Key components within the SGA include:
  - **Database Buffer Cache**: Stores copies of data blocks read from the data files.
  - **Redo Log Buffer**: Stores redo entries—a log of changes made to the data.
  - **Shared Pool**: Contains shared SQL, PL/SQL code, data dictionary cache, and other control structures.
  - **Large Pool**: Used for large memory allocations, such as Recovery Manager (RMAN) operations, parallel execution, and certain large contexts.
  - **Java Pool**: Used for all Java code and data within the JVM.
  - **Streams Pool**: Used by the Oracle Streams functionality.
- **Program Global Area (PGA)**: The PGA is a memory region that contains data and control information for each server process. Unlike the SGA, the PGA is not shared; it is allocated when a process is started and de-allocated when the process terminates. The major components of the PGA include:
  - **Sort Area**: Memory area allocated for a process to perform sorting operations.
  - **Session Memory**: Used to store session variables and other session-related data.
  - **Private SQL Area**: Contains data such as bind variable values, query execution state information.

- **Software Code Area**: This contains code that might be shared, such as PL/SQL code, and code for Oracle Database kernel.

Process Structures

Oracle Database uses various processes that handle different tasks asynchronously. These processes fall broadly under two categories: **background processes** and **server processes**.

- **Background Processes**: These processes are initiated by Oracle Database and include:
  - **Database Writer (DBWn)**: Writes modified blocks from the database buffer cache to the data files.
  - **Log Writer (LGWR)**: Writes redo log entries from the redo log buffer to the online redo log files.
  - **Checkpoint (CKPT)**: Updates file headers to indicate the location where the last checkpoint occurred.
  - **System Monitor (SMON)**: Performs crash recovery when the instance starts and cleans up temporary segments.
  - **Process Monitor (PMON)**: Cleans up failed user processes and releases resources.
  - **Recoverer (RECO)**: Handles distributed transactions.
  - **Archiver (ARCn)**: Copies redo log files to an archive location.
  - **Queue Monitor (QMNn)**: Manages advanced queuing messages.
- **Server Processes**: These processes interact with client applications and are created when a user session is established. Each user session connects to a server process which executes SQL and PL/SQL, parses queries, fetches rows, and returns results to the client.

Storage Structures

Oracle Database storage structures include physical and logical components, optimized for efficient data storage, retrieval, and management.

- **Physical Storage Structures**: These refer to the actual files on the disk that constitute the Oracle Database:

  - **Data Files**: Store user and system data. Organized by tablespaces.
  - **Redo Log Files**: Record all changes made to the data to ensure recoverability.
  - **Control Files**: Store metadata about the database and its physical structure.
  - **Archived Redo Log Files**: Copies of log files that have been filled and archived.
  - **Parameter Files**: Contain initialization parameters for configuring the database instance.
  - **Password Files**: Allow remote database startup and SYSDBA/SYSOPER connection authentication.

- **Logical Storage Structures**: Logical structures are built upon physical structures:
  - **Tablespaces**: Logical storage units composed of individual data files. Each tablespace contains various types of objects, like tables and indexes.
  - **Segments**: A set of extents allocated for a specific data structure like a table or index.
  - **Extents**: Contiguous blocks allocated for storing a specific type of information.
  - **Blocks**: The smallest units of data storage.

The interplay of these memory, process, and storage structures provides Oracle Database with the flexibility and power to handle complex data management tasks efficiently. Each component within the architecture has a specific role that ensures the database operates smoothly, maintains data integrity, and allows for scalable performance.

1.8 Oracle Database Tools and Interfaces

Oracle Database provides a comprehensive suite of tools and interfaces designed to facilitate database management, development, and monitoring. These tools are instrumental in effectively interacting with the database, performing administrative tasks, developing database applications, and monitoring performance. Understanding these tools and interfaces helps database administrators and developers to effectively harness the full potential of Oracle Database.

Oracle's primary tools and interfaces can be divided into several categories: command-line tools, graphical user interfaces (GUIs), integrated development environments (IDEs), and performance monitoring utilities.

SQL*Plus

SQL*Plus is a command-line interface used to interact with Oracle Database. It offers comprehensive facilities for executing SQL commands and PL/SQL blocks, managing database objects, and administering database systems. SQL*Plus is especially useful for scripting repetitive tasks and automating administrative procedures.

```
sqlplus username/password@database
SQL*Plus: Release 19.0.0.0.0 - Production on Thu Sep 30 11:48:16 2021

SQL> SELECT * FROM dual;
D
-
X
```

In the example above, connecting to Oracle Database with SQL*Plus allows execution of an SQL query to retrieve records from the dual table.

Oracle SQL Developer

Oracle SQL Developer is a free integrated development environment that simplifies the development and management of Oracle Database. It provides a GUI for database browsing, object management, SQL and PL/SQL execution, and debugging. SQL Developer enhances productivity with features like code insight, code formatting, and SQL tuning.

To start working with Oracle SQL Developer:

- Download and install SQL Developer from the Oracle website.
- Open SQL Developer and create a new connection by providing the necessary credentials (username, password, host, port, and SID/service name).
- Utilize the interface to browse objects, execute queries, and manage database resources.

Oracle Enterprise Manager

Oracle Enterprise Manager (OEM) is a comprehensive management tool used for monitoring and administrating Oracle Databases and associated technologies. OEM provides a single-pane-of-glass view for managing database instances, ensuring database performance, availability, and security.

Key features include:

- Performance monitoring and diagnostics
- Database administration
- Backup and recovery
- Enterprise-wide resource management

By accessing OEM through a web-based console, administrators can perform routine maintenance tasks, analyze database performance, and troubleshoot issues efficiently.

Oracle Data Pump

Oracle Data Pump is a high-speed data movement utility that provides export and import capabilities for transferring data and database objects between Oracle databases. Data Pump improves upon the older Export and Import utilities by offering better performance and extended features.

To execute a Data Pump export:

```
expdp username/password@database schemas=HR directory=dp_dir dumpfile=hr.dmp
    logfile=hr_exp.log;
```

The above command exports the HR schema to a dump file located in the dp_dir directory.

SQL*Loader

SQL*Loader is a utility for loading data from external files into Oracle Database tables. It supports a variety of data formats and provides extensive control over the loading process. SQL*Loader can handle large volumes of data efficiently.

```
sqlldr username/password control=load.ctl log=load.log;
```

This example demonstrates loading data using a control file (load.ctl) that defines the data source and loading parameters.

Oracle APEX

Oracle Application Express (APEX) is a low-code development platform enabling the creation of web applications that run on Oracle Database. APEX allows developers to build applications rapidly with a browser-based interface, leveraging SQL and PL/SQL without requiring extensive web development experience.

To create an APEX application:

- Log in to the APEX workspace.
- Choose the type of application to build.
- Use the provided wizards and tools to define the application pages.
- Deploy the application within an Oracle environment.

RMAN

Recovery Manager (RMAN) is Oracle's robust backup and recovery tool. RMAN integrates with Oracle Database and automates backup and recovery operations, making them more reliable and efficient. It supports incremental backups, backup verification, and various recovery scenarios.

Basic RMAN usage includes:

```
rman target /
RMAN> BACKUP DATABASE;
RMAN> RESTORE DATABASE;
```

These commands back up the entire database and restore it in case of failure, respectively.

Oracle REST Data Services (ORDS)

Oracle REST Data Services provides a RESTful interface for accessing Oracle Database resources. ORDS simplifies the process of developing RESTful web services, making it easier for applications to interact with Oracle Database over HTTP/HTTPS.

```
curl -X GET "http://localhost:8080/ords/hr/employees/"
```

This curl command demonstrates making a RESTful API call to fetch employee data from the HR schema.

Understanding and utilizing these tools and interfaces effectively is crucial for maximizing productivity and achieving optimal performance in an Oracle Database environment.

1.9 Getting Started with Oracle SQL*Plus and SQL Developer

Oracle SQL*Plus and SQL Developer are essential tools for interacting with Oracle Databases. SQL*Plus is a command-line utility that allows users to execute SQL and PL/SQL commands and scripts, while SQL Developer is a graphical integrated development environment (IDE) that provides a more user-friendly interface for database development tasks.

SQL*Plus is included with Oracle Database and is often the first tool used to perform administrative tasks or execute queries. It provides a robust environment for scripting and automating repetitive tasks. SQL Developer, on the other hand, offers a rich set of features for database management, including a visual interface for writing and debugging SQL and PL/SQL code, data modeling, and comprehensive reports.

To begin using these tools, it is necessary to understand how to install and configure them.

- **SQL*Plus:** Typically, SQL*Plus is installed automatically when Oracle Database is installed. It can be invoked from the command line by typing sqlplus.

- **SQL Developer:** This tool can be downloaded separately from Oracle's official website. It is a Java-based application, so ensure that Java Development Kit (JDK) is installed on the system.

Once the necessary installations are complete, connecting to the Oracle Database using SQL*Plus involves the following steps:

```
C:\> sqlplus username/password@hostname:port/servicename
```

For example, to connect as the user hr with the password oracle to a database on localhost running on the default port 1521 and with the service name orcl, the command will look like:

```
C:\> sqlplus hr/oracle@localhost:1521/orcl
```

After executing the above command, SQL*Plus will prompt with the following:

```
SQL*Plus: Release 19.0.0.0.0 - Production on Wed Sep 15 11:52:48 2023
Version 19.11.0.0.0

Copyright (c) 1982, 2023, Oracle. All rights reserved.

Connected to:
Oracle Database 19c Enterprise Edition Release 19.0.0.0.0 - Production
Version 19.11.0.0.0

SQL>
```

SQL Query Execution in SQL*Plus:

To execute a SQL query in SQL*Plus, type the query at the SQL> prompt followed by a semicolon. For instance, to retrieve all records from the employees table:

```
SQL> SELECT * FROM employees;
```

The output will be displayed immediately, and it may be formatted for better readability, depending on the width of the terminal and other settings configured within SQL*Plus.

To save a series of commands for reuse, a script file can be created. Scripts are plain text files with the extension .sql. Save the script and execute it within SQL*Plus using the @ command:

```
SQL> @path_to_script\script_name.sql
```

For example, a script named employee_query.sql stored in the C:\scripts directory can be run as follows:

```
SQL> @C:\scripts\employee_query.sql
```

Setting Up SQL Developer:

Launch SQL Developer after the installation by executing the sqldeveloper.exe file. The initial setup requires configuring the database connection. Click on the "New Connection" button and fill in the necessary details:

- **Connection Name:** A user-defined name for the connection.
- **Username:** The database username, for example, hr.
- **Password:** The corresponding password, for example, oracle.
- **Hostname:** The name or IP address of the database server, for example, localhost.
- **Port:** The port number where the database listens, typically 1521.

- **SID/Service Name:** Either the System ID (SID) or the Service Name of the database, for example, orcl.

Once the details are entered, click "Test" to verify the connection settings. If the connection is successful, click "Connect." The new connection will appear in the "Connections" panel, allowing for straightforward access to execute SQL queries, browse database objects, and manage the database.

SQL Query Execution in SQL Developer:

To execute a SQL query in SQL Developer, open a new SQL Worksheet from the "Connections" panel. Type the SQL statement and click on the "Run Script" button (the green play icon) or press F5. For example:

```
SELECT * FROM employees;
```

The results pane will display the output of the query, which can be further manipulated, exported, or analyzed using the various tools provided within SQL Developer.

Both SQL*Plus and SQL Developer are powerful tools each with unique strengths. SQL*Plus excels in scripting and command-line automation, whereas SQL Developer brings a cohesive visual and interactive experience that enhances productivity for development and administrative tasks. Understanding and leveraging both tools will provide a comprehensive capability for database management and development activities.

1.10 Basic Oracle Database Terminology

Understanding the basic terminology used in Oracle Database is essential for working effectively with the system. This section elucidates key terms and concepts that will frequently appear throughout this book.

Database: A database is a systematic collection of data. Databases support storage and manipulation of data and provide various functionalities such as data insertion, querying, updating, and deletion. In Oracle, the database refers to the collection of physical files that hold both the data and the metadata (data dictionaries).

Instance: An Oracle instance refers to the set of memory structures and background processes that Oracle Database uses to manage the database. An instance begins when it is started up and ends when it is shut down.

Schema: A schema is a collection of database objects associated with a database user. A schema contains objects, including tables, views, sequences, stored procedures, synonyms, indexes, clusters, and database links.

Table: Tables are the basic unit of data storage in an Oracle Database. They consist of rows and columns, where each column has a specific data type, and each row represents a single record of data.

Tablespace: A tablespace is a logical storage unit within an Oracle Database. It is used to group related logical structures together. Each tablespace consists of one or more data files, which physically store the data.

Data File: A data file is a physical file on disk that stores data, such as rows in tables. Data files are associated with only one tablespace and provide the physical storage for the database's data.

Control File: The control file is a small binary file that records the structure of the database, including the database name, the names and locations of associated data files and redo log files, and the timestamp of the database creation.

Redo Log: Redo logs are files that record all changes made to the data. They are critical for recovery processes, capturing changes that allow the database to be restored to a consistent state in the event of a failure.

Archive Log: Archive logs are copies of redo log files that are archived before being reused. They provide a history of the redo log files and are used for backup and recovery operations.

Backup: A backup is a copy of data from the database that can be used to reconstruct the original data in case of data loss. Backups can be full (complete snapshot) or incremental (changes since last backup).

Listener: The Oracle Listener is a server process that listens for client connection requests and directs them to the appropriate database services. It handles the network connectivity part of the client-server architecture.

Oracle Net: Oracle Net, also referred to as SQL*Net, is a component of the Oracle Database system that enables Oracle tools and applications to connect to an Oracle database. It abstracts the details of the network protocols used.

PL/SQL: PL/SQL (Procedural Language/SQL) is Oracle Corporation's procedural extension for SQL and the Oracle relational database. PL/SQL allows developers to write code to perform operations that SQL alone cannot.

Cursor: A cursor is a pointer used to fetch rows in query results one at a time. It is essential for processing individual rows returned by a query.

Index: An index is a database object that improves the speed of data retrieval. Indexes are created on one or more columns of a table and work similarly to the index in a book.

Join: A join is an SQL operation used to combine rows from two or more tables based on a related column between them. There are several types of joins, including inner join, left join, right join, and full outer join.

View: A view is a virtual table that provides a predefined SQL query on one or more tables. Views can present data from multiple tables as if they were a single table, encapsulating complex queries for easier access.

Sequence: A sequence is a database object that generates unique numeric values, typically used for primary key values. Sequences ensure that each number is unique and incremented by a defined value.

Trigger: A trigger is a stored procedure that is automatically executed in response to certain events on a table or view, such as insertions, updates, or deletions.

Synonym: A synonym is an alias or alternative name for a database object such as a table, view, sequence, stored procedure, or another synonym. Synonyms are used to provide location transparency and simplify SQL statements.

Understanding these terms is fundamental for anyone working with Oracle Database. They provide a foundation upon which more complex concepts can be built. Below is a simple example demonstrating the creation of a table and a sequence, and the insertion of data using the sequence:

```
-- Create a table called 'employees'
CREATE TABLE employees (
    employee_id NUMBER PRIMARY KEY,
    first_name VARCHAR2(50),
    last_name VARCHAR2(50)
);

-- Create a sequence for generating unique employee IDs
```

```
CREATE SEQUENCE emp_id_seq
    START WITH 1
    INCREMENT BY 1;

-- Insert a new employee using the sequence to generate the employee ID
INSERT INTO employees (employee_id, first_name, last_name)
VALUES (emp_id_seq.NEXTVAL, 'John', 'Doe');
```

Executing the above code successfully creates the employees table, a sequence named emp_id_seq, and inserts a row into the employees table with a unique employee_id generated by the sequence.

```
1 row inserted.
```

This example showcases the practical application of several key concepts, including table creation, sequence creation, and data insertion using Oracle SQL. This approach ensures that the terminology discussed is clearly illustrated through real-world use cases.

Chapter 2

Oracle Database Architecture

This chapter delves into the internal structure of Oracle Database, detailing the components that constitute its architecture. It covers database instances and structures, memory and process configurations, and storage architecture, including tablespaces and datafiles. The chapter also explores background processes, logical and physical storage structures, and offers an introduction to the multitenant architecture, providing a comprehensive understanding essential for effective database management.

2.1 Introduction to Oracle Database Architecture

Understanding the architecture of the Oracle Database is fundamental for effectively managing, tuning, and exploiting the full potential of the database system. Oracle's architecture is designed to efficiently manage large amounts of data in a multiuser environment, allowing multiple users to interact with and modify the data simultaneously while ensuring data integrity and consistency.

Oracle Database architecture consists of two main components: the database instance and the database itself. The database instance is a set of memory structures and background processes that manage database files. The database is a set of physical files, including datafiles, control files, and redo log files. To manage the data efficiently and securely, Oracle Database uses a combination of logical and physical structures.

The database instance is composed of two key memory structures: the System Global Area (SGA) and the Program Global Area (PGA). The SGA is a shared memory region that contains data and control information for the Oracle instance. It includes the database buffer cache, the redo log buffer, the shared pool, the large pool, the Java pool, and the Streams pool. The PGA, on the other hand, is a memory region that contains data and control information for a server process. Unlike the SGA, the PGA is not shared among multiple sessions; instead, it is dedicated to a single server process or a single background process.

The background processes in Oracle Database are vital for performing various tasks that ensure efficient and smooth database operation. These processes include the Database Writer (DBWn), the Log Writer (LGWR), the Checkpoint (CKPT) process, the System Monitor (SMON), the Process Monitor (PMON), and several others. Each process has a specific role, such as writing modified data from the buffer cache to the datafiles, recording redo entries, performing instance recovery, and cleaning up failed user processes.

Oracle Database also organizes its storage architecture into logical and physical structures. Logical storage units include tablespaces, segments, extents, and blocks. Tablespaces are the primary components in the logical storage structure and are used to group related logical structures together. A tablespace can contain multiple segments, where each segment contains one or more extents, and each extent contains a collection of data blocks. On the other hand, physical structures include datafiles, control files, and redo log files. Datafiles store the actual database data, control files maintain the consistency and integrity of the database, and redo log files store changes made to the database to support recovery operations.

```
-- Example: Creating a tablespace in Oracle Database
CREATE TABLESPACE example_ts
DATAFILE 'example_ts01.dbf'
SIZE 10M
EXTENT MANAGEMENT LOCAL
SEGMENT SPACE MANAGEMENT AUTO;
```

```
Tablespace created.
```

Oracle's layered architecture is designed to handle increasing workloads and concurrency in a robust manner. The statement execution process is an example of how this architecture optimizes performance and resources. When a SQL statement is executed, Oracle translates the SQL statement into a series of actions taken on the data. The parsing phase involves syntax and semantic checking, followed by the optimization phase where the Oracle optimizer determines the most efficient execution plan. The execution phase carries out the instructions within the execution plan, and the fetch phase retrieves the resulting rows.

To further enhance performance and scalability, Oracle Database implements features such as the multitenant architecture. This architecture includes Container Databases (CDBs) and Pluggable Databases (PDBs), allowing a single CDB to host multiple PDBs. PDBs can be managed independently yet share the resources provided by the CDB. This approach reduces resource overhead and simplifies database consolidation.

```
-- Example: Creating a pluggable database in Oracle Database
CREATE PLUGGABLE DATABASE example_pdb
ADMIN USER pdb_admin IDENTIFIED BY password
ROLES = (DBA)
DEFAULT TABLESPACE users
DATAFILE 'example_pdb_users01.dbf'
SIZE 10M
AUTOEXTEND ON;
```

```
Pluggable database created.
```

Understanding the foundational elements of Oracle Database architecture enables database administrators, developers, and users to interact with the system more effectively. The ability to manage resources, optimize performance, and ensure data integrity stems from a deep comprehension of these fundamental components and their interactions. This architecture supports Oracle's goal of providing a versatile, efficient, and reliable database system suited for a wide range of applications.

2.2 Database Instance and Database Structure

The Oracle Database system is fundamentally divided into two key components: the database instance and the database itself. These components function together to manage and store the data efficiently, ensuring the integrity and usability for various applications.

An **Oracle Database Instance** consists of the set of memory structures and background processes that manage database files. The instance is dynamic and transient, existing as the intermediary between the physical files on disk and the database users' queries. Each instance is associated with a specific database and is responsible for allocating memory structures and managing the processes that perform numerous tasks, such as writing data to disk, managing user sessions, and handling requests.

Database Structure refers to the physical and logical components that store and organize the data within the database. Comprising several essential elements, it includes data files, control files, redo log files, and, optionally, archive log files. These elements together ensure that data is stored in an organized and recoverable manner, guaranteeing integrity and performance.

Database Instance Components: The instance consists of the System Global Area (SGA) and a set of background processes.

System Global Area (SGA): This shared memory region contains data and control information for the Oracle Database instance. It includes the following components:

- **Database Buffer Cache**: Stores copies of data blocks read from data files. It serves as the primary location for caching data.
- **Redo Log Buffer**: Temporarily stores redo records generated by transactions before they are written to the redo log files.
- **Shared Pool**: Caches various structures such as SQL and PL/SQL statements, data dictionary cache, and more to enhance system performance.
- **Large Pool**: Optional memory area that provides large allocations for certain large processes, like Recovery Manager (RMAN) operations.
- **Java Pool**: Used for Java-based applications within Oracle.
- **Streams Pool**: Allocates memory for Oracle Streams operations, which provide data replication and streaming capabilities.
- **Fixed SGA**: Contains general information about the state of the instance, such as initialization parameters.

Background Processes: These are essential for the functioning of the instance, performing tasks such as writing, cleaning, and monitoring the database:

- **DBWn (Database Writer)**: Writes modified data from the database buffer cache to the data files.
- **LGWR (Log Writer)**: Writes redo log buffer contents to the redo log files.
- **CKPT (Checkpoint)**: Updates the control files and data files with checkpoint information.
- **SMON (System Monitor)**: Performs recovery operations, such as instance recovery, after a crash.
- **PMON (Process Monitor)**: Cleans up processes that have terminated abnormally.
- **ARCn (Archiver)**: Archives redo log files when the database is in ARCHIVELOG mode.
- **RECO (Recoverer)**: Manages distributed transactions and resolves in-doubt transactions.
- **MMAN (Memory Manager)**: Manages the SGA's memory allocation.

Database Structure Components: The logical structure of an Oracle Database is abstracted from the physical structure to provide flexibility and ease of management. The core elements of the database structure include:

- **Data Files**: These store the database's actual data. Data files are grouped into tablespaces, which logically partition the database.
- **Control Files**: Essential for database startup, control files maintain the state of the database, including the location of data files and redo logs, the current log sequence number, and checkpoint information.
- **Redo Log Files**: Record changes made to the data, providing the ability to recover the database in case of a failure.
- **Archive Log Files**: An optional component, primarily used for backup and recovery purposes. They store historical redo logs, vital for recovering previous states of the database.

- **Temporary Files**: Used for managing temporary segments, especially during large sort operations.

A clear understanding of these core components is crucial for effective management, optimization, and maintenance of an Oracle Database system. Each element, whether part of the dynamic instance or the structured database, plays a specific role, ensuring data reliability, consistency, and availability. Through this, the Oracle Database consistently upholds its performance and integrity, meeting the diverse demands of modern data-driven applications.

2.3 Memory Structures in Oracle Database

Oracle Database employs a sophisticated memory structure to manage and optimize the performance of database operations. The memory architecture is bifurcated into two primary sections: the System Global Area (SGA) and the Program Global Area (PGA). Each of these memory segments plays a critical role in ensuring the efficiency and stability of database operations.

The **System Global Area (SGA)** is a group of shared memory structures that contain data and control information for one Oracle database instance. This memory area is shared by all server and background processes, making it central to the functioning of the Oracle Database. The principal components of the SGA include:

- **Database Buffer Cache**: Used to store data blocks read from disk.
- **Shared Pool**: Contains shared SQL, PL/SQL code, data dictionary cache, and other control structures.
- **Redo Log Buffer**: Holds redo entries, which are a record of changes made to the database.
- **Large Pool**: Used for large memory allocations, relieving the burden on the Shared Pool.
- **Java Pool**: Used for all session-specific Java code and data.
- **Streams Pool**: Utilized by Oracle Streams to manage data capture, staging, and propagation.

- **Fixed SGA**: Contains general information about the state of the database and the instance, which the background processes need to access.

Database Buffer Cache is a critical component for optimizing physical I/O operations. When a query requests data, it is first searched within the Database Buffer Cache; if the data is found (cache hit), it is retrieved quickly without accessing the disk, considerably improving performance. Cache management employs a Least Recently Used (LRU) algorithm to ensure that frequently accessed data remains in memory. You can control its size by setting the DB_CACHE_SIZE initialization parameter.

```
ALTER SYSTEM SET db_cache_size = 512M;
```

The **Shared Pool** is another integral part of the SGA, encompassing various caches, the most important being the library cache and the data dictionary cache. The **Library Cache** stores parsed SQL statements and PL/SQL code. When a new SQL query is executed, Oracle first checks the library cache to see if an identical statement already exists. If it does, Oracle uses the parsed representation from the cache, saving the parsing time. The **Data Dictionary Cache** holds key metadata such as information about tables, columns, users, and privileges. The size of the Shared Pool can be adjusted using the SHARED_POOL_SIZE parameter.

```
ALTER SYSTEM SET shared_pool_size = 256M;
```

The **Redo Log Buffer** temporarily stores redo information (change vectors) generated by DML and DDL operations. This buffer is cyclic and written to the online redo log files by the Log Writer (LGWR) process to ensure that all transaction changes are saved, providing a means for recovery in case of a failure. The size of this buffer is configured by the LOG_BUFFER parameter.

```
ALTER SYSTEM SET log_buffer = 8M;
```

The **Large Pool** is optional but beneficial for systems requiring large memory allocations typical in operations like RMAN backup and restore, parallel queries, and message buffers in shared server configurations. By configuring a Large Pool, you can offload memory requirements from the Shared Pool, minimizing its fragmentation. Use the LARGE_POOL_SIZE parameter to set its size.

```
ALTER SYSTEM SET large_pool_size = 128M;
```

Java Pool memory is allocated specifically for Java code execution and parsing within the Oracle JVM environment. The JAVA_POOL_SIZE parameter is used to manage its capacity.

```
ALTER SYSTEM SET java_pool_size = 64M;
```

The **Streams Pool** is used exclusively by Oracle Streams to manage memory for capture processes, apply processes, and propagation. The STREAMS_POOL_SIZE parameter can be set to allocate the required memory for these operations.

```
ALTER SYSTEM SET streams_pool_size = 32M;
```

The **Fixed SGA** is a small, non-configurable part of the SGA that contains essential information about the state of the database and the instance. This area stores data such as the size of each component within the SGA, internal database instance states, and process control information. Although the Fixed SGA's size is predetermined by Oracle and cannot be altered, understanding its function is crucial for a complete grasp of SGA operations.

The **Program Global Area (PGA)** is a non-shared memory region that contains data and control information exclusive to a single server process or background process. The PGA memory structure is crucial for individual operations and is dynamically allocated as needed. Elements include:

- **Private SQL Area**: Stores bind variable values and runtime execution information.
- **Session Memory**: Holds session-specific variables such as logon information.
- **Sort Area**: Utilized during sort operations, managing the sort data.

Administrators do not directly control PGA allocations; instead, they influence it via the PGA_AGGREGATE_TARGET initialization parameter. This parameter specifies the target aggregate PGA memory available to all server processes attached to an instance.

```
ALTER SYSTEM SET pga_aggregate_target = 1G;
```

Optimizing memory usage within Oracle Database necessitates thoroughly understanding and configuring these memory structures, ensuring that each component is adequately sized to handle the operational workload.

2.4 Process Structures in Oracle Database

In Oracle Database, processes are fundamental to the operation and management of the database. They execute database operations, manage memory structures, and ensure data consistency and concurrent access. Oracle Database uses various types of processes, primarily categorized into user processes, server processes, and background processes.

A **user process** is initiated when a user connects to the Oracle Database, typically through an Oracle client. This process is responsible for running the user's application or request. However, it does not directly interact with the Oracle Database. Instead, communication is mediated through server processes.

A **server process** is dedicated to serving user processes. It handles the execution of SQL statements and returns results to the user processes. In a dedicated server configuration, each user process has a corresponding server process. Conversely, in a shared server configuration, multiple user processes can share a small pool of server processes. Shared server configuration is especially useful in environments with a large number of users, reducing the overall resource consumption.

```
-- Example SQL for setting a database to dedicated or shared server mode
ALTER SYSTEM SET SHARED_SERVERS = 0; -- Dedicated Server Mode
ALTER SYSTEM SET SHARED_SERVERS = 5; -- Shared Server Mode
```

Oracle Background Processes handle various maintenance and administrative tasks required for Oracle Database to function efficiently. These processes form the backbone of Oracle's database management and automation capabilities. Key background processes include:

Database Writer (DBWn): This process handles writing modified (dirty) buffers from the database buffer cache to the datafiles. By doing so, it ensures that sufficient clean buffers are available in the buffer cache for new transactions.

```
-- Query to check the status of the DBWn process
SELECT STATUS
FROM V$BGPROCESS
WHERE NAME = 'DBW0';
```

Log Writer (LGWR): This process writes redo log entries from the redo log buffer to the redo log files. Redo logs contain a record of changes made to the database, ensuring that these changes can be replayed or rolled back if necessary.

```
-- Query to check the status of the LGWR process
SELECT STATUS
FROM V$BGPROCESS
WHERE NAME = 'LGWR';
```

System Monitor (SMON): This process performs recovery operations when a database is started or an instance crashes. It may also perform certain space management tasks, such as coalescing free space in tablespaces.

```
-- Query to check the status of the SMON process
SELECT STATUS
FROM V$BGPROCESS
WHERE NAME = 'SMON';
```

Process Monitor (PMON): This process cleans up after failed processes. It frees resources held by those processes and recovers their transactions.

```
-- Query to check the status of the PMON process
SELECT STATUS
FROM V$BGPROCESS
WHERE NAME = 'PMON';
```

Checkpoint (CKPT): This process updates datafile headers and control files to reflect that a checkpoint has occurred. A checkpoint ensures that all modified buffers are written to the datafiles, reducing the time required for recovery.

```
-- Query to check the status of the CKPT process
SELECT STATUS
FROM V$BGPROCESS
WHERE NAME = 'CKPT';
```

Archiver (ARCn): This process copies filled redo log files to the archive log destination. It is essential for enabling the recovery of the database in case of media failure.

```
-- Query to check the status of the ARCn process
SELECT STATUS
FROM V$BGPROCESS
WHERE NAME = 'ARC0';
```

Recovery Writer (RVWR): This process writes flashback logs in Oracle's Flashback feature, enabling the database to be rewound to a previous state.

```
-- Query to check the status of the RVWR process
SELECT STATUS
FROM V$BGPROCESS
WHERE NAME = 'RVWR';
```

These processes interact through shared memory structures like the System Global Area (SGA) and Program Global Area (PGA). The efficient functioning of these processes ensures high performance, reliability, and scalability of the Oracle Database. Understanding the role and monitoring the status of these processes are vital for database administrators to maintain the health of the database environment.

Each background process is integral to the overall architecture, playing a specialized role to ensure the integrity and availability of the database system. Proper configuration and management of these processes can significantly impact the performance and reliability of the Oracle Database. Monitoring and tuning these processes are routine tasks for a database administrator, which involve analyzing dynamic performance views and adjusting initialization parameters.

2.5 Storage Architecture: Tablespaces and Datafiles

Oracle Database storage architecture is a critical component in the efficient management and performance of the database. The storage architecture encompasses tablespaces and datafiles, which are fundamental building blocks for the physical and logical storage in Oracle databases.

Tablespaces are logical storage units that consist of one or more datafiles. Each tablespace in Oracle Database is used to group related logical structures together. Tablespaces facilitate database administration by enabling the management of storage allocation for different types of data, enhancing data organization, and optimizing performance.

Datafiles are physical files on the disk that store the actual data within the Oracle Database. They are associated with a specific tablespace, and each datafile can belong to only one tablespace. Datafiles contain user data, system data, metadata, and indexes. The structure and management of datafiles are essential for ensuring data integrity and performance.

To create and manage tablespaces and datafiles, Oracle provides several SQL commands and options. Below, we explore the various types of tablespaces, the role and creation of datafiles, and the management practices for both.

Types of Tablespaces

Oracle Database supports several types of tablespaces, each serving different purposes:

- **System Tablespace**: This is a mandatory tablespace that contains the data dictionary, which is the core metadata for the database. The system tablespace is critical for the database's operational integrity.
- **User Tablespaces**: These tablespaces store the various user-generated objects such as tables, indexes, and clusters. Different user tablespaces can be created to organize and manage user data efficiently.
- **Temporary Tablespaces**: Temporary tablespaces are used for storing temporary data generated by SQL operations that require additional space, such as sorting or joining operations.
- **Undo Tablespaces**: Undo tablespaces are used for storing undo data, which is essential for providing read consistency, rolling back transactions, and supporting Oracle's Flashback technologies.
- **Default Permanent Tablespaces**: This serves as the default location for non-system schemas to store permanent objects.

Creating a Tablespace

Creating a tablespace involves defining its name, specifying the datafiles associated with it, and setting various storage parameters. Here is an example of how to create a user tablespace:

```
-- Create a new tablespace named 'app_data'
CREATE TABLESPACE app_data
DATAFILE '/u01/app/oracle/oradata/app_data01.dbf' SIZE 100M
AUTOEXTEND ON NEXT 10M MAXSIZE UNLIMITED
LOGGING
EXTENT MANAGEMENT LOCAL
SEGMENT SPACE MANAGEMENT AUTO;
```

This SQL statement creates a tablespace named app_data with an initial datafile size of 100 MB. It sets the datafile to auto-extend in increments of 10 MB without any maximum size limit. The LOGGING clause specifies that logging is enabled for this tablespace, while EXTENT MANAGEMENT LOCAL specifies that extent management is local to the tablespace, and SEGMENT SPACE MANAGEMENT AUTO means that segment space management is automated.

Datafiles

Datafiles are the physical files where the database stores its data. Every tablespace comprises one or more datafiles, which are automatically created when a tablespace is created. Additional datafiles can be added to a tablespace when the storage requirement increases.

To add a datafile to an existing tablespace, use the ALTER TABLESPACE command:

```
-- Add a new datafile to the 'app_data' tablespace
ALTER TABLESPACE app_data
ADD DATAFILE '/u01/app/oracle/oradata/app_data02.dbf' SIZE 100M
AUTOEXTEND ON NEXT 10M MAXSIZE 500M;
```

This command adds a new datafile to the app_data tablespace with an initial size of 100 MB and allows it to auto-extend by 10 MB increments until it reaches a maximum size of 500 MB.

Managing Tablespaces and Datafiles

Over time, it may be necessary to manage tablespace and datafile storage to ensure optimal database performance and storage utilization. Essential management tasks include monitoring tablespace usage, resizing tablespaces, and managing datafile attributes.

Resizing a Datafile

If a datafile needs to be resized, it can be done using the RESIZE clause:

```
-- Resize the datafile to 200 MB
ALTER DATABASE DATAFILE '/u01/app/oracle/oradata/app_data01.dbf' RESIZE
    200M;
```

Dropping a Tablespace

To drop a tablespace along with its associated datafiles, use the DROP TABLESPACE command:

```
-- Drop the tablespace 'app_data' and delete its datafiles
DROP TABLESPACE app_data INCLUDING CONTENTS AND DATAFILES;
```

The INCLUDING CONTENTS AND DATAFILES clause ensures that both the tablespace and its datafiles are removed.

Understanding the storage architecture of Oracle Database, particularly tablespaces and datafiles, is crucial for efficient data management and optimization of database operations. Effective use of tablespaces enhances data organization and performance, while proper management of datafiles ensures consistent data integrity and availability.

2.6 System Global Area (SGA) and Program Global Area (PGA)

Understanding the memory structures in Oracle Database is pivotal for database performance and management. This section covers the two main areas of memory: the System Global Area (SGA) and the Program Global Area (PGA), elucidating their purposes, components, and configurations.

The **System Global Area (SGA)** is a shared memory region that contains data and control information for an Oracle Database instance. The SGA is divided into several sub-components, each with a specific role in database operation. Being shared, the SGA is accessible by multiple Oracle processes, enabling efficient data caching and management of internal structures.
Key components of the SGA include:

- **Database Buffer Cache**: This cache stores copies of data blocks read from datafiles. Its purpose is to optimize read and write operations by minimizing physical I/O. When a user modifies a database block, the changes are made in the buffer cache before being written to the disk.
- **Redo Log Buffer**: This buffer holds redo entries—a log of changes made to the database. Redo entries are essential for database recovery. These changes are periodically written to the redo log files by the Log Writer process (LGWR).
- **Shared Pool**: This pool stores various structures, such as SQL executables, parsed SQL statements, and data dictionary cache information. The shared pool ensures that frequently executed SQL statements and data dictionary objects are readily accessible, reducing the need for repetitive parsing and compilation.

- **Large Pool**: This optional memory area is used for large memory allocations, such as backup and recovery operations and I/O server processes. By offloading large allocations from the shared pool, the large pool helps prevent fragmentation.
- **Java Pool**: Required if the Oracle Database includes JVM (Java Virtual Machine) support, the Java Pool is used for all session-specific Java code and data within the JVM.
- **Streams Pool**: Used exclusively by Oracle Streams, it provides memory needed for capture and apply operations.

Configuring the SGA properly is crucial for optimal database performance. The parameters that dictate the size of the SGA components include DB_CACHE_SIZE, SHARED_POOL_SIZE, LARGE_POOL_SIZE, JAVA_POOL_SIZE, and STREAMS_POOL_SIZE. Oracle's Automatic Shared Memory Management (ASMM) allows for dynamic adjustment of these parameters based on workload requirements.

```
ALTER SYSTEM SET DB_CACHE_SIZE = 2G SCOPE=BOTH;
ALTER SYSTEM SET SHARED_POOL_SIZE = 1G SCOPE=BOTH;
ALTER SYSTEM SET LARGE_POOL_SIZE = 512M SCOPE=BOTH;
```

Output:

```
System altered.
```

The **Program Global Area (PGA)** differs from the SGA as it is specific to a server process and is not shared. Each server process and background process has its own PGA. The PGA contains data and control information exclusively for a single process, which is essential for database tasks like sorting operations and running user queries.

Components of the PGA include:

- **Sort Area**: Used for sorting operations during query execution, index creation, etc.
- **Session Memory**: Contains session-specific information for dedicated connections.
- **Private SQL Area**: Holds information about binding variables and query execution for a specific SQL statement.

The size of the PGA can be managed automatically by Oracle using the PGA_AGGREGATE_TARGET parameter. Oracle's Automatic Memory Management (AMM) dynamically adjusts the PGA size according to workload demands.

```
ALTER SYSTEM SET PGA_AGGREGATE_TARGET = 1G SCOPE=BOTH;
```

Output:

```
System altered.
```

Evaluating the effectiveness of PGA usage can be done using Oracle's dynamic performance view, V$PGASTAT. This view provides insights into the amount of memory used and the efficiency of memory distribution across operations.

```
SELECT * FROM V$PGASTAT;
```

Output:

```
NAME                                    VALUE           UNIT
--------------------------------------- --------------- -----------
aggregate PGA target parameter          1073741824      bytes
aggregate PGA auto target               805306368       bytes
global memory bound                     268435456       bytes
total PGA inuse                         524288000       bytes
total PGA allocated                     536870912       bytes
PGA used for auto workareas             104857600       bytes
PGA used for manual workareas           0               bytes
over allocation count                   0               count
bytes processed                         0               bytes
extra bytes read/written                0               bytes
cache hit percentage                    100             percent
```

The effective management of the SGA and PGA is fundamental for database performance, as improper configurations can lead to resource bottlenecks, increased I/O operations, and suboptimal query performance. With a comprehensive understanding of these memory structures and their configurations, database administrators can ensure that Oracle Databases operate efficiently, handling workloads proficiently.

2.7 Background Processes

In Oracle Database, background processes are essential for the smooth functioning and efficient management of the database. These processes work in synergy to perform a variety of tasks such as managing memory structures, handling I/O operations, and providing recoverability. Understanding these background processes is crucial for effective database administration and troubleshooting.

Oracle background processes can be broadly categorized into mandatory and optional ones. The mandatory processes are essential for database operation, whereas optional processes provide additional functionalities that might not be needed in all environments.

Mandatory Background Processes:

- **Database Writer Process (DBWn)**: The primary role of the Database Writer process is to write modified (dirty) buffers in the database buffer cache to datafiles. This write operation is critical to ensure that data changes are permanently stored on disk to maintain data consistency. DBWn processes function in the background, asynchronously writing dirty buffers to avoid delays in user transactions. Oracle can use multiple DBWn processes (DBW0 through DBW9 and DBWa through DBWj) depending on the workload and system architecture.

- **Log Writer Process (LGWR)**: The Log Writer process is responsible for writing redo log entries from the redo log buffer in the System Global Area (SGA) to online redo log files. LGWR ensures that redo information pertaining to committed transactions is safely logged to disk, providing the foundation for Oracle's transaction recovery mechanism. LGWR writes redo entries in a circular fashion and is crucial for maintaining the integrity of the database in the event of a failure.

- **System Monitor Process (SMON)**: The System Monitor process performs instance recovery at database startup if the instance was previously shut down abnormally. SMON's tasks include recovering transactions pending due to instance failures, cleaning up temporary segments that are no longer in use, and coalescing contiguous free space in the tablespace to ensure optimal space utilization.

- **Process Monitor Process (PMON)**: The Process Monitor process is responsible for cleaning up after failed user processes, releasing resources such as locks and freeing up memory segments allocated to user processes. PMON also restarts failed background processes deemed essential by Oracle.

- **Checkpoint Process (CKPT)**: The Checkpoint process is responsible for signaling DBWn to write dirty buffers to disk at regular intervals. Additionally, CKPT updates the headers of datafiles and control files to reflect recent checkpoint information, speeding up data recovery during database startup. The checkpoint process ensures that Oracle can quickly recover and resume operations following a crash.

- **Archiver Process (ARCn)**: The Archiver processes are involved in copying filled redo log files to archive log destinations when the database operates in ARCHIVELOG mode. This process ensures that redo logs are available for point-in-time recovery by keeping a history of all transactions executed in the database. Oracle can spawn up to ten ARCn processes (ARC0 through ARC9) to handle heavy workloads.

Optional Background Processes:

- **Recoverer Process (RECO)**: The Recoverer process automatically resolves distributed transactions that are pending due to network or system failures in a distributed database environment. RECO coordinates with other databases to ensure that distributed transactions are either fully committed or rolled back.
- **Job Queue Processes (CJQ0 and Jnnn)**: Job Queue processes handle the execution of scheduled jobs in the database. CJQ0 coordinates job scheduling, while Jnnn processes execute the scheduled jobs. These processes facilitate the automation of maintenance tasks, data collection, and reporting.
- **Automatic Database Diagnostic Monitor (ADDM) Process**: The ADDM process analyzes system performance data collected by Automatic Workload Repository (AWR) and provides actionable recommendations for improving database performance. This process runs periodically to help database administrators identify and address performance bottlenecks.
- **Shared Server Processes and Dispatcher Processes**: These processes facilitate the handling of user connections in environments configured for shared server architecture. The dispatcher (Dnnn) processes route user requests to shared server (Snnn) processes, which manage database operations. This architecture allows for scalable handling of large numbers of concurrent connections by reducing the memory overhead associated with dedicating server processes to each user.

```
SELECT p.spid, p.program
FROM v$process p
JOIN v$session s
ON p.addr = s.paddr
WHERE s.type = 'BACKGROUND'
ORDER BY p.spid;
```

The command above lists the operating system process identifiers (SPID) and the corresponding Oracle programs for all background processes currently running in the database environment.

The background processes ensure database efficiency by automating routine maintenance tasks, managing system resources, and ensuring fault tolerance. They form a critical part of Oracle Database internals, interfacing with various memory and storage structures to maintain smooth operations. Proper understanding and monitoring of these processes are key to proficient database administration, which ultimately supports the reliability and performance of the database system.

2.8 Logical and Physical Storage Structures

Oracle Database storage architecture is divided into two primary categories: logical and physical storage structures. Each category serves distinct functions and operates at different levels of abstraction to manage data efficiently within the database environment.

Logical storage structures in Oracle Database provide an abstraction layer that helps in the organization and manipulation of data. These structures include tablespaces, segments, extents, and data blocks. Each logical storage unit is built upon the preceding unit, forming a hierarchy that supports the overall data storage mechanism.

Tablespaces are the highest level of logical storage. A tablespace can contain various types of database objects, such as tables, indexes, and large objects (LOBs). It acts as a logical container for these objects and can span multiple physical datafiles. Oracle employs tablespaces to manage storage allocation and retrieval more efficiently. Typical examples include the SYSTEM and SYSAUX tablespaces, which store system-related data and user-defined tablespaces for application-specific data.

Segments represent a logical storage structure within a tablespace. Each database object that requires storage space belongs to a segment. Common types of segments include table segments, index segments, rollback segments, and temporary segments. For instance, a table segment stores the data of a database table, whereas an index segment stores the data of an index. Segments are further divided into extents.

Extents are a collection of contiguous data blocks within a segment. When a segment requires more space, the Oracle Database allocates an extent. Extents help manage storage allocation by ensuring that large amounts of contiguous space are available for objects. They enable the database to minimize fragmentation and optimize space usage. Extents are dynamically allocated as the objects grow over time.

Data blocks, or database blocks, are the smallest unit of data storage in Oracle Database. When Oracle reads or writes data, it moves it in blocks. A data block corresponds to a specific number of bytes of physical database space on the disk. The size of the data blocks is defined at the time of database creation and can vary depending on the needs of the database. Typical block sizes are 4KB, 8KB, 16KB, and 32KB. Data blocks form the foundation of logical storage in the Oracle Database.

Physical storage structures, on the other hand, refer to the actual files on the file system that store the database's data. These structures include datafiles, redo log files, and control files. They interact directly with the storage hardware to store and manage data.

Datafiles are the physical files that store the data of all logical structures within a tablespace. Each tablespace consists of at least one datafile, but it can contain multiple datafiles as well. Datafiles hold the actual data designed for the database objects. They are stored on disk and managed by the operating system. The storage capacity of a datafile can be adjusted by the database administrator (DBA) as needed.

Redo log files store a record of changes made to the database. They are crucial for database recovery, ensuring that any changes made to the data are not lost in the event of a failure. The redo logs capture both committed and uncommitted transactions, aiding in the restoration of the database to a consistent state during recovery operations. Oracle Database uses a group of redo log files, typically organized into redo log groups to provide redundancy and ensure data integrity.

Control files serve as metadata repositories that track the physical structure of the database. They contain crucial information such as the database name, datafile locations, redo log file locations, and the timestamps of the last backups. Control files are essential for the startup and operation of the Oracle Database. Multiple copies of control files are usually maintained to safeguard against data loss due to corruption or hardware failure.

The interaction between logical and physical storage structures ensures that the Oracle Database operates efficiently, maintaining data integrity and performance. Logical structures provide an organized framework for data management, while physical structures facilitate actual data storage and retrieval on the hardware. Understanding this distinction is fundamental for database administration and optimization.

```
CREATE TABLESPACE example_tblspace
  DATAFILE 'example_datafile.dbf' SIZE 100M
  AUTOEXTEND ON
  NEXT 10M;
```

```
Tablespace created.
```

The SQL code above demonstrates the creation of a tablespace named example_tblspace and an associated datafile named example_datafile.dbf. The AUTOEXTEND clause allows the datafile to grow automatically in increments of 10MB, ensuring that the tablespace can accommodate more data as needed. This example illustrates how logical storage structures extend down to physical datafiles.

Understanding both logical and physical storage structures is essential for effective database management. These layers enable the Oracle Database to efficiently handle data storage, retrieval, and maintenance, ensuring robust performance and data integrity. Through meticulous design and management, administrators can leverage these structures to optimize database operations.

2.9 Oracle Data Dictionary and Metadata

The Oracle data dictionary is a comprehensive set of read-only tables and views that provide metadata about the database. Metadata, in the context of databases, refers to the data about data; essentially, it is information that describes and provides information about the database objects. The data dictionary is a crucial aspect of the Oracle database, as it holds the definitions of all schema objects such as tables, indexes, views, and procedures, as well as user information, and system configuration parameters.

At the core of Oracle's metadata management, the data dictionary is maintained automatically by the Oracle Database when data structures are updated. This section delves into the structure, usage, and significance of the data dictionary and metadata in Oracle Database.

The data dictionary's primary role is to store database metadata. The dictionary is itself composed of a set of tables and views owned by the database user SYS. The structure and contents of these tables are the foundation for much of the Oracle Database's operation. Key components of the data dictionary include:

- User and Role Information
- Object Metadata such as Tables, Indexes, and Views
- System Parameters and Settings
- Storage Structures and Space Usage
- Performance Statistics

Queries on the data dictionary are internally redirected to base tables owned by the SYS user and these queries are processed by the Oracle SQL engine. For end-user convenience, Oracle categorizes dictionary views into three main groups:

DBA Views: These views provide metadata across the entire database and are accessible only by users with the DBA role or SELECT ANY DICTIONARY system privilege. They are prefixed with DBA_, such as DBA_TABLES, DBA_INDEXES, and DBA_USERS.

ALL Views: These views provide metadata concerning all objects that the current user has permissions to access, regardless of ownership. They are prefixed with ALL_, such as ALL_TABLES, ALL_INDEXES, and ALL_USERS.

USER Views: These views provide metadata concerning objects owned by the current user. They are prefixed with USER_, such as USER_TABLES, USER_INDEXES, and USER_USERS.

Here is an example to list all tables owned by the current user:

```
SELECT table_name
FROM user_tables;
```

When this query is executed, Oracle internally translates it into more complex queries involving base tables in the SYS schema to retrieve the requested metadata.

For instance, to list all users in the database, the below query can be used:

```
SELECT username
FROM dba_users;
```

Understanding the data dictionary's metadata architecture is fundamental for database management. Let's consider the DBA_TABLES view, which provides metadata about tables. This view includes columns such as TABLE_NAME, OWNER, TABLESPACE_NAME, NUM_ROWS, and many other attributes conveying detailed information about each table.

Example of exploring DBA_TABLES:

```
SELECT table_name, owner, tablespace_name, num_rows
FROM dba_tables
WHERE owner = 'HR';
```

Output:

```
TABLE_NAME  OWNER  TABLESPACE_NAME  NUM_ROWS
---------- ------ --------------- --------
EMPLOYEES   HR      USERS          107
DEPARTMENTS HR      USERS           27
JOBS        HR      USERS          19
...
```

Additionally, the metadata structure also plays a pivotal role in database security, helping administrators grant and revoke object privileges, track users' activity, and audit database usage. Utilizing the data dictionary views, an administrator can easily track object dependencies and avoid potential pitfalls during database changes.

Behind these views, Oracle maintains base tables located in the SYS schema, such as SYS.TS$, SYS.OBJ$, and SYS.USER$. These base tables store the low-level details from which the user-friendly views derive their information.

The data dictionary is supplemented by dynamic performance views, also known as V$ views, providing real-time or near-real-time database performance statistics and operational state. For instance, V$TABLESPACE provides information about table spaces, whereas V$SESSION gives insights into active sessions.

Metadata retrieval and analysis are automated and integral to tasks like optimizing performance, managing storage, and ensuring database security compliance. Hence, mastering the Oracle data dictionary is essential for proficiently managing and troubleshooting Oracle databases.

Understanding how to efficiently query and utilize the Oracle Data Dictionary ensures that database administrators and developers can maintain a deep awareness of the database's structure and health, enabling high levels of optimization and proactive management.

2.10 Overview of Multitenant Architecture

Oracle Database 12c introduced the multitenant architecture, a significant advancement that enables a single Oracle database instance to host multiple pluggable databases (PDBs). This architecture simplifies database consolidation, improves resource utilization, and enhances manageability. The multitenant architecture has two primary components: the Container Database (CDB) and the Pluggable Databases (PDBs).

Container Database (CDB): The CDB is the core of the multitenant architecture. It contains the root container, known simply as the root, which stores the Oracle System Metadata like common users and roles, as well as the data dictionary that is shared among all PDBs. The root also holds the shared memory and background processes that service all the pluggable databases within the container.

Pluggable Databases (PDBs): PDBs are the portable subsets of the Oracle Database that reside within the CDB. Each PDB appears to applications as a separate database, but they share the infrastructure of the CDB, including resources, security, and memory management. PDBs are isolated from each other, providing security and manageability. However, they are not completely independent; they share some common properties and resources of the CDB.

To illustrate, consider the following SQL query that demonstrates creating a CDB with one root and one PDB:

```
CREATE DATABASE cdb1
USER SYS IDENTIFIED BY Pa55w0rd
USER SYSTEM IDENTIFIED BY Pa55w0rd
ENABLE PLUGGABLE DATABASE
SEED
FILE_NAME_CONVERT = ('/u01/app/oracle/oradata/CDB1/', '/u01/app/oracle/
    oradata/PDBSEED/');
```

The query creates a Container Database named cdb1 with the root container and a seed PDB. The PDBSEED serves as a template for creating new PDBs. To create a new PDB from the seed, you can use the following command:

```
CREATE PLUGGABLE DATABASE pdb1
ADMIN USER pdb_adm IDENTIFIED BY Pa55w0rd
ROLES = (DBA)
FILE_NAME_CONVERT = ('/u01/app/oracle/oradata/PDBSEED/', '/u01/app/
    oracle/oradata/PDB1/');
```

Here, pdb1 is a new pluggable database created from the PDBSEED, and pdb_adm is the administrative user for the PDB.

Benefits of Multitenant Architecture:

- **Resource Management**: The multitenant architecture allows for efficient resource management through Resource Manager plans, which can be used to allocate CPU, IO, and parallel execution resources among PDBs.
- **Cost Efficiency**: Consolidating multiple databases into a single CDB reduces hardware and operational costs significantly.
- **Ease of Deployment and Management**: Deploying and managing multiple databases becomes easier because they share a single set of system services and memory structures.
- **Rapid PDB Provisioning and Cloning**: Provisioning new databases and cloning existing ones can be achieved swiftly using the CREATE PLUGGABLE DATABASE commands.
- **Seamless PDB Migration**: Moving a PDB between CDBs is straightforward, enabling workload distribution and resource optimization.

Security and Isolation: Each PDB operates in its own namespace and has its own set of data files. Users from one PDB cannot access the objects in another PDB unless explicitly granted permissions, which ensures a high level of security and isolation.

Backup and Recoverability: Backup and recovery operations are performed at the CDB level, but can also be performed for individual PDBs if required. RMAN (Recovery Manager) supports PDB-level backup and restore operations, offering flexibility and granularity in data protection.

```
RMAN> BACKUP PLUGGABLE DATABASE pdb1;
```

PDB Hot Cloning and Relocation: PDBs can be cloned while they are open and in use, a feature known as hot cloning. Additionally, PDBs can be relocated from one CDB to another with minimal downtime, providing agility in database management.

```
CREATE PLUGGABLE DATABASE pdb2 FROM pdb1 @remote_cdb_link;
```

In summary, the multitenant architecture of Oracle Database facilitates database consolidation, optimization of resource usage, and simplifies database lifecycle management. This architecture provides a robust platform for cloud computing and enterprise environments, where flexibility and scalability are crucial.

Chapter 3

SQL Basics with Oracle

This chapter introduces the foundational concepts of SQL within the Oracle Database environment. It covers connecting to the database, executing basic SELECT statements, and applying filters, sorting, and aggregate functions. Readers will also learn to group and join tables, use subqueries and set operators, and perform data manipulation tasks such as inserting, updating, and deleting data, establishing a solid groundwork for proficient SQL use.

3.1 Introduction to SQL

Structured Query Language (SQL) is a robust domain-specific language used in programming and designed for managing data held in a relational database management system (RDBMS) or for stream processing in a relational data stream management system (RDSMS). SQL comprises a data definition language (DDL), a data manipulation language (DML), and a data control language (DCL), making it a comprehensive tool for database interaction and management.

SQL's syntax and commands are designed to facilitate a highly intuitive interface for users, abstracting complex database operations into readable and explanatory commands. Oracle Database, a leading RDBMS, extensively employs SQL to interact with its datasets, providing enhanced tools and functionalities for enterprise-scale data management.

SQL operates on sets of data and is declarative, meaning that SQL statements define what to retrieve rather than how to retrieve it, allowing the underlying RDBMS to optimize the processes involved. To efficiently utilize SQL within Oracle, one must understand the core principles, functions, and capabilities offered by SQL.

The fundamental SQL commands can be classified broadly into four categories:

- **Data Query Language (DQL):** Primarily consists of the SELECT statement used to query the database and retrieve data.
- **Data Definition Language (DDL):** Includes statements such as CREATE, ALTER, DROP, and TRUNCATE, which define and modify database structures.
- **Data Manipulation Language (DML):** Comprises commands like INSERT, UPDATE, DELETE, and MERGE that enable manipulation of data within the database.
- **Data Control Language (DCL):** Encompasses the GRANT and REVOKE statements to control access to data stored in the database.

Key Characteristics of SQL

SQL is not case-sensitive, though it is customary to write SQL keywords in uppercase to distinguish them from user-defined names such as column names and table names. SQL statements can be written on one line or multiple lines, enhancing readability without affecting execution.

Example SQL Statement:

Here is an example of a simple SELECT statement which retrieves a list of all employees from an employees table:

```
SELECT *
FROM employees;
```

This SQL query instructs Oracle Database to select all columns (denoted by the asterisk) from the employees table.

Understanding SQL Statements

An SQL statement comprises clauses, expressions, predicates, and queries. A clause is a constituent component of a statement, typically starting with a keyword like SELECT, FROM, WHERE, etc. For instance, in the example above:

- **SELECT Clause:** Specifies the columns to be displayed in the query result.
- **FROM Clause:** Indicates the table from which to retrieve the data.

SQL Syntax Rules

To write effective SQL statements, one must adhere to specific syntax rules:

- Keywords must be used appropriately.
- Column names and table names follow user-defined naming conventions but must be consistent and unique.
- Statements must end with a semicolon (;) for proper execution in Oracle.

Data Types

Each column in a SQL table is assigned a data type defining the kind of data the column can hold. Common data types in SQL include:

- VARCHAR2 - Variable-length character string.
- NUMBER - Numeric data with optional precision and scale.
- DATE - Date and time values.
- BLOB - Binary Large Object for storing large binary data.

Null Values

In SQL, a null value represents missing or unknown data. It is distinct from zero or an empty string and needs to be handled explicitly in queries.

Example of a table creation statement illustrating data types:

```
CREATE TABLE employees (
    employee_id NUMBER PRIMARY KEY,
    first_name VARCHAR2(50),
    last_name VARCHAR2(50),
    hire_date DATE
);
```

The above statement creates an employees table with specific columns, each assigned a data type and a constraint (primary key for employee_-id).

Having a thorough comprehension of SQL is crucial for proficient database management and data manipulation within Oracle Database. By mastering the basic SQL commands and understanding their application, one can efficiently query, define, manipulate, and control data in a relational database environment.

3.2 Connecting to an Oracle Database

Establishing a connection to an Oracle Database is a critical first step that enables users to execute SQL statements and interact with the database. This section provides detailed instructions on connecting to an Oracle Database using various methods, including SQL*Plus, SQL Developer, and JDBC (Java Database Connectivity).

To connect to an Oracle Database, you must have the database installed and properly configured, alongside having the necessary user credentials.

SQL*Plus Connection

SQL*Plus is a command-line tool provided by Oracle to interact with the database. To establish a connection using SQL*Plus, follow the steps below:

1. Open a terminal or command prompt. 2. Execute the ‘sqlplus‘ command and provide the username, password, and database connection string as shown in the example below:

```
sqlplus username/password@//hostname:port/SERVICENAME
```

For example, suppose the username is **scott**, the password is **tiger**, the hostname is **localhost**, the port is **1521**, and the service name is **ORCL**. The command will be:

```
sqlplus scott/tiger@//localhost:1521/ORCL
```

Upon successful execution, you will be connected to the Oracle Database and will see a SQL prompt where you can start executing SQL commands.

SQL Developer Connection

Oracle SQL Developer is a graphical user interface that simplifies database management and development tasks. To connect using SQL Developer:

1. Open Oracle SQL Developer. 2. In the "Connections" tab, click the green plus icon to create a new connection. 3. Enter the connection details in the dialog:

- **Connection Name**: A descriptive name for the connection.
- **Username**: The database user name, for example, **scott**.
- **Password**: The corresponding password, for example, **tiger**.
- **Hostname**: The database server hostname, for example, **localhost**.
- **Port**: The port number, typically **1521**.
- **SID/Service Name**: Either the system identifier (SID) or the service name of the database, for example, **ORCL**.

4. Click the "Test" button to verify the connection details. 5. If the test succeeds, click "Connect."

Once connected, the database connection will appear under the "Connections" tab, allowing you to browse schemas, inspect tables, and execute SQL queries.

JDBC Connection

Java Database Connectivity (JDBC) provides a standard API for connecting Java applications to a database. To establish a JDBC connection to an Oracle Database, follow these steps:

1. Ensure that the Oracle JDBC driver (ojdbc8.jar) is included in your project's classpath. 2. Use the following code snippet to establish a connection:

```
import java.sql.Connection;
import java.sql.DriverManager;
import java.sql.SQLException;

public class OracleDBConnection {
    public static void main(String[] args) {
        Connection connection = null;
        try {
            // Load Oracle JDBC Driver
            Class.forName("oracle.jdbc.driver.OracleDriver");

            // Connect to the database
```

```
            connection = DriverManager.getConnection(
                "jdbc:oracle:thin:@localhost:1521:ORCL", "scott", "tiger");

            if (connection != null) {
                System.out.println("Connected to the database!");
            } else {
                System.out.println("Failed to make connection!");
            }
        } catch (ClassNotFoundException e) {
            System.out.println("Oracle JDBC Driver not found.");
            e.printStackTrace();
        } catch (SQLException e) {
            System.out.println("Connection failed.");
            e.printStackTrace();
        } finally {
            try {
                if (connection != null && !connection.isClosed()) {
                    connection.close();
                }
            } catch (SQLException e) {
                e.printStackTrace();
            }
        }
    }
}
```

The above program includes:

- Loading the Oracle JDBC driver with Class.forName("oracle.jdbc.driver.OracleDriver").
- Establishing a database connection using DriverManager.getConnection.
- Connection details such as URL "jdbc:oracle:thin:@localhost:1521:ORCL", username "scott", and password "tiger".
- Proper exception handling and resource cleanup.

```
Connected to the database!
```

Using these methods, one can efficiently connect to an Oracle Database and start performing a variety of database operations. Each method serves different purposes, from command-line interfacing with SQL*Plus to using graphical tools like SQL Developer, and integrating with applications via JDBC.

3.3 Basic SQL SELECT Statements

The foundational operation in SQL for querying data from a database is the SELECT statement. SQL stands for Structured Query Language, and it allows users to specify the data they wish to retrieve in a highly structured format. In an Oracle Database environment, the SELECT statement is essential for extracting meaningful data from tables. This section explores the syntax and usage of the SELECT statement, providing examples and explanations to solidify understanding.

A SELECT statement's primary components are the SELECT keyword, the column names or expressions to retrieve, the FROM keyword, and the table name from which to retrieve the data. The basic syntax of a SELECT statement is as follows:

```
SELECT column1, column2, ...
FROM table_name;
```

In this SQL query:

- The SELECT keyword indicates that a query is being performed.
- column1, column2, ... represent the columns that are being retrieved from the table.
- The FROM keyword specifies the table from which the data is being selected.
- table_name is the name of the table in the database.

To illustrate the use of a SELECT statement, consider a table named employees with the following columns: employee_id, first_name, last_name, department_id, and salary. To retrieve all the columns for all the employees from this table, one would construct the following query:

```
SELECT employee_id, first_name, last_name, department_id, salary
FROM employees;
```

An execution of the preceding query might produce an output resembling:

```
EMPLOYEE_ID FIRST_NAME LAST_NAME DEPARTMENT_ID SALARY
----------- ---------- --------- ------------- -------
101         John       Smith     10            60000
102         Jane       Doe       20            75000
103         Emily      Brown     10            72000
104         Michael    Johnson   30            80000
```

Enumerating all columns using the column names can become cumbersome, especially when dealing with tables that have numerous columns. SQL offers a shorthand to retrieve all columns from a table using the asterisk (*) wildcard:

```
SELECT *
FROM employees;
```

This query returns the same result as explicitly listing all column names.

The SELECT statement also allows for the inclusion of expressions, literals, and functions in the result set. For example, one can concatenate columns and literals to form a full name and apply arithmetic operations directly within the SELECT clause:

```
SELECT first_name || ' ' || last_name AS full_name, salary * 12 AS annual_salary
FROM employees;
```

In the aforementioned query:

- first_name || ' ' || last_name concatenates first and last names with a space in between to form a full name. This is given the alias full_name using the AS keyword.
- salary * 12 calculates the annual salary by multiplying the monthly salary by 12 and renames it to annual_salary.

An output for this query might appear as:

```
FULL_NAME              ANNUAL_SALARY
---------------------- -------------
John Smith              720000
Jane Doe               900000
Emily Brown             864000
Michael Johnson         960000
```

Additionally, SQL allows aliasing columns and tables to make queries more readable and manageable. Aliasing can be particularly helpful when dealing with column names that are long or when performing joins between tables, as will be seen in later sections.

Using distinct values in the result set can be achieved by the DISTINCT keyword, which eliminates duplicates from the result set. For instance, to retrieve distinct department IDs from the employees table:

```
SELECT DISTINCT department_id
FROM employees;
```

This would yield a list of unique department IDs.

```
DEPARTMENT_ID
-------------
10
20
30
```

The DISTINCT keyword affects all columns listed in the SELECT clause and ensures that each row in the output is unique.

Finally, the order in which columns are specified in the SELECT clause determines the order in which they appear in the result set. This ordering of columns is essential to ensure the data is presented in a meaningful way according to the requirements of the query context. As we progress in complexity with the SQL language, understanding these fundamentals provides the necessary foundation for more advanced querying techniques.

3.4 Filtering Data with WHERE Clause

The WHERE clause is fundamental for filtering data in SQL queries. By specifying conditions within the WHERE clause, users can limit the rows returned by a query to those that meet the desired criteria. This section delves into the syntax and usage of the WHERE clause within the Oracle Database environment, illustrating various conditional expressions and their applicability.

The basic syntax of the WHERE clause in an SQL SELECT statement is as follows:

```
SELECT column1, column2, ...
FROM table_name
WHERE condition;
```

condition is an expression that evaluates to true or false. Only rows for which the condition is true are included in the result set. Conditions can include comparisons, various operators, and logical combinations of multiple conditions.

Consider the following example. To retrieve records from an employees table where the last_name is 'Smith', the query will be:

```
SELECT first_name, last_name, email
FROM employees
WHERE last_name = 'Smith';
```

```
FIRST_NAME  LAST_NAME  EMAIL
----------- ---------- ----------------
John        Smith      john.smith@oracle.com
Anna        Smith      anna.smith@oracle.com
```

Comparison Operators

Comparison operators in the WHERE clause include the following: - =: Equal to - <> or !=: Not equal to - >: Greater than - <: Less than -

>=: Greater than or equal to - <=: Less than or equal to

For example, to find employees with a salary greater than 60000:

```
SELECT first_name, last_name, salary
FROM employees
WHERE salary > 60000;
```

```
FIRST_NAME  LAST_NAME  SALARY
------------- ------------- ---------
Jane        Doe        75000
Mark        Brown      85000
```

Logical Operators

Logical operators enable the combination of multiple conditions: - AND: All conditions must be true. - OR: At least one condition must be true. - NOT: Reverses the truth value of the condition.

To retrieve employees whose salary is greater than 60000 and department id is 10:

```
SELECT first_name, last_name, salary, department_id
FROM employees
WHERE salary > 60000 AND department_id = 10;
```

```
FIRST_NAME  LAST_NAME  SALARY  DEPARTMENT_ID
------------- ------------- --------- --------------
Jane        Doe        75000   10
```

Pattern Matching with LIKE

The LIKE operator and wildcards are used for pattern matching. The percent sign (%) represents zero, one, or multiple characters, and the underscore (_) represents a single character. For example, to find employees whose last names start with 'Sm':

```
SELECT first_name, last_name
FROM employees
WHERE last_name LIKE 'Sm%';
```

```
FIRST_NAME  LAST_NAME
------------- -------------
John        Smith
Anna        Smith
```

Null Values with IS NULL

To filter rows with null values in a column, the IS NULL condition is used. Conversely, IS NOT NULL checks for non-null values. For instance, to retrieve employees without a manager:

```
SELECT first_name, last_name
FROM employees
WHERE manager_id IS NULL;
```

```
FIRST_NAME LAST_NAME
------------- -------------
Linda       King
```

Filtering with IN and BETWEEN

The IN operator allows specification of multiple values in a WHERE clause, whereas BETWEEN bounds the range of values. To find employees in departments 10, 20, or 30:

```
SELECT first_name, last_name, department_id
FROM employees
WHERE department_id IN (10, 20, 30);
```

```
FIRST_NAME LAST_NAME DEPARTMENT_ID
------------- ------------- --------------
Jane        Doe         10
John        Irish       20
Anne        Brown       30
```

To retrieve employees with salaries between 50000 and 80000:

```
SELECT first_name, last_name, salary
FROM employees
WHERE salary BETWEEN 50000 AND 80000;
```

```
FIRST_NAME LAST_NAME SALARY
------------- ------------- ---------
John        Irish       55000
Anna        Lee         70000
```

Combining Conditions

Combining conditions using parentheses ensures correct evaluation order. For example:

```
SELECT first_name, last_name, salary, department_id
FROM employees
WHERE (department_id = 10 OR department_id = 20)
AND salary > 60000;
```

```
FIRST_NAME LAST_NAME SALARY DEPARTMENT_ID
------------- ------------- --------- --------------
Jane        Doe         75000   10
Anne        Smith       65000   20
```

These capabilities of the WHERE clause enhance query precision, enabling selective data retrieval based on diverse criteria. By leveraging conditional expressions and operators, meaningful and relevant data subsets can be efficiently isolated within the Oracle Database environment.

3.5 Sorting Data with ORDER BY Clause

The query result set in SQL is inherently unordered; thus, to present data in a desired sequence, we employ the ORDER BY clause. This clause allows us to sort the rows returned from a SELECT statement based on one or more columns. Understanding this concept is pivotal as it helps in arranging data meaningfully for reporting and analysis purposes.

Syntax:

```
SELECT column1, column2, ...
FROM table_name
ORDER BY column1 [ASC|DESC], column2 [ASC|DESC], ...;
```

Here, ASC specifies ascending order, which is the default, and DESC specifies descending order.

Example:

Consider a table named employees with columns employee_id, first_name, last_name, and salary. To sort all employees by last_name in ascending order:

```
SELECT employee_id, first_name, last_name, salary
FROM employees
ORDER BY last_name ASC;
```

This will yield:

```
| employee_id | first_name | last_name | salary |
|-------------|------------|-----------|--------|
| 102         | Kate       | Adams     | 60000  |
| 101         | John       | Doe       | 50000  |
| 103         | Mike       | Smith     | 70000  |
```

Sorting by Multiple Columns:

In cases where sorting by a single column does not suffice, multiple columns can be specified in the ORDER BY clause. For instance, to sort first by last_name in ascending order and for employees with the same last_name, sort by first_name in descending order:

```
SELECT employee_id, first_name, last_name, salary
FROM employees
ORDER BY last_name ASC, first_name DESC;
```

Let's amend the employees table to have another employee with the last name Adams:

```
INSERT INTO employees (employee_id, first_name, last_name, salary)
VALUES (104, 'John', 'Adams', 55000);
```

Executing the preceding ORDER BY clause would now yield:

employee_id	first_name	last_name	salary
104	John	Adams	55000
102	Kate	Adams	60000
101	John	Doe	50000
103	Mike	Smith	70000

Null Values in Sorting:

Handling of NULL values in sorting can vary by SQL implementation. In Oracle, NULL values are treated as the lowest possible values by default. To illustrate:

```
SELECT employee_id, first_name, last_name, salary
FROM employees
ORDER BY salary ASC;
```

If the employees table includes a row with NULL salary:

```
INSERT INTO employees (employee_id, first_name, last_name, salary)
VALUES (105, 'Alice', 'Brown', NULL);
```

The ORDER BY results would be:

employee_id	first_name	last_name	salary
105	Alice	Brown	NULL
101	John	Doe	50000
104	John	Adams	55000
102	Kate	Adams	60000
103	Mike	Smith	70000

To treat NULL values as the highest values, the ORDER BY clause can be modified as:

```
SELECT employee_id, first_name, last_name, salary
FROM employees
ORDER BY salary ASC NULLS LAST;
```

This yields:

employee_id	first_name	last_name	salary
101	John	Doe	50000
104	John	Adams	55000
102	Kate	Adams	60000
103	Mike	Smith	70000
105	Alice	Brown	NULL

Understanding the flexible and precise ways to control sorting in SQL with the ORDER BY clause empowers users to organize returned data effectively for analysis and presentation. Proper usage of this clause facilitates not only basic listing but also complex ordered datasets for in-depth querying and reporting.

3.6 Using Aggregate Functions

Aggregate functions are instrumental in SQL for performing calculations on a set of values and returning a single value. These functions are commonly utilized for summarizing or aggregating the data within a table, and they often appear with the GROUP BY clause to provide meaningful insights from the data. The primary aggregate functions available in SQL, and supported by Oracle Database, include COUNT, SUM, AVG, MIN, and MAX.

Consider the following definitions and examples for each aggregate function.

COUNT: This function returns the number of rows that match a specified criterion. It can count all rows in a table or only those rows where a specified column has non-NULL values.

```
SELECT COUNT(*) FROM employees;
SELECT COUNT(department_id) FROM employees;
```

In the first query, COUNT(*) returns the total number of rows in the employees table. The second query, COUNT(department_id), returns the number of rows where department_id is not NULL.

```
SELECT COUNT(*) FROM employees;
---------
| 107   |
---------

SELECT COUNT(department_id) FROM employees;
---------
| 106   |
---------
```

SUM: This function calculates the total sum of a numeric column.

```
SELECT SUM(salary) FROM employees;
```

This query results in the total sum of all employees' salaries within the employees table.

```
SELECT SUM(salary) FROM employees;
------------
| 691400   |
------------
```

AVG: This function calculates the average value of a numeric column.

```
SELECT AVG(salary) FROM employees;
```

This query computes the average salary of the employees.

```
SELECT AVG(salary) FROM employees;
------------
| 6461.68  |
------------
```

MIN and MAX: These functions return the minimum and maximum values of a specified column, respectively.

```
SELECT MIN(salary), MAX(salary) FROM employees;
```

The above query simultaneously calculates the minimum and maximum salaries from the employees table.

```
SELECT MIN(salary), MAX(salary) FROM employees;
------------------
| 2100   | 24000 |
------------------
```

When using aggregate functions in queries, it is imperative to understand how they interact with the GROUP BY clause. The GROUP BY clause groups rows that have the same values in specified columns into summary rows. An example to illustrate this interaction involves calculating the total salary paid to employees in each department:

```
SELECT department_id, SUM(salary)
FROM employees
GROUP BY department_id;
```

This query segments the data by department_id, then calculates the sum of salaries within each department.

```
SELECT department_id, SUM(salary)
FROM employees
GROUP BY department_id;
-------------------------------
| DEPARTMENT_ID | SUM(SALARY) |
-------------------------------
| 10            | 4400        |
| 20            | 19000       |
| 30            | 24900       |
-------------------------------
```

The HAVING clause is another critical component when working with aggregate functions and GROUP BY. It allows filtering of group rows after the aggregate functions are applied, unlike the WHERE clause, which filters rows before aggregation. Consider the following query that selects departments with total salaries greater than 30000:

```
SELECT department_id, SUM(salary)
FROM employees
GROUP BY department_id
```

```
HAVING SUM(salary) > 30000;
```

The resulting output will only include departments where the sum of salaries exceeds 30000.

```
SELECT department_id, SUM(salary)
FROM employees
GROUP BY department_id
HAVING SUM(salary) > 30000;
-------------------------------
| DEPARTMENT_ID | SUM(SALARY) |
-------------------------------
| 50            | 156400      |
| 80            | 304500      |
-------------------------------
```

Understanding and utilizing aggregate functions effectively enables more complex data analysis and reporting capabilities within SQL, providing valuable insights and summaries of your dataset.

3.7 Group By and Having Clauses

The GROUP BY clause in SQL is essential for aggregating data into multiple records and grouping these records based on a common attribute. This clause is often used in conjunction with aggregate functions such as COUNT, SUM, AVG, MAX, and MIN. The primary purpose of the GROUP BY clause is to condense detailed data into a summary form.

Consider a scenario where we have a table named sales that records sales transactions with the following structure:

```
CREATE TABLE sales (
    transaction_id NUMBER PRIMARY KEY,
    sale_date DATE,
    product_id NUMBER,
    sales_amount NUMBER
);
```

We might want to know the total sales amount for each product. To achieve this, we would employ the GROUP BY clause as follows:

```
SELECT product_id, SUM(sales_amount) AS total_sales
FROM sales
GROUP BY product_id;
```

The query groups the records in the sales table by the product_id and then calculates the sum of sales_amount for each product. The result of this query would be a list of each product_id and the corresponding total_sales:

```
PRODUCT_ID  TOTAL_SALES
1           1500
2           2750
3           900
```

It is critical to understand that every column in the SELECT statement that is not encapsulated by an aggregate function must be included in the GROUP BY clause. Failure to do so will result in an SQL error, as the database system would not know how to group non-aggregated columns.

Furthermore, when filtering aggregated data, the HAVING clause is used. The HAVING clause operates similarly to the WHERE clause but is specifically designed to work with the results of aggregate functions. The HAVING clause is applied after the GROUP BY clause and is used to filter the grouped results.

Suppose we wish to identify only those products whose total sales exceed 1000. We can use the following query:

```
SELECT product_id, SUM(sales_amount) AS total_sales
FROM sales
GROUP BY product_id
HAVING SUM(sales_amount) > 1000;
```

The HAVING clause filters the aggregated results returned from the GROUP BY clause to include only those groups where the total sales amount exceeds 1000. The output might be something like:

```
PRODUCT_ID  TOTAL_SALES
1           1500
2           2750
```

To illustrate the practical utility of the GROUP BY and HAVING clauses, let's consider a more complex use case. Assume we have another table named products with the schema:

```
CREATE TABLE products (
    product_id NUMBER PRIMARY KEY,
    product_name VARCHAR2(50),
    category VARCHAR2(50)
);
```

A typical use case might be to find the total sales per product category for categories where the total sales amount is above a certain threshold. We can achieve that by using the JOIN clause in conjunction with GROUP BY and HAVING:

```
SELECT p.category, SUM(s.sales_amount) AS total_sales
FROM sales s
JOIN products p ON s.product_id = p.product_id
```

```
GROUP BY p.category
HAVING SUM(s.sales_amount) > 5000;
```

In this example, we are joining the sales and products tables on the product_id field, grouping the results by the category, summing the sales_amount, and then filtering to include only those categories where the total sales amount exceeds 5000. The output might look like:

```
CATEGORY    TOTAL_SALES
Electronics 13000
Furniture   7800
```

It is essential to carefully plan the use of the HAVING clause as it can significantly impact the performance of the query due to its filtering at the summary level, which often involves large datasets. In contrast, the WHERE clause filters records before any grouping and aggregation occurs.

In summary, the GROUP BY clause is a robust feature for aggregating data, and the HAVING clause extends its functionality by providing a means to filter these aggregated results. Mastering these clauses is crucial for performing sophisticated data analysis and reporting within Oracle databases. Proper application of these concepts ensures efficient data retrieval and leveraging Oracle's powerful SQL capabilities to their fullest extent.

3.8 Joining Tables with SQL

In relational database systems, the JOIN operation is integral to querying data that is spread across multiple tables. Oracle Database, like other relational database management systems, supports a variety of join operations that enable efficient and flexible data retrieval. This section explores the different types of joins available in SQL, focusing on syntactical structure and practical applications.

A join operation combines rows from two or more tables based on a related column. The most common types of joins include INNER JOIN, LEFT JOIN (commonly referred to as LEFT OUTER JOIN), RIGHT JOIN (or RIGHT OUTER JOIN), and FULL JOIN (or FULL OUTER JOIN).

An INNER JOIN returns only the rows where there is a match in both tables. To illustrate, consider two tables: employees and departments.

```
CREATE TABLE employees (
   employee_id NUMBER PRIMARY KEY,
```

```
    first_name VARCHAR2(50),
    last_name VARCHAR2(50),
    department_id NUMBER
);

CREATE TABLE departments (
    department_id NUMBER PRIMARY KEY,
    department_name VARCHAR2(100)
);
```

To retrieve a list of employees along with the names of their respective departments, an INNER JOIN is employed as follows:

```
SELECT employees.first_name, employees.last_name, departments.department_name
FROM employees
INNER JOIN departments ON employees.department_id = departments.
    department_id;
```

The INNER JOIN keyword selects rows that have matching values in both tables. The SQL statement above returns only those employees who are associated with a department.

A LEFT JOIN returns all rows from the left table and the matched rows from the right table. If there is no match, the result is NULL on the side of the right table. Here's how a LEFT JOIN can be performed:

```
SELECT employees.first_name, employees.last_name, departments.department_name
FROM employees
LEFT JOIN departments ON employees.department_id = departments.department_id;
```

In this query, all employees will be listed even if they do not belong to any department. The department_name will be displayed as NULL for those employees without an assigned department.

Conversely, a RIGHT JOIN returns all rows from the right table and the matched rows from the left table, with NULL values in the left table columns when there is no match. The following query demonstrates a RIGHT JOIN:

```
SELECT employees.first_name, employees.last_name, departments.department_name
FROM employees
RIGHT JOIN departments ON employees.department_id = departments.
    department_id;
```

In the case of the RIGHT JOIN, all departments are displayed, including those without employees.

Lastly, a FULL JOIN combines the results of both LEFT JOIN and RIGHT JOIN. It returns all rows from both tables, with NULL values where there is no match. Here's an example of a FULL JOIN:

```
SELECT employees.first_name, employees.last_name, departments.department_name
```

```
FROM employees
FULL JOIN departments ON employees.department_id = departments.department_id;
```

This FULL JOIN would return a comprehensive list covering all employees and all departments, including unmatched entries from each table with NULL values for missing data from the other table.

Understanding which join to use depends on the specific dataset and query requirements. Each join operation aligns with different relational algebra constructs, helping to build queries that are both efficient and expressive.

Beyond simple joins, Oracle SQL provides enhanced join capabilities like CROSS JOIN, which is used for the Cartesian product of two tables, and SELF JOIN, which joins a table to itself. Here is an example of a CROSS JOIN that returns a Cartesian product of the employees and departments tables:

```
SELECT employees.first_name, departments.department_name
FROM employees
CROSS JOIN departments;
```

Each row from employees is combined with each row from departments, resulting in a potentially large result set.

A SELF JOIN can be employed to find related data within the same table. For example, consider finding employees who work under the same department.

```
SELECT e1.first_name AS Employee, e2.first_name AS Manager
FROM employees e1
INNER JOIN employees e2 ON e1.department_id = e2.department_id AND e1.
    employee_id != e2.employee_id;
```

In this self-join query, the employees table is joined with itself to list employees alongside their colleagues in the same department, excluding themselves.

Mastering join operations in SQL is essential for combining data from multiple tables and establishing comprehensive queries in Oracle Database, enabling nuanced data analysis and manipulation within complex relational schemas.

```
Employee     | Manager
-------------|-------------
John         | Mike
Alice        | Bob
David        | Sarah
```

These various types of joins provide a versatile set of tools for SQL practitioners to manipulate and retrieve data according to specific criteria directly reflective of the multi-faceted relationships inherent in relational databases.

3.9 Subqueries and Nested Queries

Subqueries, also known as inner queries or nested queries, are employed to perform operations in multiple steps, where the result of one query is used as an input for another query. This mechanism enables complex filtering, aggregations, and transformations that may not be straightforward when using simple SQL queries. A subquery is a select statement within a select, insert, update, or delete statement or inside an expression.

A subquery is enclosed within parentheses and usually appears in the WHERE clause. It can also be placed in the FROM clause or the SELECT clause and can return either a single scalar value or multiple rows and columns. Let's explore various scenarios where subqueries are useful, including filtering data based on aggregated subquery results and using correlated subqueries.

Consider the following example:

```
SELECT employee_id, first_name, last_name
FROM employees
WHERE department_id = (SELECT department_id
                       FROM departments
                       WHERE department_name = 'Sales');
```

In this query, the subquery finds the department ID corresponding to the 'Sales' department, and the main query retrieves details of employees in that department. This type of subquery is known as a single-row subquery, as it returns only one row.

When a subquery is expected to return more than one row, we can use it with operators like IN, ANY, or ALL. For instance:

```
SELECT product_name, list_price
FROM products
WHERE list_price > ALL (SELECT AVG(list_price)
                        FROM products
                        GROUP BY category_id);
```

This query selects the products with a list price higher than the average list price of any product category. The ALL operator ensures that the product's list price is compared with every average list price among the grouped categories.

Correlated subqueries are another powerful feature of SQL. Unlike regular subqueries, correlated subqueries reference columns from the outer query. They are evaluated once for each row processed by the outer query.

```
SELECT employee_id, first_name, last_name
FROM employees e
WHERE salary > (SELECT AVG(salary)
                FROM employees
                WHERE department_id = e.department_id);
```

In this case, the subquery calculates the average salary within the same department of each employee, and the main query returns employees who earn more than this average.

When used inside the FROM clause, subqueries are referred to as inline views. Inline views help simplify complex queries by breaking them into manageable parts. Here's an example:

```
SELECT dept_name, avg_salary
FROM (SELECT department_name AS dept_name,
          AVG(salary) AS avg_salary
    FROM employees e
        JOIN departments d ON e.department_id = d.department_id
    GROUP BY department_name)
WHERE avg_salary > 50000;
```

The inner query acts as a derived table that summarizes the average salary per department. The outer query filters departments with an average salary above 50,000.

Another application of subqueries is within the SELECT clause. These subqueries must return a single value that can be incorporated directly into the result set.

```
SELECT employee_id, first_name, last_name,
       (SELECT department_name
        FROM departments
        WHERE department_id = e.department_id) AS department
FROM employees e;
```

In the above example, the subquery runs for each employee and fetches the department name corresponding to the employee's department ID.

Subqueries can also be used in INSERT, UPDATE, and DELETE statements to dynamically determine values. Here's an example within an INSERT statement:

```
INSERT INTO employees_archive
```

```
SELECT *
FROM employees
WHERE department_id IN (SELECT department_id
                        FROM departments
                        WHERE location_id = 1700);
```

This statement archives employee records working in the departments located at a specific location.

Finally, nested queries can also be employed to perform conditional updates:

```
UPDATE employees
SET salary = salary * 1.1
WHERE department_id IN (SELECT department_id
                        FROM departments
                        WHERE department_name = 'IT');
```

This command applies a 10

Using subqueries and nested queries allows for greater flexibility and the ability to perform complex data retrieval and manipulation tasks effectively. They are essential tools for advanced SQL proficiency in Oracle Database environments.

3.10 Using Set Operators

SQL set operators allow the combination of results from two or more SELECT queries. Set operators facilitate advanced data analysis by enabling the merging, intersecting, and differentiation of SQL query results. In Oracle SQL, the primary set operators are UNION, UNION ALL, INTERSECT, and MINUS. These set operators enable more sophisticated queries, providing the flexibility to generate complex data sets from multiple tables or queries.

UNION merges distinct results from two or more SELECT statements into a single result set, removing duplicate rows. Each SELECT statement within the UNION must have the same number and compatible types of columns. The basic syntax is as follows:

```
SELECT column_list1
FROM table1
UNION
SELECT column_list2
FROM table2;
```

Consider the following example, which retrieves unique department IDs from the employees and departments tables:

```
SELECT department_id
FROM employees
UNION
SELECT department_id
FROM departments;
```

If both tables have departments in common, those department IDs will appear only once in the final result set.

UNION ALL is similar to UNION, but it includes all results from the SELECT statements, retaining duplicates. This operator is useful when the presence of duplicates is meaningful for the analysis:

```
SELECT column_list1
FROM table1
UNION ALL
SELECT column_list2
FROM table2;
```

Applying UNION ALL to the previous example, every occurrence of department IDs, including duplicates, is included in the output:

```
SELECT department_id
FROM employees
UNION ALL
SELECT department_id
FROM departments;
```

INTERSECT returns only the rows that are present in both SELECT statements. Similar to UNION, the columns in each SELECT statement must be the same in number and data type:

```
SELECT column_list1
FROM table1
INTERSECT
SELECT column_list2
FROM table2;
```

For practical application, this example retrieves department IDs that exist in both employees and departments tables:

```
SELECT department_id
FROM employees
INTERSECT
SELECT department_id
FROM departments;
```

The intersected result contains only the department IDs common to both tables.

MINUS returns the rows from the first SELECT statement that are not in the second SELECT statement. It is also subject to the same requirements regarding matching numbers and types of columns:

```
SELECT column_list1
FROM table1
MINUS
SELECT column_list2
FROM table2;
```

This example shows how to get department IDs from the employees table that are not found in the departments table:

```
SELECT department_id
FROM employees
MINUS
SELECT department_id
FROM departments;
```

Here, the result set will exclude any department IDs that appear in both tables, showing only the department IDs unique to the employees table.

To illustrate how set operators integrate within more complex queries, consider a scenario where results from multiple queries need merging for a detailed analysis. Suppose you need to find the unique list of all job IDs appearing either in the employees or the job_history tables, while also identifying any common job IDs. The following SQL combines UNION, UNION ALL, and INTERSECT for this purpose:

```
-- Unique job IDs combining both tables
SELECT job_id
FROM employees
UNION
SELECT job_id
FROM job_history;

-- All job IDs including duplicates
SELECT job_id
FROM employees
UNION ALL
SELECT job_id
FROM job_history;

-- Common job IDs in both tables
SELECT job_id
FROM employees
INTERSECT
SELECT job_id
FROM job_history;
```

Selection of the appropriate set operator depends on the data analysis requirements. Use UNION when the uniqueness of dataset matters, UNION ALL for complete datasets, INTERSECT for commonality, and MINUS for differences.

Understanding set operators is vital in performing comprehensive data analysis in SQL, providing tools for merging and filtering data from disparate sources effectively.

3.11 Inserting Data into Tables

Inserting data into tables is a fundamental operation in SQL, particularly within the Oracle Database environment. This operation is essential for populating tables with initial data, adding new records as they become available, and testing various database functionalities. The primary SQL command used for this purpose is the INSERT statement, which allows the insertion of new rows into a table. This section delves into the syntax, usage, and various methodologies for inserting data, ensuring a thorough understanding of the command and its practical applications.

The basic syntax for the INSERT statement is as follows:

```
INSERT INTO table_name (column1, column2, column3, ...)
VALUES (value1, value2, value3, ...);
```

Explanation:

- table_name: The name of the table where the data will be inserted.
- column1, column2, column3, ...: The columns in the table that will receive the values.
- value1, value2, value3, ...: The values to be inserted into the corresponding columns.

If inserting values into all columns of the table, there is an abbreviated form where the column list can be omitted. The values must be provided in the order in which the columns appear in the table's structure:

```
INSERT INTO table_name
VALUES (value1, value2, value3, ...);
```

Consider a table named employees with the following structure:

```
CREATE TABLE employees (
  employee_id NUMBER PRIMARY KEY,
  first_name VARCHAR2(50),
  last_name VARCHAR2(50),
  email VARCHAR2(100),
```

```
  hire_date DATE,
  job_id VARCHAR2(10)
);
```

To insert a new employee's data into this table:

```
INSERT INTO employees (employee_id, first_name, last_name, email, hire_date,
      job_id)
VALUES (101, 'John', 'Doe', 'john.doe@example.com', TO_DATE('2023-10-01', '
      YYYY-MM-DD'), 'IT_PROG');
```

In this example:

- employee_id is set to 101.
- first_name is set to 'John'.
- last_name is set to 'Doe'.
- email is set to 'john.doe@example.com'.
- hire_date is set to October 1, 2023, using the TO_DATE function to convert the string to a valid date.
- job_id is set to 'IT_PROG'.

Inserting Multiple Rows in a Single Statement

Oracle SQL allows for the insertion of multiple rows in a single INSERT statement using the ALL or ANY keyword:

```
INSERT ALL
  INTO employees (employee_id, first_name, last_name, email, hire_date, job_id)
  VALUES (102, 'Jane', 'Smith', 'jane.smith@example.com', TO_DATE('2023-10-02', '
      YYYY-MM-DD'), 'HR_REP')
  INTO employees (employee_id, first_name, last_name, email, hire_date, job_id)
  VALUES (103, 'Sam', 'Brown', 'sam.brown@example.com', TO_DATE('2023-10-03', '
      YYYY-MM-DD'), 'MK_MAN')
SELECT * FROM dual;
```

In the example above, two new records are inserted into the employees table in a single operation. The SELECT * FROM dual statement is used to satisfy the requirement for a query to accompany the INSERT ALL statement; dual is a special dummy table available in Oracle Database.

Using Subqueries in INSERT Statements

Instead of supplying static values, an INSERT statement can dynamically insert data from another table using a subquery:

```
INSERT INTO employees (employee_id, first_name, last_name, email, hire_date,
    job_id)
SELECT employee_seq.NEXTVAL, first_name, last_name, email, hire_date, '
    IT_PROG'
FROM candidates
WHERE status = 'Hired';
```

In this scenario:

- The SELECT query retrieves data from the candidates table.
- The employee_id is set using a sequence (employee_seq.NEXTVAL) to generate a unique identifier.
- Only candidates with a status of 'Hired' are selected for insertion.

This method is valuable for bulk data migration or transformation tasks where data from one table is inserted into another based on specific criteria.

Handling NULL Values

Columns may permit NULL values unless explicitly defined as NOT NULL. Insertion can either provide NULL explicitly or omit the column from the list if it has a default value or allows NULL values:

```
INSERT INTO employees (employee_id, first_name, last_name, email, hire_date)
VALUES (104, 'Alice', 'Green', 'alice.green@example.com', TO_DATE('2023-10-04', '
    YYYY-MM-DD'));
```

Here, the job_id is omitted, implicitly setting it to NULL.

Mastering the INSERT statement and its various applications is crucial for effective data management in Oracle Databases. This knowledge forms the bedrock for more advanced data manipulation techniques, ensuring the integrity and precision of data operations.

3.12 Updating and Deleting Data

Updating and deleting data are critical operations in any database environment. These operations allow for the modification and removal of records, ensuring that the database remains dynamic and current. Understanding how to efficiently update and delete data contributes to maintaining database integrity and performance.

The UPDATE and DELETE statements in SQL are used to modify existing records and remove unwanted records, respectively. It is important to use these operations cautiously, especially in a production environment, to prevent accidental data loss or corruption.

Updating Data with the UPDATE Statement

The UPDATE statement is employed to modify existing records in a table. The syntax for the UPDATE statement is straightforward:

```
UPDATE table_name
SET column1 = value1, column2 = value2, ...
WHERE condition;
```

- table_name: Specifies the table containing the records to be updated. - column1, column2, ...: Indicates the columns to be updated. - value1, value2, ...: Denotes the new values to be assigned to the columns. - condition: Defines which records should be updated. Omitting the WHERE clause will update all records in the table.

Consider a table named employees with the following structure:

```
+-------------+------------+-----------+----------+
| employee_id | first_name | last_name | salary   |
+-------------+------------+-----------+----------+
|           1 | John       | Doe       | 60000    |
|           2 | Jane       | Smith     | 70000    |
|           3 | Alice      | Brown     | 80000    |
+-------------+------------+-----------+----------+
```

To increase the salary of the employee with employee_id 1 to 65000, the UPDATE statement is used as follows:

```
UPDATE employees
SET salary = 65000
WHERE employee_id = 1;
```

Executing this statement will modify the record for employee 1:

```
+-------------+------------+-----------+----------+
| employee_id | first_name | last_name | salary   |
+-------------+------------+-----------+----------+
|           1 | John       | Doe       | 65000    |
|           2 | Jane       | Smith     | 70000    |
|           3 | Alice      | Brown     | 80000    |
+-------------+------------+-----------+----------+
```

It is essential to ensure the WHERE clause is specific enough to avoid unintended modifications. For instance, omitting the WHERE clause will set the salary for all employees to 65000, which could be detrimental:

```
UPDATE employees
SET salary = 65000;
```

To update multiple columns in a single statement, separate the column-value pairs with commas. For example, to change the first_name and last_name of employee 2:

```
UPDATE employees
SET first_name = 'Janet', last_name = 'Smythe'
WHERE employee_id = 2;
```

Deleting Data with the DELETE Statement

The DELETE statement is used to remove records from a table. The basic syntax for the DELETE statement is:

```
DELETE FROM table_name
WHERE condition;
```

- table_name: Specifies the table from which the records will be deleted.
- condition: Specifies which records should be deleted. Omitting the WHERE clause will delete all records in the table.

Consider the following employees table:

```
+-------------+------------+-----------+----------+
| employee_id | first_name | last_name | salary   |
+-------------+------------+-----------+----------+
|           1 | John       | Doe       | 65000    |
|           2 | Janet      | Smythe    | 70000    |
|           3 | Alice      | Brown     | 80000    |
+-------------+------------+-----------+----------+
```

To delete the record of employee 3, the DELETE statement is executed as follows:

```
DELETE FROM employees
WHERE employee_id = 3;
```

The table will then be:

```
+-------------+------------+-----------+----------+
| employee_id | first_name | last_name | salary   |
+-------------+------------+-----------+----------+
|           1 | John       | Doe       | 65000    |
|           2 | Janet      | Smythe    | 70000    |
+-------------+------------+-----------+----------+
```

Similar to the UPDATE statement, it is crucial to specify an accurate and detailed WHERE clause to avoid deleting more records than intended. For instance, executing a DELETE statement without the WHERE clause will remove all records from the table, resulting in an empty table:

```
DELETE FROM employees;
```

Combining Conditions in UPDATE and DELETE Statements

Both UPDATE and DELETE statements can utilize complex conditions in the WHERE clause to target specific records. SQL supports logical operators such as AND, OR, and NOT to combine multiple conditions.

For example, to update the salary of employees who have a salary less than 70000 and the last name 'Doe':

```
UPDATE employees
SET salary = 70000
WHERE salary < 70000 AND last_name = 'Doe';
```

To delete records of employees who have a salary greater than 75000 or last name 'Brown':

```
DELETE FROM employees
WHERE salary > 75000 OR last_name = 'Brown';
```

This level of specificity provides powerful tools for database management, ensuring precise control over data modifications and deletions. Avoiding broad or ambiguous criteria maintains data integrity and prevents accidental data loss, particularly in large and complex databases.

Chapter 4

Advanced SQL Techniques

This chapter explores sophisticated SQL techniques within the Oracle Database. It includes advanced joins, unions, complex subqueries, hierarchical queries, and analytical functions. Topics such as pivoting data, managing tables and views, and working with large datasets are discussed. Techniques for using cursors, handling advanced data types, optimizing SQL, and error handling are also covered, enhancing the reader's ability to perform complex database operations.

4.1 Advanced Joins and Unions

Advanced SQL techniques in Oracle Database facilitate the handling and manipulation of complex datasets. This section delves into advanced joins and unions, enabling the synthesis of nuanced datasets by leveraging multiple tables efficiently. Understanding these concepts is fundamental for conducting in-depth data analysis and generating comprehensive reports.

Joins are used to combine rows from two or more tables based on a related column between them. In advanced SQL, various types of joins, such as inner joins, outer joins, cross joins, and self joins, are used to fetch data adhering to specific conditions. Additionally, the union operator combines the result sets of two or more queries into a single result set, eliminating any duplicate rows.

Inner Join: An inner join retrieves records that have matching values in both tables. It is the most commonly used join type and is specified using the INNER JOIN clause or simply JOIN.

```
SELECT a.column1, b.column2
FROM table1 a
INNER JOIN table2 b
ON a.common_column = b.common_column;
```

Left (Outer) Join: A left join returns all records from the left table (table1), and the matched records from the right table (table2). The result is NULL on the side where there is no match.

```
SELECT a.column1, b.column2
FROM table1 a
LEFT JOIN table2 b
ON a.common_column = b.common_column;
```

Right (Outer) Join: A right join returns all records from the right table (table2), and the matched records from the left table (table1). The result is NULL on the side where there is no match.

```
SELECT a.column1, b.column2
FROM table1 a
RIGHT JOIN table2 b
ON a.common_column = b.common_column;
```

Full (Outer) Join: A full join returns all records when there is a match in either left (table1) or right (table2) table. Records not matching in either table will display NULL values.

```
SELECT a.column1, b.column2
FROM table1 a
FULL OUTER JOIN table2 b
ON a.common_column = b.common_column;
```

Cross Join: A cross join returns the Cartesian product of the two tables, meaning it returns all possible combinations of rows.

```
SELECT a.column1, b.column2
FROM table1 a
CROSS JOIN table2 b;
```

Self Join: A self join is a regular join but the table is joined with itself. It is useful for querying hierarchical data or comparing rows within the same table.

```
SELECT a.column1, b.column2
FROM table1 a, table1 b
```

```
WHERE a.common_column = b.common_column;
```

Union: The UNION operator combines the result sets of two or more SELECT statements, keeping only distinct values.

```
SELECT column1 FROM table1
UNION
SELECT column2 FROM table2;
```

Union All: The UNION ALL operator is similar to UNION, but it includes all duplicates.

```
SELECT column1 FROM table1
UNION ALL
SELECT column2 FROM table2;
```

Combining joins and unions can intersect complex datasets efficiently. This hybrid approach is useful for creating extensive reporting and analyzing interrelated datasets from different sources.

Given two queries:

```
SELECT a.column1, b.column2
FROM table1 a
INNER JOIN table2 b
ON a.common_column = b.common_column;

SELECT c.column3, d.column4
FROM table3 c
LEFT JOIN table4 d
ON c.common_column = d.common_column;
```

Using UNION:

```
SELECT a.column1, b.column2
FROM table1 a
INNER JOIN table2 b
ON a.common_column = b.common_column

UNION

SELECT c.column3, d.column4
FROM table3 c
LEFT JOIN table4 d
ON c.common_column = d.common_column;
```

This query merges the results of an INNER JOIN and a LEFT JOIN operation into a single result set. Optimum performance and accurate data retrieval are achieved through precise use of join conditions and union operations, which prevent redundant data and ensure meaningful results.

Proficiency in using advanced joins and unions is a significant skill in Oracle Database, offering robust data manipulation capabilities for complex, multi-dimensional analyses.

4.2 Complex Subqueries and Correlated Subqueries

Subqueries, also known as inner queries or nested queries, are a powerful feature in SQL that allow a query to select data based on the result of another query. Subqueries can be categorized into simple subqueries and complex subqueries. The latter includes correlated subqueries, which refer to elements in the outer query and therefore are evaluated once for each row processed by the outer query, making them more sophisticated but also more computationally intensive.

Creating complex subqueries entails leveraging nested SELECT statements to retrieve data based on intricate conditions or aggregations. Complex subqueries can appear in the SELECT, FROM, WHERE, or HAVING clause of an SQL statement.

Consider the following example, where we need to find employees with a salary greater than the average salary of their respective departments. The complex subquery here is used in the WHERE clause:

```
SELECT employee_id, employee_name, salary
FROM employees e
WHERE salary >
      (SELECT AVG(salary)
       FROM employees
       WHERE department_id = e.department_id);
```

In this example, the subquery SELECT AVG(salary) FROM employees WHERE department_id = e.department_id computes the average salary within the same department as each employee. This subquery is executed for each employee to determine whether their salary exceeds their department's average. This is a classic example of a correlated subquery because the inner query depends on the e.department_id value from the outer query.

Another example of a complex subquery is when combining the results of multiple subqueries. Consider finding customers who have placed more orders than the average number of orders placed by all customers:

```
SELECT customer_id, customer_name, total_orders
FROM customers c
```

```
WHERE (SELECT COUNT(order_id)
       FROM orders
       WHERE customer_id = c.customer_id) >
      (SELECT AVG(order_count)
       FROM
           (SELECT customer_id, COUNT(order_id) AS order_count
            FROM orders
            GROUP BY customer_id));
```

Here, the subquery within the WHERE clause calculates the total number of orders for a specific customer and compares it to the average order count per customer calculated in the nested subquery within the FROM clause. The use of nested subqueries allows complex data retrieval operations based on multiple aggregated calculations.

Correlated subqueries can also be used in the SELECT clause to return additional computed columns. For example, we can append the average department salary as a column in our result set:

```
SELECT employee_id, employee_name, salary,
       (SELECT AVG(salary)
        FROM employees
        WHERE department_id = e.department_id) AS avg_dept_salary
FROM employees e;
```

This query includes a correlated subquery in the SELECT clause to compute the average salary for each employee's department and adds it as a column in the result set. The subquery recalculates the department's average salary for each row in the employees' table.

Complex and correlated subqueries can also be employed in data modification operations. For instance, to increase the salary of employees whose salary is below the average salary of their department by 10%, the following SQL statement could be used:

```
UPDATE employees e1
SET salary = salary * 1.10
WHERE salary <
      (SELECT AVG(salary)
       FROM employees e2
       WHERE e1.department_id = e2.department_id);
```

In this update statement, the correlated subquery determines which employees' salaries are increased by 10% based on their department's average salary. This approach ensures only those employees with below-average salaries are affected by the update.

The understanding and use of complex and correlated subqueries greatly enhance the capability to perform sophisticated data retrieval and manipulation tasks in Oracle SQL. By mastering these techniques, users can efficiently handle intricate requirements involving multiple tables, conditions, and aggregates, significantly optimizing the database operations and ensuring accurate results.

4.3 Hierarchical Queries

Hierarchical queries allow the retrieval of data from a self-referential table where rows have a parent-child relationship. In Oracle SQL, the hierarchical query syntax enables the representation of hierarchical data structures directly within SQL queries. Such data is prevalent in organizational structures, bill-of-materials, and tree-structured data.

To construct a hierarchical query, the CONNECT BY clause is used to define the relationship between parent and child rows. The query often starts with the START WITH clause, specifying the root(s) of the hierarchy. The LEVEL pseudo-column can be used to indicate the depth of the hierarchy, starting from 1 for root nodes.

Consider the table EMPLOYEES with columns EMPLOYEE_ID, MANAGER_ID, and NAME, representing an organizational hierarchy:

```
CREATE TABLE EMPLOYEES (
  EMPLOYEE_ID NUMBER PRIMARY KEY,
  MANAGER_ID NUMBER,
  NAME VARCHAR2(100)
);
```

For demonstration, populate this table with sample data:

```
INSERT INTO EMPLOYEES VALUES (1, NULL, 'CEO');
INSERT INTO EMPLOYEES VALUES (2, 1, 'CTO');
INSERT INTO EMPLOYEES VALUES (3, 1, 'CFO');
INSERT INTO EMPLOYEES VALUES (4, 2, 'Engineering Manager');
INSERT INTO EMPLOYEES VALUES (5, 2, 'Technical Lead');
INSERT INTO EMPLOYEES VALUES (6, 4, 'Software Engineer');
INSERT INTO EMPLOYEES VALUES (7, 3, 'Finance Manager');
```

The following query retrieves the hierarchy starting from the CEO:

```
SELECT
  LEVEL,
  EMPLOYEE_ID,
  NAME,
  SYS_CONNECT_BY_PATH(NAME, '/') AS PATH
FROM
  EMPLOYEES
START WITH
  MANAGER_ID IS NULL
CONNECT BY
```

```
PRIOR EMPLOYEE_ID = MANAGER_ID;
```

The output of the above query will be:

```
LEVEL  EMPLOYEE_ID  NAME                 PATH
--------------------------------------------------------------------------
1      1            CEO                  /CEO
2      2            CTO                  /CEO/CTO
3      4            Engineering Manager  /CEO/CTO/Engineering Manager
4      6            Software Engineer    /CEO/CTO/Engineering Manager/Software Engineer
3      5            Technical Lead       /CEO/CTO/Technical Lead
2      3            CFO                  /CEO/CFO
3      7            Finance Manager      /CEO/CFO/Finance Manager
```

LEVEL indicates the depth of each row in the hierarchy. The SYS_-CONNECT_BY_PATH function concatenates the path from the root to the current row, using the specified delimiter.

The direction of traversal can be influenced by the CONNECT BY condition. An important aspect is the PRIOR keyword, indicating a directed relationship between parent and child nodes. For instance, CONNECT BY PRIOR EMPLOYEE_ID = MANAGER_ID navigates from manager to subordinate.

To prevent cycles in hierarchical querying, utilize the NOCYCLE keyword. Omitting NOCYCLE can lead to infinite loops if cyclic relationships are present in the data:

```
SELECT
  LEVEL,
  EMPLOYEE_ID,
  NAME,
  SYS_CONNECT_BY_PATH(NAME, '/') AS PATH
FROM
  EMPLOYEES
START WITH
  MANAGER_ID IS NULL
CONNECT BY NOCYCLE
  PRIOR EMPLOYEE_ID = MANAGER_ID;
```

This query is similar to the previous one but will gracefully handle cycles by terminating the loop and continuing with the next set of relationships.

By employing hierarchical queries, complex structures can be flattened to represent the hierarchy in a tabular format, facilitating analysis and reporting in scenarios where hierarchical data is essential for conveying nested relationships.

When dealing with deeply nested structures, ensure optimal performance by indexing the key columns used in the CONNECT BY clause, such as EMPLOYEE_ID and MANAGER_ID. Proper indexing is crucial for efficient execution of hierarchical queries, particularly with extensive datasets commonly found in enterprise environments.

Hierarchical queries form a vital component of SQL, enabling intuitive operations over data models with built-in parent-child relationships. Employing CONNECT BY, LEVEL, and SYS_CONNECT_BY_PATH, among others, these queries transform hierarchical data into actionable insights.

4.4 Analytical Functions

Analytical functions in Oracle SQL provide powerful capabilities for performing complex calculative and data analysis tasks directly within SQL queries. These functions allow for sophisticated computations over a set of rows, returning a single result for each row. They are particularly useful in scenarios involving ranking, averaging, summing, and performing statistical calculations across result sets without the need for complex subqueries or procedural code.

Analytical functions are evaluated after the FROM, WHERE, GROUP BY, and HAVING clauses but before the ORDER BY clause, preserving the sequence of rows. The basic syntax for an analytical function is as follows:

$$\text{analytic\_function\_name(arguments)} \quad \text{OVER} \quad \text{(analytic\_clause)}$$

The analytic_clause can further be broken down into four main components:

- **Partitioning Clause**
- **Ordering Clause**
- **Windowing Clause**
- **Window Frame Clause**

Partitioning Clause: The PARTITION BY clause defines how the result set is divided into partitions, within which the analytical function is applied independently. For example:

```
SELECT employee_id, department_id, salary,
RANK() OVER (PARTITION BY department_id ORDER BY salary DESC) AS
    sal_rank
FROM employees;
```

This query ranks employees within each department based on their salary in descending order.

Ordering Clause: The ORDER BY clause specifies the order in which data is processed within each partition. For example:

```
SELECT employee_id, department_id, salary,
SUM(salary) OVER (ORDER BY salary) AS cumulative_salary
FROM employees;
```

This query calculates a cumulative sum of salaries ordered by salary across the entire dataset.

Windowing Clause: The ROWS or RANGE clause, sometimes referred to as the window frame, defines the set of rows used for calculations for each row in the partition. By default, this considers all rows within a partition.

Types of Analytical Functions:

Ranking Functions:

- RANK(): Assigns a rank to each row within a partition, with gaps in ranks where there are ties.
- DENSE_RANK(): Similar to RANK(), but without gaps in ranks.
- ROW_NUMBER(): Assigns a unique sequential integer to rows within a partition.

Example:

```
SELECT employee_id, department_id, salary,
ROW_NUMBER() OVER (PARTITION BY department_id ORDER BY salary DESC
    ) AS row_num
FROM employees;
```

This assigns sequential numbers to employees within their departments based on salary in descending order.

Aggregate Functions:

- SUM(): Calculates the sum.
- AVG(): Computes the average.
- MIN() and MAX(): Return the minimum and maximum values, respectively.

Example:

```
SELECT employee_id, department_id, salary,
SUM(salary) OVER (PARTITION BY department_id ORDER BY salary DESC) AS
    cumulative_salary
FROM employees;
```

This computes a running total of salaries within each department in descending salary order.

Window Functions:

- LAG(): Accesses data from a previous row within the same result set.
- LEAD(): Provides access to subsequent rows.
- FIRST_VALUE() and LAST_VALUE(): Return the first and last value in an ordered set.

Example:

```
SELECT employee_id, department_id, salary,
LAG(salary, 1, 0) OVER (PARTITION BY department_id ORDER BY salary) AS
    previous_salary
FROM employees;
```

This retrieves the salary from the previous row within each department, with a default value of 0 if there is no previous row.

Statistical Functions:

- STDDEV(): Computes the standard deviation.
- VARIANCE(): Calculates the variance of a set of rows.

Example:

```
SELECT department_id,
STDDEV(salary) OVER (PARTITION BY department_id) AS salary_stddev
FROM employees;
```

This calculates the standard deviation of salaries within each department.

Practical Usage: Analytical functions can be nested within other SQL constructs such as views, subqueries, and inline views to produce complex analytical queries without excessive code. They are particularly useful in business intelligence and reporting applications, enabling quick and efficient data analysis.

Example:

```
SELECT department_id, last_name, salary, avg_salary,
CASE
    WHEN salary < avg_salary THEN 'Below Average'
    WHEN salary = avg_salary THEN 'Average'
    ELSE 'Above Average'
END AS salary_level
FROM (
    SELECT department_id, last_name, salary,
    AVG(salary) OVER (PARTITION BY department_id) AS avg_salary
    FROM employees
) e;
```

This nested query categorizes employee salaries compared to the departmental average.

4.5 Pivot and Unpivot Operations

Pivot and unpivot operations transform data sets, facilitating powerful data analyses and reporting in Oracle databases. Pivoting data rotates row data into columnar format, thus improving readability and data structuring for various analytical tasks. Conversely, unpivoting transposes columns back into rows, enabling valid normalization and simplified processing.

Pivot Operations

The pivot operation in SQL is an explicit mechanism to convert data from rows to columns. This action is particularly useful when dealing with summarized data, transforming it into a format appropriate for reporting tools or dashboards.

Consider a table sales capturing quarterly sales data:

```
CREATE TABLE sales (
    product_id NUMBER,
    quarter VARCHAR2(2),
    sales_amount NUMBER
);

INSERT INTO sales VALUES (1, 'Q1', 100);
INSERT INTO sales VALUES (1, 'Q2', 150);
INSERT INTO sales VALUES (1, 'Q3', 200);
INSERT INTO sales VALUES (1, 'Q4', 250);
INSERT INTO sales VALUES (2, 'Q1', 300);
INSERT INTO sales VALUES (2, 'Q2', 350);
INSERT INTO sales VALUES (2, 'Q3', 400);
INSERT INTO sales VALUES (2, 'Q4', 450);
```

To pivot this data, converting row values under the quarter column into separate columns (Q1, Q2, Q3, Q4):

```
SELECT product_id, Q1, Q2, Q3, Q4
FROM (
    SELECT product_id, quarter, sales_amount
    FROM sales
)
PIVOT(
    MAX(sales_amount)
    FOR quarter IN ('Q1' AS Q1, 'Q2' AS Q2, 'Q3' AS Q3, 'Q4' AS Q4)
);
```

The resulting output organizes sales data with each quarter represented as a distinct column:

```
PRODUCT_ID  Q1   Q2   Q3   Q4
---------- ---- ---- ---- ----
    1       100  150  200  250
    2       300  350  400  450
```

Key elements of this transformation include the subquery, which retrieves the relevant columns (product_id, quarter, sales_amount), and the PIVOT clause, specifying the aggregation function MAX() and target columns.

Unpivot Operations

Unpivot operations reverse the effects of pivot operations, converting columns back into rows. This operation is vital for data preparation, enabling further normalization and simplified manipulation in subsequent processes.

Given the pivoted sales data, unpivoting it would return to its original tabular form:

```
CREATE TABLE pivoted_sales (
    product_id NUMBER,
    Q1 NUMBER,
    Q2 NUMBER,
    Q3 NUMBER,
    Q4 NUMBER
);

INSERT INTO pivoted_sales VALUES (1, 100, 150, 200, 250);
INSERT INTO pivoted_sales VALUES (2, 300, 350, 400, 450);
```

To unpivot this data:

```
SELECT product_id, quarter, sales_amount
FROM pivoted_sales
UNPIVOT (
    sales_amount FOR quarter IN (Q1 AS 'Q1', Q2 AS 'Q2', Q3 AS 'Q3', Q4 AS 'Q4')
);
```

This command yields the original sales dataset:

```
PRODUCT_ID QUARTER SALES_AMOUNT
---------- ------- ------------
         1 Q1      100
         1 Q2      150
         1 Q3      200
         1 Q4      250
         2 Q1      300
         2 Q2      350
         2 Q3      400
         2 Q4      450
```

In the unpivot process, the UNPIVOT clause reconfigures data, explicitly mapping columns (Q1, Q2, Q3, Q4) back into row values under the quarter column. This inverse transformation is critical to return pivoted data to its relational, row-based structure.

Practical Considerations

- *Performance*: Pivot and unpivot operations can be resource-intensive, especially with significant datasets. Optimization strategies include indexing critical columns and minimizing intermediate data redundancy. - *Data Integrity*: Ensure null and empty values are correctly managed, as they can heavily influence the transformational logic's correctness. - *Aggregation Functions*: Non-summarized columns necessitate defined aggregation functions (e.g., SUM(), AVG()) to avoid logical errors and maintain consistent results.

Consider the pivotal role these operations play in data warehousing and business intelligence environments, where data is frequently restructured for reporting and analytical applications. Understanding and correctly utilizing pivot and unpivot functions drive more effective data management and insightful data-driven decisions.

4.6 Table and View Management

Effective table and view management are fundamental skills for any database administrator or developer working with Oracle databases. This section delves into the creation, maintenance, and optimization of tables and views, key operations that underpin advanced SQL techniques.

Creating and Managing Tables

Tables are the basic unit of data storage in Oracle databases. A table is defined by a set of columns and constraints, with each column having a specified data type. The standard SQL command to create a table is the CREATE TABLE statement.

```
CREATE TABLE employees (
    employee_id NUMBER PRIMARY KEY,
    first_name VARCHAR2(50),
    last_name VARCHAR2(50),
    email VARCHAR2(100) UNIQUE,
    hire_date DATE,
    salary NUMBER(8, 2),
    department_id NUMBER
);
```

This command defines a table named employees with seven columns. The employee_id column is specified as the primary key, and the email column is unique. Proper definition of columns and constraints is crucial for data integrity and performance optimization.

Altering Tables

Tables are often subject to changes as the database evolves. The ALTER TABLE statement allows modification of an existing table structure without dropping and re-creating the table. Common operations include adding, deleting, and modifying columns:

```
ALTER TABLE employees
ADD phone_number VARCHAR2(20);

ALTER TABLE employees
MODIFY salary NUMBER(10, 2);

ALTER TABLE employees
DROP COLUMN phone_number;
```

These commands add a column (phone_number), modify the data type of an existing column (salary), and drop a column (phone_number).

Dropping Tables

Dropping a table permanently removes the table's structure and data from the database. Use the DROP TABLE statement with caution:

```
DROP TABLE employees;
```

Be aware that this action cannot be undone, and all data within the table will be lost.

Creating and Managing Views

Views are virtual tables representing the result of a query. They do not store data themselves but provide a way to encapsulate complex queries, enhance security, and simplify data access. The CREATE VIEW statement is used to define a view:

```
CREATE VIEW employee_details AS
```

```
SELECT e.employee_id,
       e.first_name,
       e.last_name,
       e.email,
       d.department_name
FROM employees e
JOIN departments d ON e.department_id = d.department_id;
```

This view, employee_details, encapsulates a join operation between the employees and departments tables, making it easier for users to query employee information along with their respective department names.

Altering Views

Views can be altered by redefining them using the CREATE OR REPLACE VIEW statement. This allows changes to the view's query without dropping it:

```
CREATE OR REPLACE VIEW employee_details AS
SELECT e.employee_id,
       e.first_name,
       e.last_name,
       e.email
FROM employees e;
```

This command redefines the employee_details view, now excluding the department_name column.

Dropping Views

Dropping a view is straightforward and can be done using the DROP VIEW statement:

```
DROP VIEW employee_details;
```

This removes the view from the database, but the underlying data in the referenced tables remains intact.

Indexed Views

In Oracle, materialized views (also known as indexed views) store the actual data returned by the query, rather than just the query itself. They can significantly improve performance for complex queries that aggregate large amounts of data:

```
CREATE MATERIALIZED VIEW emp_dept_summary
AS
SELECT d.department_id,
       d.department_name,
       COUNT(e.employee_id) AS employee_count,
       AVG(e.salary) AS avg_salary
FROM employees e
JOIN departments d ON e.department_id = d.department_id
GROUP BY d.department_id, d.department_name;
```

Materialized views like emp_dept_summary are periodically refreshed to keep the data current. The refresh can be automatic or manual, depending on the application need.

Maintaining Materialized Views

Proper maintenance of materialized views is essential for data accuracy and performance. This can involve setting up periodic refreshes and ensuring that the view's query is optimized. The following command sets a materialized view to refresh daily:

```
CREATE MATERIALIZED VIEW emp_dept_summary
REFRESH COMPLETE START WITH SYSDATE NEXT SYSDATE + 1
AS
SELECT d.department_id,
       d.department_name,
       COUNT(e.employee_id) AS employee_count,
       AVG(e.salary) AS avg_salary
FROM employees e
JOIN departments d ON e.department_id = d.department_id
GROUP BY d.department_id, d.department_name;
```

This configuration specifies that the emp_dept_summary materialized view should be completely refreshed every day.

Querying Views

Querying data from a view is identical to querying data from a table. This makes views a powerful tool for simplifying query complexity and improving security by controlling access to specific data:

```
SELECT * FROM employee_details
WHERE last_name = 'Smith';
```

Such practices ensure data consistency while abstracting the complexity of underlying tables.

Accurate table and view management are indispensable for maintaining the integrity, performance, and efficiency of databases. Mastery of these operations supports robust database design and streamlined data retrieval.

4.7 Manipulating Large Data Sets

Managing and manipulating large datasets efficiently is paramount in any enterprise environment where data volume can pose significant challenges. Employing SQL in Oracle to handle substantial amounts of data requires an in-depth understanding of efficient techniques and strategies to minimize resource consumption and maximize performance.

Bulk Collect and Forall

One effective method to handle large datasets in Oracle is using *Bulk Collect* and *Forall* constructs within PL/SQL. These constructs allow the processing of multiple rows in a single fetch, reducing the context switches between SQL and PL/SQL engines.

```
DECLARE
    TYPE t_employee_ids IS TABLE OF employees.employee_id%TYPE;
    l_employee_ids t_employee_ids;
BEGIN
    SELECT employee_id
    BULK COLLECT INTO l_employee_ids
    FROM employees;

    FORALL i IN l_employee_ids.FIRST..l_employee_ids.LAST
        UPDATE employees
        SET salary = salary * 1.10
        WHERE employee_id = l_employee_ids(i);
END;
```

The example above demonstrates how *Bulk Collect* fetches multiple rows into a PL/SQL collection and *Forall* subsequently processes the collection with a single context switch.

Partitioning

Partitioning is another crucial technique when handling large tables. By dividing a table into smaller, more manageable pieces, Oracle optimizes the performance and maintenance of large datasets. There are various partitioning methods, including range, list, hash, and composite.

```
CREATE TABLE sales (
    sale_id NUMBER NOT NULL,
    sale_date DATE NOT NULL,
    amount NUMBER
)
PARTITION BY RANGE (sale_date) (
    PARTITION sales_q1 VALUES LESS THAN (TO_DATE('01-APR-2023', 'DD-
        MON-YYYY')),
    PARTITION sales_q2 VALUES LESS THAN (TO_DATE('01-JUL-2023', 'DD-
        MON-YYYY')),
    PARTITION sales_q3 VALUES LESS THAN (TO_DATE('01-OCT-2023', 'DD-
        MON-YYYY')),
    PARTITION sales_q4 VALUES LESS THAN (TO_DATE('01-JAN-2024', 'DD-
        MON-YYYY'))
);
```

Range partitioning enables segmenting the sales table by quarters, each partition containing data for respective quarters. Queries that filter by sale_date can quickly access the relevant partition, improving query performance.

Parallel Execution

For scenarios involving massive queries or updates, leveraging Oracle's parallel execution capabilities can drastically decrease processing time by distributing the workload across multiple CPUs.

```
ALTER SESSION ENABLE PARALLEL DML;

SELECT /*+ PARALLEL(employees, 4) */
    employee_id, first_name, last_name, salary
FROM employees
ORDER BY salary DESC;
```

The hint PARALLEL(employees, 4) specifies that the operation on the employees table should use four parallel execution servers.

Materialized Views

Materialized views can significantly enhance performance when dealing with large datasets by storing the result of a query and periodically refreshing the data. They are particularly useful for queries that aggregate or join large volumes of data.

```
CREATE MATERIALIZED VIEW sales_summary
BUILD IMMEDIATE
REFRESH FAST ON COMMIT
AS
SELECT product_id, SUM(amount) as total_sales, COUNT(*)
FROM sales
GROUP BY product_id;
```

This sales_summary materialized view stores the aggregated sales data and ensures it is refreshed immediately upon any transaction commit affecting the sales table.

Indexing Strategies

Appropriate indexing on large tables can yield substantial performance benefits. Composite indexes, bitmap indexes, and function-based indexes are some advanced options that may be applied to large databases to optimize searches and joins.

```
CREATE INDEX idx_employee_name
ON employees (last_name, first_name);
```

A composite index on last_name and first_name enhances search efficiencies for queries filtering by both columns.

Manipulating Large Data With SQL Loader

Oracle SQL*Loader efficiently loads external data into Oracle Database. It is particularly beneficial for handling bulk imports of data.

```
sqlldr userid=your_username/your_password control=loader.ctl
```

An essential component is the control file (loader.ctl) specifying how to parse and insert the data.

```
LOAD DATA
INFILE 'data.csv'
INTO TABLE employees
FIELDS TERMINATED BY ','
(employee_id, first_name, last_name, hire_date, salary)
```

Using SQL*Loader can lead to substantial time savings compared to conventional insert operations for large datasets.

As these techniques and tools illustrate, managing and manipulating large datasets within Oracle Database involves a blend of efficient SQL coding practices, strategic use of database features, and leveraging the computational power inherent in Oracle's architecture.

4.8 Using Cursors in SQL

Using cursors in SQL is essential for handling query results that return multiple rows. A cursor allows row-by-row processing of query results, which is particularly useful for operations where set-based processing is either insufficient or impossible. This section details the types of cursors, how to declare and use them, and offers examples to elucidate the concepts.

A cursor is essentially a pointer to the result set of a query. The main types of cursors include:

- **Implicit Cursors**: Automatically created by Oracle whenever an SQL statement is executed.
- **Explicit Cursors**: Defined and controlled by the programmer for processing individual rows returned by a query.

Implicit cursors are straightforward and require minimal coding effort. They are handled automatically by the Oracle engine during SQL operations like INSERT, UPDATE, DELETE, or SELECT INTO. However, explicit cursors provide greater control and flexibility, allowing operations to be performed on each row individually.

To declare and use an explicit cursor, follow these steps:

- **Declare the Cursor**: State the SELECT statement that will be executed.
- **Open the Cursor**: Execute the query and establish the result set.
- **Fetch from the Cursor**: Retrieve the rows in the result set one at a time.
- **Close the Cursor**: Release the cursor resources.

Here is an example of how to declare and use an explicit cursor in PL/SQL:

```
DECLARE
   CURSOR emp_cursor IS
      SELECT employee_id, first_name, last_name, salary
      FROM employees
      WHERE department_id = 10;

   v_employee_id employees.employee_id%TYPE;
   v_first_name employees.first_name%TYPE;
   v_last_name employees.last_name%TYPE;
   v_salary employees.salary%TYPE;
BEGIN
   OPEN emp_cursor;
   LOOP
      FETCH emp_cursor INTO v_employee_id, v_first_name, v_last_name,
            v_salary;
      EXIT WHEN emp_cursor%NOTFOUND;

      DBMS_OUTPUT.PUT_LINE('ID: ' || v_employee_id || ' Name: ' ||
            v_first_name || ' ' || v_last_name || ' Salary: ' || v_salary);
   END LOOP;
   CLOSE emp_cursor;
END;
```

In the example above:

- DECLARE section is used to define the cursor and the variables for holding the fetched values.
- The OPEN statement executes the SELECT query, and prepares the result set for fetching.
- A LOOP with FETCH retrieves each row from the cursor and assigns the values to the declared variables. The loop exits when there are no more rows to fetch, determined by emp_cursor%NOTFOUND.

- CLOSE statement releases the cursor, freeing up system resources.

Explicit cursors also support cursor attributes, which provide additional information about the cursor state. Key cursor attributes include:

- %ISOPEN: Returns TRUE if the cursor is open.
- %NOTFOUND: Returns TRUE if the last fetch did not return a row.
- %FOUND: Returns TRUE if the last fetch returned a row.
- %ROWCOUNT: Returns the number of rows fetched so far.

Another powerful feature is the use of parameterized cursors, which allow the passing of variables to the cursor's query. This is beneficial when the cursor needs to be reused with different criteria. Here is an example of a parameterized cursor:

```
DECLARE
  CURSOR emp_cursor (p_department_id NUMBER) IS
    SELECT employee_id, first_name, last_name, salary
    FROM employees
    WHERE department_id = p_department_id;

  v_employee_id employees.employee_id%TYPE;
  v_first_name employees.first_name%TYPE;
  v_last_name employees.last_name%TYPE;
  v_salary employees.salary%TYPE;
BEGIN
  OPEN emp_cursor(20);
  LOOP
    FETCH emp_cursor INTO v_employee_id, v_first_name, v_last_name,
        v_salary;
    EXIT WHEN emp_cursor%NOTFOUND;

    DBMS_OUTPUT.PUT_LINE('ID: ' || v_employee_id || ' Name: ' ||
        v_first_name || ' ' || v_last_name || ' Salary: ' || v_salary);
  END LOOP;
  CLOSE emp_cursor;
END;
```

In the parameterized cursor example:

- The cursor emp_cursor is declared with a parameter p_department_id.
- The cursor is opened with the department ID 20, enabling dynamic row fetching based on this parameter.

Cursors are indispensable for procedural logic within PL/SQL, enabling granular control over query results. Proper management of cursors, including ensuring they are closed after use, is vital for memory management and resource utilization within Oracle Database applications.

4.9 Advanced Data Types

Oracle Database supports a variety of complex data types beyond the standard number, date, and varchar2 types. Advanced data types allow for the representation of more complex structures, such as collections, object types, and large objects (LOBs), which are essential for handling sophisticated database designs and operations.

Collections: Collections in Oracle are composite data types that serve to hold multiple values of the same type. Collections can be of three types: nested tables, varrays (variable-size arrays), and associative arrays.

Nested Tables: These are unordered collections that can be stored in database columns. Each element in a nested table is stored in a separate row in a storage table.

```
CREATE TYPE NumList AS TABLE OF NUMBER;
/
CREATE TABLE orders (
  order_id NUMBER,
  product_ids NumList
) NESTED TABLE product_ids STORE AS product_tab;
```

When a query is executed, the nested table values can be manipulated using operations like CAST and table functions. For example:

```
SELECT o.order_id, p.COLUMN_VALUE AS product_id
FROM orders o, TABLE(CAST(o.product_ids AS NumList)) p;
```

Varrays: Varrays, or variable-size arrays, have a maximum specified number of elements. They store elements in the order they are added, and this order is preserved.

```
CREATE TYPE VarChar2List AS VARRAY(10) OF VARCHAR2(50);
/
CREATE TABLE students (
  student_id NUMBER,
  courses VarChar2List
);
```

Data in varrays is accessed and modified in-place using SQL operations:

```
INSERT INTO students VALUES (1, VarChar2List('Math', 'Science'));
SELECT s.student_id, c.COLUMN_VALUE AS course
FROM students s, TABLE(s.courses) c;
```

Associative Arrays: Unlike nested tables and varrays, associative arrays (formerly index-by tables) are only available in PL/SQL and are not stored in the database. They offer a flexible and efficient means of handling collections indexed by either numbers or strings.

```
DECLARE
  TYPE AssocArray IS TABLE OF VARCHAR2(50) INDEX BY PLS_INTEGER;
  courses AssocArray;
BEGIN
  courses(1) := 'Math';
  courses(2) := 'Science';

  FOR idx IN 1..courses.COUNT LOOP
    DBMS_OUTPUT.PUT_LINE(courses(idx));
  END LOOP;
END;
```

Object Types: Object types allow the creation of complex data structures that include both attributes (data) and methods (procedures/functions) to operate on the data. This approach is fundamental for implementing object-relational database design.

```
CREATE TYPE Address AS OBJECT (
  street VARCHAR2(50),
  city VARCHAR2(50),
  state VARCHAR2(2),
  zip_code VARCHAR2(10)
);
/
CREATE TYPE Employee AS OBJECT (
  emp_id NUMBER,
  name VARCHAR2(100),
  address Address,
  MEMBER FUNCTION get_full_address RETURN VARCHAR2
);
```

Methods within object types can be defined using specific member functions.

```
CREATE TYPE BODY Employee AS
  MEMBER FUNCTION get_full_address RETURN VARCHAR2 IS
  BEGIN
    RETURN address.street || ', ' || address.city || ', ' ||
           address.state || ' ' || address.zip_code;
  END;
END;
```

To utilize these object types within a table:

```
CREATE TABLE employees (
  emp Employee
);
INSERT INTO employees VALUES (Employee(1, 'John Doe',
  Address('123 Main St', 'Anytown', 'CA', '12345')));
```

Advanced data types enhance the ability to handle complex and hierarchical data models in Oracle Database environments, enabling refined data relationships and operations.

4.10 SQL Optimization Techniques

SQL optimization is an essential skill for ensuring high performance and efficiency in an Oracle Database environment. This section delves into various techniques and practices aimed at enhancing the execution speed and resource utilization of SQL queries.

A fundamental concept in SQL optimization is understanding and interpreting the **execution plan**, which Oracle generates to represent the steps it will take to execute a query. The plan includes operations like table scans, index usage, joins, and sorts. Grasping the nuances of these operations can significantly impact optimization strategies.

To examine an execution plan, the EXPLAIN PLAN statement is used. It provides a detailed breakdown of the query execution steps:

```
EXPLAIN PLAN FOR
SELECT * FROM employees e, departments d
WHERE e.department_id = d.department_id;
```

To visualize the execution plan, one can query the PLAN_TABLE:

```
SELECT * FROM TABLE(DBMS_XPLAN.DISPLAY);
```

Useful metrics such as COST, CARDINALITY, and BYTES in the execution plan help infer the resource requirements and potential performance efficacy.

```
-----------------------------------------------------------------------------------
| Id  | Operation              | Name        | Rows  | Bytes | Cost (%CPU)| Time     |
-----------------------------------------------------------------------------------
|   0 | SELECT STATEMENT       |             |   107 |  5885 |    18   (0)| 00:00:01 |
|*  1 |  HASH JOIN             |             |   107 |  5885 |    18   (0)| 00:00:01 |
|   2 |   TABLE ACCESS FULL    | DEPARTMENTS |    27 |   621 |     3   (0)| 00:00:01 |
|   3 |   TABLE ACCESS FULL    | EMPLOYEES   |   107 |  2140 |    14   (0)| 00:00:01 |
-----------------------------------------------------------------------------------
```

Analyzing this plan, one identifies that a HASH JOIN operation takes place, indicating a join condition favorable for such a method, often efficient for medium-sized datasets.

Indexing is another pivotal optimization technique. Properly utilized indexes reduce the amount of data to be scanned, greatly enhancing query performance. Oracle supports several types of indexes, including:

- - **B-trees**: Optimal for high-cardinality columns.
- - **Bitmap indexes**: Suitable for low-cardinality columns.
- - **Function-based indexes**: Useful when querying with expressions.

Consider indexing to optimize a query. For example, creating an index on the department_id column:

```
CREATE INDEX idx_department_id ON employees(department_id);
```

Once this index is in place, a query filtering by department_id can benefit from reduced scan times.

Query rewriting involves transforming a query into a more efficient version without compromising the results. Common practices include:

- **Using EXISTS** over IN for subqueries when dealing with large datasets. - **Applying join predicates and filters as early as possible in the execution plan.**

A practical example contrasts a typical subquery with its more efficient form using EXISTS:

```
-- Suboptimal query with IN
SELECT * FROM employees
WHERE department_id IN (SELECT department_id FROM departments WHERE
      location_id = 1700);

-- Optimized query with EXISTS
SELECT * FROM employees e
WHERE EXISTS (
  SELECT 1
  FROM departments d
  WHERE e.department_id = d.department_id AND d.location_id = 1700);
```

In the optimized query, using EXISTS allows the database to terminate the subquery once a match is found, thereby saving execution time.

Partitioning large tables and indexes is another technique that can significantly enhance performance, especially with queries that target specific range partitions. Oracle supports various partitioning methods:

- - **Range partitioning**: Useful for date ranges.
- - **List partitioning**: Ideal for a set of discrete values.
- - **Hash partitioning**: Suitable for evenly distributing load across partitions.

An example of range partitioning:

```
CREATE TABLE sales (
  sale_id NUMBER,
  sale_date DATE,
  amount NUMBER
)
PARTITION BY RANGE (sale_date) (
  PARTITION sales_q1 VALUES LESS THAN (TO_DATE('01-APR-2023', 'DD-MON-
       YYYY')),
  PARTITION sales_q2 VALUES LESS THAN (TO_DATE('01-JUL-2023', 'DD-MON-
       YYYY')),
  PARTITION sales_q3 VALUES LESS THAN (TO_DATE('01-OCT-2023', 'DD-MON
       -YYYY')),
  PARTITION sales_q4 VALUES LESS THAN (TO_DATE('01-JAN-2024', 'DD-MON-
       YYYY'))
);
```

Additionally, leveraging **Oracle optimizer hints** can influence the execution path chosen by the SQL optimizer. Hints are directives specified in comments within the query to alter its processing strategy.

For instance, to force the use of a specific index:

```
SELECT /*+ INDEX(e idx_department_id) */ *
FROM employees e
WHERE department_id = 10;
```

Employing hints judiciously can guide the optimizer to more efficient query plans, but it's crucial to use them with deep understanding of the underlying data and workloads.

Finally, **Database statistics gathering** is critical. The Oracle optimizer relies on up-to-date statistics to make informed decisions. Automating statistics collection ensures that these are regularly refreshed:

```
BEGIN
  DBMS_STATS.GATHER_SCHEMA_STATS('HR', cascade => TRUE);
END;
```

Through these techniques—interpreting execution plans, indexing, query rewriting, partitioning, using optimizer hints, and regularly gathering statistics—developers and database administrators can significantly optimize SQL queries, contributing to the overall performance and efficiency of Oracle databases.

4.11 Error Handling and Debugging in SQL

Effective error handling and debugging are essential skills for any practitioner working with SQL and Oracle databases. This section delves into the mechanisms and best practices for managing errors and debugging SQL code to ensure robust and resilient database applications.

Oracle SQL provides a variety of tools and techniques for error handling and debugging, including exceptions handling, the use of built-in error functions, and the DBMS_OUTPUT package for debugging output. Understanding how to utilize these resources efficiently can greatly enhance the reliability and maintainability of SQL scripts.

Exceptions handling in Oracle SQL is primarily facilitated through the use of PL/SQL blocks. Within these blocks, exceptions can be caught and managed using the EXCEPTION section. To illustrate this, consider the following PL/SQL block that attempts to divide a number by zero, capturing the resulting exception:

```
DECLARE
  num1 NUMBER := 10;
  num2 NUMBER := 0;
  result NUMBER;
BEGIN
  result := num1 / num2;
EXCEPTION
  WHEN ZERO_DIVIDE THEN
    DBMS_OUTPUT.PUT_LINE('Error: Division by zero encountered.');
END;
/
```

In this example, the ZERO_DIVIDE exception is specifically caught, and a user-friendly message is output using the DBMS_OUTPUT.PUT_LINE procedure. This approach ensures that the script fails gracefully, providing meaningful feedback instead of an abrupt termination.

The EXCEPTION section can handle multiple error types. A comprehensive handling mechanism could look like this:

```
DECLARE
  val1 NUMBER := 100;
  val2 NUMBER := NULL;
  result NUMBER;
BEGIN
  result := val1 / val2;
EXCEPTION
  WHEN ZERO_DIVIDE THEN
    DBMS_OUTPUT.PUT_LINE('Error: Division by zero encountered.');
  WHEN VALUE_ERROR THEN
    DBMS_OUTPUT.PUT_LINE('Error: Invalid value encountered.');
```

```
  WHEN OTHERS THEN
    DBMS_OUTPUT.PUT_LINE('Error: An unexpected error has occurred.');
END;
/
```

Here, the VALUE_ERROR exception is also managed, which handles scenarios where operations involve invalid or null values. The WHEN OTHERS clause acts as a catch-all for any other exceptions not explicitly handled, ensuring no error goes unnoticed.

Beyond exception handling, Oracle's DBMS_OUTPUT package serves as a valuable tool for debugging. By using DBMS_OUTPUT.PUT_LINE, developers can output variable values and informative messages at crucial points in the script:

```
DECLARE
  num1 NUMBER := 20;
  num2 NUMBER := 5;
  result NUMBER;
BEGIN
  DBMS_OUTPUT.PUT_LINE('Starting calculation...');
  DBMS_OUTPUT.PUT_LINE('num1: ' || num1 || ' num2: ' || num2);
  result := num1 / num2;
  DBMS_OUTPUT.PUT_LINE('Result: ' || result);
EXCEPTION
  WHEN OTHERS THEN
    DBMS_OUTPUT.PUT_LINE('Error encountered during calculation.');
END;
/
```

Incorporating such debug outputs can trace the script's execution flow and isolate issues effectively. Additionally, SQL error functions like SQLCODE and SQLERRM provide detailed information about errors. SQLCODE returns the error number, while SQLERRM returns the associated message. These functions can enhance exception messages, making them more descriptive:

```
DECLARE
  num1 NUMBER := 20;
  num2 NUMBER := 0;
  result NUMBER;
BEGIN
  result := num1 / num2;
EXCEPTION
  WHEN OTHERS THEN
    DBMS_OUTPUT.PUT_LINE('Error ' || SQLCODE || ': ' || SQLERRM);
END;
/
```

This technique not only captures the error but also provides the SQL error code and message, aiding in swift diagnosis and resolution.

To further refine the debugging process, Oracle SQL Developer offers a rich suite of tools, including breakpoints, variable watches, and step execution similar to those found in standard IDEs. This integrated environment allows for intricate analysis and fine-tuning of SQL scripts.

Lastly, logging mechanisms can be employed to persist error information, facilitating long-term monitoring and analysis. Implementing logging involves custom procedures to write error details to a logging table:

```
CREATE TABLE error_log (
  error_date DATE,
  error_code NUMBER,
  error_message VARCHAR2(4000)
);

CREATE OR REPLACE PROCEDURE log_error(p_code NUMBER, p_message
     VARCHAR2) IS
BEGIN
  INSERT INTO error_log (error_date, error_code, error_message)
  VALUES (SYSDATE, p_code, p_message);
  COMMIT;
END;
/
```

Within the main PL/SQL block, call this logging procedure upon error detection:

```
DECLARE
  num1 NUMBER := 30;
  num2 NUMBER := 0;
  result NUMBER;
BEGIN
  result := num1 / num2;
EXCEPTION
  WHEN OTHERS THEN
    log_error(SQLCODE, SQLERRM);
    DBMS_OUTPUT.PUT_LINE('Error logged: ' || SQLERRM);
END;
/
```

Overall, a structured approach to error handling and debugging fosters robust and resilient database operations, enabling developers to identify, manage, and rectify errors efficiently.

Chapter 5

PL/SQL Programming

This chapter covers the essentials of PL/SQL programming within Oracle Database. It introduces the PL/SQL block structure, variables, data types, and control structures. The chapter further explores creating procedures, functions, cursors, and handling exceptions. Additionally, it delves into modular programming with packages, triggers, dynamic SQL execution, and best practices for error handling and optimization, equipping readers with a comprehensive understanding of PL/SQL development.

5.1 Introduction to PL/SQL

PL/SQL, which stands for Procedural Language extensions to SQL, is Oracle Corporation's procedural extension for SQL and the Oracle relational database. PL/SQL includes procedural constructs such as loops and conditional statements, allowing developers to build complex business logic into their applications. This section provides a meticulous examination of the foundational concepts of PL/SQL, enabling a comprehensive understanding of its capabilities and utilization within the Oracle Database environment.

PL/SQL allows for the integration of SQL statements with procedural constructs. This amalgamation enables the creation of dynamic and flexible database applications. By embedding PL/SQL code blocks within SQL statements or Oracle forms, developers can enhance the database's capability to process transactions efficiently while maintaining robust control over error handling and execution flow.

Key Characteristics of PL/SQL:

- **Tight Integration with SQL:** PL/SQL seamlessly integrates with SQL, allowing SQL statements to be included directly within PL/SQL programs.
- **High Performance:** PL/SQL improves performance by sending a single block of statements to the Oracle engine from an application, reducing network overhead.
- **Portability:** PL/SQL code runs on any Oracle Database, ensuring portability across different platforms.
- **Block Structure:** PL/SQL uses a structured block format that encapsulates declarations, executable commands, and exception handling in logical units.

PL/SQL Block Structure:

PL/SQL code is structured into logical blocks. Each block can include declarations, executable commands, and exception handling.

The generalized structure of a PL/SQL block is as follows:

```
DECLARE
  -- Declarations
BEGIN
  -- Executable statements
EXCEPTION
  -- Exception handling
END;
```

Components of a PL/SQL Block:

- **Declarations:** Declares variables, constants, cursors, and subprograms.

```
DECLARE
    v_employee_id NUMBER;
    v_employee_name VARCHAR2(50);
```

- **Executable Statements:** Contains the logic of the program, including SQL statements and procedural constructs.

```
BEGIN
    SELECT employee_id, employee_name
    INTO v_employee_id, v_employee_name
    FROM employees
    WHERE employee_email = 'john.doe@example.com';
```

- **Exception Handling:** Handles runtime errors, providing a mechanism to gracefully manage exceptions.

```
EXCEPTION
    WHEN NO_DATA_FOUND THEN
        DBMS_OUTPUT.PUT_LINE('No such employee.');
    WHEN OTHERS THEN
        DBMS_OUTPUT.PUT_LINE('An unexpected error occurred.');
END;
```

Advantages of Using PL/SQL:

- **Improved Performance:** By allowing multiple SQL statements to be passed as a single block, PL/SQL minimizes the network traffic between applications and the Oracle Database.
- **Code Reusability:** Encapsulating logic in stored procedures and functions promotes code reuse and modular programming.
- **Error Management:** PL/SQL provides extensive error handling features, enabling developers to manage exceptions effectively and ensure the robustness of applications.
- **High Security:** Stored PL/SQL code can run with higher security privilege levels as compared to individual SQL statements issued directly from applications.

A simple example of a PL/SQL block delivering a basic operation is illustrated below. This block retrieves and prints out an employee's name based on their email:

```
DECLARE
    v_employee_name VARCHAR2(50);
BEGIN
    SELECT employee_name
    INTO v_employee_name
    FROM employees
    WHERE employee_email = 'john.doe@example.com';

    DBMS_OUTPUT.PUT_LINE('Employee Name: ' || v_employee_name);
EXCEPTION
    WHEN NO_DATA_FOUND THEN
        DBMS_OUTPUT.PUT_LINE('No such employee.');
    WHEN OTHERS THEN
        DBMS_OUTPUT.PUT_LINE('An unexpected error occurred.');
END;
```

```
Employee Name: John Doe
```

This example demonstrates how PL/SQL effectively combines SQL queries with procedural logic. The use of exception handling ensures that any potential errors, such as no matching employee being found, are managed gracefully.

As we delve deeper into PL/SQL, understanding its architecture, block structure, and fundamental syntax is crucial in leveraging its full potential for building robust and efficient database applications.

5.2 PL/SQL Block Structure

PL/SQL (Procedural Language/Structured Query Language) is Oracle Corporation's procedural extension for SQL and the Oracle relational database. The fundamental building block of PL/SQL is the block itself, which is the central unit of execution and organization. Each PL/SQL program consists of logical blocks, and a block can contain nested sub-blocks. Understanding the structure of these blocks is essential for mastering PL/SQL programming.

A PL/SQL block consists of three main sections: the declaration section, the executable section, and the exception handling section. These sections are organized as follows:

- **Declaration Section (Optional)**: This section is where variables, cursors, types, and other local programming constructs are defined. It begins with the keyword DECLARE.
- **Executable Section (Mandatory)**: This is the core of the PL/SQL block where the executable statements (SQL and PL/SQL statements) are written. This section starts with the keyword BEGIN.
- **Exception Handling Section (Optional)**: This section handles exceptions (errors) that occur during the execution of the block. It starts with the keyword EXCEPTION.

A typical PL/SQL block has the following structure:

```
DECLARE
   -- Declaration of variables, cursors, etc.
BEGIN
   -- Executable statements
EXCEPTION
   -- Exception handling statements
END;
```

Declaration Section:

The declaration section is used to define variables, constants, types, cursors, and other elements that will be used within the block. This section is optional but if necessary precedes the executable section. For example:

```
DECLARE
   v_employee_id NUMBER(6);
   v_employee_name VARCHAR2(50);
   v_salary NUMBER(8, 2)
BEGIN
   -- Executable statements
EXCEPTION
   -- Exception handling
END;
```

In this example, three variables v_employee_id, v_employee_name, and v_salary are declared.

Executable Section:

The executable section contains the actual code that needs to be executed. This section is mandatory in a PL/SQL block. The statements within this section involve assignments, control statements, SQL queries, and procedural constructs. For instance:

```
BEGIN
   v_employee_id := 101;
   SELECT first_name INTO v_employee_name FROM employees WHERE
         employee_id = v_employee_id;
   v_salary := v_salary * 1.10;
END;
```

Here, the employee's name is fetched from the database based on the employee ID, and the salary is updated.

Exception Handling Section:

The exception handling section is used to manage runtime errors, ensuring that the block does not abruptly terminate on encountering an error. This section is optional but is highly recommended for making the block resilient and robust. Exception handlers are defined using the WHEN keyword followed by an appropriate exception name or condition.

```
EXCEPTION
   WHEN NO_DATA_FOUND THEN
      v_employee_name := 'Unknown';
   WHEN TOO_MANY_ROWS THEN
      v_employee_name := 'Multiple employees found';
   WHEN OTHERS THEN
      v_employee_name := 'Error fetching employee name';
END;
```

In the example above, three exceptions are handled: NO_DATA_FOUND, TOO_MANY_ROWS, and OTHERS. The OTHERS handler is a catch-all that handles any exceptions not explicitly handled by preceding WHEN clauses.

Blocks can be nested to create composite logic:

```
BEGIN
   BEGIN
      -- Nested Block
      v_employee_id := 102;
      SELECT first_name INTO v_employee_name FROM employees WHERE
            employee_id = v_employee_id;
   EXCEPTION
      WHEN NO_DATA_FOUND THEN
         v_employee_name := 'Nested - No Data Found';
   END;
   -- Outer Block Continuation
   v_salary := v_salary * 1.10;
END;
```

Nesting allows for a high level of modularity and granularity in handling exceptions and managing workflows within a PL/SQL block. This capability is crucial for constructing complex applications where various operations must be encapsulated and controlled within different scopes.

Different types of PL/SQL blocks include anonymous blocks, named blocks (procedures and functions), and triggers. The structure remains consistent across these block types, but certain elements, such as parameters for procedures and functions, add complexity.

A comprehensive understanding of the PL/SQL block structure, including the declaration, executable, and exception handling sections, is instrumental for developing robust and maintainable Oracle database applications. This knowledge forms the foundation upon which advanced PL/SQL concepts, such as cursors, packages, and triggers, are built. A correct implementation ensures that programs are scalable, efficient, and capable of managing exceptions gracefully, providing a robust solution to business logic within the Oracle database environment.

5.3 Variables and Data Types in PL/SQL

In PL/SQL, variables and data types form the foundation for writing robust and flexible code. Variables introduce flexibility into a program by allowing it to store and manipulate data. Understanding the various data types available in PL/SQL is crucial to effective programming.

PL/SQL variables must be declared in the declarative section of a PL/SQL block, subprogram, or package. Variables can be used to store temporary results, manipulate data in a formula, or pass it as an argument to procedures and functions. Variable declaration follows the syntax:

```
variable_name [CONSTANT] datatype [NOT NULL] [:= expression];
```

Example

```
DECLARE
    employee_name VARCHAR2(50);
    employee_id NUMBER := 1001;
    hire_date DATE := SYSDATE;
BEGIN
    -- Variable usage examples
END;
```

Data Types

PL/SQL offers various data types to handle different kinds of data precisely:

1. Scalar Data Types: These data types hold a single value and include:

- **Number Types:** Used for numeric operations.
  - **NUMBER:** A broadly used data type for storing fixed and floating-point numbers.
  - **PLS_INTEGER:** A high-performance integer type for integers within the range of -2,147,483,647 to 2,147,483,647.
  - **BINARY_INTEGER:** Synonym for PLS_INTEGER but mainly used for backward compatibility.
  - **BINARY_FLOAT and BINARY_DOUBLE:** Represent single and double precision floating-point numbers respectively, commonly used for scientific computations.
- **Character Types:** Handle alphanumeric data.
  - **CHAR:** A fixed-length character data type.
  - **VARCHAR2:** A variable-length data type, most commonly used for strings. The maximum length can be set up to 32767 bytes (for PL/SQL) or 4000 bytes (for SQL).
- **Date/Time Types:** Encapsulate dates and times.

- **DATE:** Stores date and time information, accurate to a second.
- **TIMESTAMP:** An extension of the DATE data type with fractional seconds.
- **TIMESTAMP WITH TIME ZONE, TIMESTAMP WITH LOCAL TIME ZONE:** Extend TIMESTAMP to include timezone information, useful for global applications.

- **Boolean Type:** Represents logical values.
  - **BOOLEAN:** Can hold the values TRUE, FALSE, or NULL.

2. **Composite Data Types:** These allow for storing collections of data.

- **Records:** Enable you to manage values of different types as a single unit.

```
DECLARE
    TYPE EmployeeRec IS RECORD (
        employee_id NUMBER,
        employee_name VARCHAR2(50),
        hire_date DATE
    );
    emp_rec EmployeeRec;
BEGIN
    -- Usage of record
END;
```

- **Collections:** Arrays (nested tables and VARRAYs) and associative arrays (index-by tables).
  - **Nested Tables:** A set whose size is not fixed, dynamically extendable.

```
DECLARE
    TYPE NumTable IS TABLE OF NUMBER;
    num_list NumTable := NumTable(1, 2, 3, 4, 5);
BEGIN
    -- Manipulation of nested table
END;
```

  - **VARRAYs:** A fixed-size array.

```
DECLARE
    TYPE NumVarray IS VARRAY(5) OF NUMBER;
    num_varray NumVarray := NumVarray(1, 2, 3, 4, 5);
BEGIN
    -- Manipulation of VARRAY
END;
```

- **Associative Arrays:** Key-value pairs where keys do not need to be consecutive.

```
DECLARE
    TYPE AssocArray IS TABLE OF VARCHAR2(100) INDEX
        BY PLS_INTEGER;
    varray AssocArray;
BEGIN
    varray(1) := 'Item 1';
    varray(2) := 'Item 2';
    -- Manipulation of associative array
END;
```

3. Reference Data Types: These types store pointers to other data items.

- **REF CURSOR:** A cursor variable, offering dynamic cursor capabilities for flexible result sets.

```
DECLARE
    TYPE EmpCurType IS REF CURSOR RETURN employees%
        ROWTYPE;
    emp_cv EmpCurType;
BEGIN
    OPEN emp_cv FOR SELECT * FROM employees;
    -- Usage of ref cursor
END;
```

4. Large Object (LOB) Data Types: Allow storage of large blocks of unstructured data, such as texts or binary files.

- **BLOB:** Binary Large Object, suitable for binary data.
- **CLOB:** Character Large Object, suitable for text data.
- **NCLOB:** National Character Large Object, for multi-byte character data.
- **BFILE:** Holds a pointer to an external binary file which is stored outside the database.

```
DECLARE
    my_blob BLOB;
    my_clob CLOB;
    my_nclob NCLOB;
    my_bfile BFILE;
BEGIN
    -- Usage of LOBs
END;
```

Variables in PL/SQL enable sophisticated data handling essential for program logic, making comprehension of their declaration and types fundamental for both novice and seasoned developers.

5.4 Control Structures in PL/SQL

Control structures in PL/SQL provide the foundation for implementing conditional logic and control flow in your programs. These structures are essential for creating robust and dynamic applications. PL/SQL supports a variety of control structures including conditional statements, iterative statements, and sequential control.

Conditional Statements

Conditional statements allow the execution of code based on the evaluation of a condition. PL/SQL provides several constructs for implementing conditional logic, including IF-THEN, IF-THEN-ELSE, IF-THEN-ELSIF, and CASE statements.

IF-THEN Statement

The IF-THEN statement evaluates a condition. If the condition is true, the associated block of code is executed.

```
IF condition THEN
    -- Statements to execute when condition is true
END IF;
```

IF-THEN-ELSE Statement

The IF-THEN-ELSE statement provides an alternative block of code to execute if the condition is false.

```
IF condition THEN
    -- Statements to execute when condition is true
ELSE
    -- Statements to execute when condition is false
END IF;
```

IF-THEN-ELSIF Statement

The IF-THEN-ELSIF statement allows for multiple conditions to be evaluated in sequence.

```
IF condition1 THEN
    -- Statements to execute when condition1 is true
ELSIF condition2 THEN
```

```
    -- Statements to execute when condition2 is true
ELSE
    -- Statements to execute when no conditions are true
END IF;
```

CASE Statement

The CASE statement is used for choosing among several possible values of an expression.

```
CASE expression
    WHEN value1 THEN
        -- Statements to execute when value1 matches expression
    WHEN value2 THEN
        -- Statements to execute when value2 matches expression
    ELSE
        -- Statements to execute when no values match expression
END CASE;
```

Alternatively, the searched CASE statement can be used to check multiple conditions.

```
CASE
    WHEN condition1 THEN
        -- Statements to execute when condition1 is true
    WHEN condition2 THEN
        -- Statements to execute when condition2 is true
    ELSE
        -- Statements to execute when no conditions are true
END CASE;
```

Iterative Control

Iterative control structures are used to execute a sequence of statements multiple times. PL/SQL provides various loop constructs, including the LOOP, WHILE-LOOP, and FOR-LOOP.

Simple LOOP Statement

The LOOP statement executes a block of code repeatedly until an EXIT statement is encountered.

```
LOOP
    -- Statements to execute
    EXIT WHEN condition;
END LOOP;
```

WHILE-LOOP Statement

The WHILE-LOOP statement executes a block of code as long as the specified condition is true.

```
WHILE condition LOOP
    -- Statements to execute
END LOOP;
```

FOR-LOOP Statement

The FOR-LOOP statement iterates over a specified range of values.

```
FOR counter IN lower_bound..upper_bound LOOP
    -- Statements to execute
END LOOP;
```

The counter automatically increases after each iteration. The bounds can be specified in both ascending (e.g., 1..10) and descending (e.g., 10..1) order.

Sequential Control

Sequential control structures direct the flow of program execution. The GOTO statement provides unconditional branching to a labeled instruction.

GOTO Statement

The GOTO statement transfers control to a labeled block of code.

```
<Goto_Label>
GOTO <Goto_Label>;
-- More statements
<<Goto_Label>>
    -- Labeled block of code
```

Though the GOTO statement can make code harder to read and maintain, it can be useful in specific scenarios for breaking out of deeply nested loops or error handling.

Control structures enhance the flexibility and robustness of PL/SQL programs by directing the flow of execution, allowing conditions to be evaluated and blocks of code to be repeated. They are pivotal for building compound logic and optimizing code execution paths. When combined with properly scoped variables and error handling mechanisms, control structures contribute to creating efficient, maintainable, and well-structured PL/SQL applications.

5.5 Procedures and Functions

Procedures and functions are fundamental building blocks in PL/SQL, allowing for modularity, reusability, and a more structured approach to programming. While both procedures and functions serve to encapsulate PL/SQL code for reusability and organization, they have distinct characteristics and use cases. Understanding these distinctions, as well as how to create and utilize them effectively, is crucial for proficient PL/SQL development.

Procedures perform an action, potentially affecting the database or performing complex computations, and do not return a value directly. Functions, conversely, are designed to return a value and are often utilized within expressions.

Creating Procedures

A procedure is a named PL/SQL block that performs one or more specific tasks. The syntax for creating a procedure is as follows:

```
CREATE [OR REPLACE] PROCEDURE procedure_name
  [ (parameter1 [mode1] datatype1 [, parameter2 [mode2] datatype2, ...]) ]
IS
  -- Declarations
BEGIN
  -- Executable statements
EXCEPTION
  -- Exception handling
END procedure_name;
```

Example Procedure

Below is an example of a simple procedure that accepts two input parameters and updates a record in a table.

```
CREATE OR REPLACE PROCEDURE update_employee_salary (
  emp_id IN NUMBER,
  new_salary IN NUMBER
)
IS
BEGIN
  UPDATE employees
  SET salary = new_salary
  WHERE employee_id = emp_id;

  COMMIT;
END update_employee_salary;
```

To invoke this procedure, use the 'EXEC' command:

```
EXEC update_employee_salary(101, 60000);
```

Creating Functions

A function, similar to a procedure, is a subprogram that performs a specific task. However, a function must return a value. The syntax for creating a function is:

```
CREATE [OR REPLACE] FUNCTION function_name
  [ (parameter1 [mode1] datatype1 [, parameter2 [mode2] datatype2, ...]) ]
RETURN return_datatype
IS
  -- Declarations
BEGIN
  -- Executable statements
  -- Return statement
  RETURN return_value;
EXCEPTION
  -- Exception handling
END function_name;
```

Example Function

Here is an example of a function that calculates the total salary of an employee including a bonus:

```
CREATE OR REPLACE FUNCTION calculate_total_salary (
  emp_id IN NUMBER,
  bonus IN NUMBER
) RETURN NUMBER
IS
  total_salary NUMBER;
BEGIN
  SELECT salary + bonus INTO total_salary
  FROM employees
  WHERE employee_id = emp_id;

  RETURN total_salary;
END calculate_total_salary;
```

To invoke this function, it can be used in a SQL statement such as:

```
SELECT calculate_total_salary(101, 5000) AS total_compensation FROM dual;
```

Parameter Modes

There are three types of parameter modes in PL/SQL:

- **IN**: This mode allows a parameter to be passed to the subprogram. Default mode if none is specified.
- **OUT**: This mode allows a parameter to be returned from the subprogram. The actual parameter must be a variable.
- **IN OUT**: This mode allows a parameter to be passed to the subprogram and returned after execution.

An example to illustrate different parameter modes:

```
CREATE OR REPLACE PROCEDURE process_bonus (
  emp_id IN NUMBER,
  bonus OUT NUMBER,
  total_salary IN OUT NUMBER
)
IS
BEGIN
  SELECT salary + 1000 INTO bonus
  FROM employees
  WHERE employee_id = emp_id;

  total_salary := total_salary + bonus;
END process_bonus;
```

Invocation example with local variables:

```
DECLARE
  e_id NUMBER := 101;
  bns NUMBER;
  tot_sal NUMBER := 50000;
BEGIN
  process_bonus(e_id, bns, tot_sal);
  DBMS_OUTPUT.PUT_LINE('Bonus: ' || bns);
  DBMS_OUTPUT.PUT_LINE('Total Salary: ' || tot_sal);
END;
```

Creating and Using Recursive Functions

PL/SQL supports recursive functions, allowing a function to call itself. This can be useful in scenarios such as calculating factorial or traversing a hierarchy.

Example of a recursive function to calculate factorial:

```
CREATE OR REPLACE FUNCTION factorial (n NUMBER) RETURN NUMBER
IS
BEGIN
  IF n = 1 THEN
    RETURN 1;
  ELSE
    RETURN n * factorial(n - 1);
  END IF;
END factorial;
```

Calling the recursive function:

```
SELECT factorial(5) AS result FROM dual;
```

```
RESULT
-------
    120
```

Understanding how to effectively create and invoke procedures and functions, including the use of parameter modes and recursive calls, is essential for PL/SQL developers in building robust, maintainable, and efficient database applications.

5.6 Cursors and Process Control

Cursors in PL/SQL play a pivotal role in the efficient manipulation and retrieval of data from the database. Cursors, essentially, act as pointers or handles to the result set of a query. There are two main types of cursors in PL/SQL: implicit and explicit cursors. This section will delve into both types, their use cases, and the control structures essential for process control within PL/SQL code.

Implicit Cursors: These are automatically created by Oracle whenever a SQL statement is executed. They are designed for single-row SELECT statements, DML operations (INSERT, UPDATE, DELETE), and control statements (COMMIT, ROLLBACK). Implicit cursors are managed internally by Oracle, abstracting the complexities of cursor management from the programmer.

Consider the following example of an implicit cursor with a SELECT INTO statement:

```
DECLARE
  v_employee_name VARCHAR2(50);
BEGIN
  SELECT employee_name INTO v_employee_name
  FROM employees
  WHERE employee_id = 100;
  DBMS_OUTPUT.PUT_LINE('Employee Name: ' || v_employee_name);
END;
```

In this example, an implicit cursor is used to select the employee name for the employee with ID 100 and store it in the variable v_employee_name. The result is then printed using DBMS_OUTPUT.PUT_LINE.

Explicit Cursors: These are defined and controlled by the programmer. Explicit cursors are essential for handling multi-row result sets fetched from the database. The lifecycle of an explicit cursor consists of three main operations: declaration, opening, fetching, and closing.

- **Cursor Declaration**: Defined in the declarative section using the CURSOR keyword.
- **Cursor Opening**: Initialized using the OPEN statement.
- **Cursor Fetching**: Rows are retrieved one at a time using the FETCH statement.

- **Cursor Closing**: Freed using the CLOSE statement.

Below is an example demonstrating the use of an explicit cursor:

```
DECLARE
  CURSOR c_employee IS
    SELECT employee_id, employee_name
    FROM employees;

  v_employee_id employees.employee_id%TYPE;
  v_employee_name employees.employee_name%TYPE;
BEGIN
  OPEN c_employee;

  LOOP
    FETCH c_employee INTO v_employee_id, v_employee_name;
    EXIT WHEN c_employee%NOTFOUND;

    DBMS_OUTPUT.PUT_LINE('Employee ID: ' || v_employee_id ||
                         ', Employee Name: ' || v_employee_name);
  END LOOP;

  CLOSE c_employee;
END;
```

This example declares a cursor c_employee that selects employee_id and employee_name from the employees table. The cursor is opened, and a LOOP statement fetches each row and prints the result until no more rows are found.

Cursor Attributes: Oracle provides several useful cursor attributes to check the status of cursor operations:

- %FOUND: Returns TRUE if the last fetch returns a row.
- %NOTFOUND: Returns TRUE if the last fetch does not return a row.
- %ISOPEN: Returns TRUE if the cursor is open.
- %ROWCOUNT: Returns the number of rows fetched so far.

Integrating cursors with control structures like loops and conditional statements provides powerful mechanisms for complex data processing tasks.

Parameterized Cursors: These cursors accept parameters, allowing for more dynamic and flexible queries. Parameters are defined at cursor declaration and are supplied when the cursor is opened. Parameterized cursors enhance reusability.

```
DECLARE
  CURSOR c_dept_employees (p_department_id departments.department_id%TYPE
       ) IS
    SELECT employee_id, employee_name
    FROM employees
    WHERE department_id = p_department_id;

  v_employee_id employees.employee_id%TYPE;
  v_employee_name employees.employee_name%TYPE;
BEGIN
  OPEN c_dept_employees(10); -- Open cursor for department_id 10

  LOOP
    FETCH c_dept_employees INTO v_employee_id, v_employee_name;
    EXIT WHEN c_dept_employees%NOTFOUND;

    DBMS_OUTPUT.PUT_LINE('Employee ID: ' || v_employee_id ||
                     ', Employee Name: ' || v_employee_name);
  END LOOP;

  CLOSE c_dept_employees;
END;
```

This example utilizes a parameterized cursor c_dept_employees to fetch employees from a specified department, providing flexible query execution.

FOR Loops with Cursors: Oracle simplifies cursor handling with FOR loops, eliminating the need for explicit open, fetch, and close operations. The FOR loop implicitly manages the cursor lifecycle.

```
BEGIN
  FOR rec IN (SELECT employee_id, employee_name FROM employees)
  LOOP
    DBMS_OUTPUT.PUT_LINE('Employee ID: ' || rec.employee_id ||
                     ', Employee Name: ' || rec.employee_name);
  END LOOP;
END;
```

In this case, the query result is treated as a cursor, iterated automatically by the FOR loop, and individual row data is accessed through the loop index rec.

Cursor FOR UPDATE and WHERE CURRENT OF Clause: The FOR UPDATE clause marks the selected rows with row locks to ensure exclusive updates. The WHERE CURRENT OF clause facilitates updates or deletions on the current row of the cursor.

```
DECLARE
  CURSOR c_employees IS
    SELECT employee_id, salary
    FROM employees
    FOR UPDATE OF salary;

  v_employee_id employees.employee_id%TYPE;
```

```
  v_salary employees.salary%TYPE;
BEGIN
  OPEN c_employees;

  LOOP
    FETCH c_employees INTO v_employee_id, v_salary;
    EXIT WHEN c_employees%NOTFOUND;

    UPDATE employees
    SET salary = salary * 1.10
    WHERE CURRENT OF c_employees;
  END LOOP;

  CLOSE c_employees;
END;
```

In this script, the cursor c_employees selects employee_id and salary from the employees table for update. Each fetched row's salary is incremented by 10% using the UPDATE WHERE CURRENT OF statement.

Control structures and cursors provide a symbiotic relationship in PL/SQL, promoting efficient data manipulation, encapsulation, and robust error handling. Combining implicit and explicit cursors with loops and conditional statements offers a powerful toolkit for database interaction and process control.

5.7 Exception Handling in PL/SQL

Exception handling in PL/SQL is a crucial aspect that ensures robust and reliable database applications. An exception is a runtime error or warning condition that disrupts the normal flow of execution. PL/SQL provides a mechanism to capture and manage these exceptions, enabling developers to respond appropriately and maintain control over program flow.

PL/SQL supports both predefined and user-defined exceptions. Predefined exceptions are automatically raised by the runtime system when a standard error occurs. User-defined exceptions are explicitly defined and raised by the developer within the PL/SQL block.

The syntax for handling exceptions in PL/SQL consists of the following blocks: *DECLARE*, *BEGIN*, *EXCEPTION*, and *END*. The *EXCEPTION* block is the key segment where different exceptions are handled.

```
DECLARE
   -- Variable declarations
BEGIN
```

```
    -- Executable statements
EXCEPTION
    WHEN exception_name1 THEN
        -- Exception handling statements
    WHEN exception_name2 THEN
        -- Exception handling statements
    WHEN OTHERS THEN
        -- Default exception handling statements
END;
```

Predefined Exceptions

Oracle provides a set of predefined exceptions that cover common error conditions. Each predefined exception has a corresponding named identifier. Some commonly used predefined exceptions include:

- NO_DATA_FOUND: Raised when a SELECT INTO statement returns no rows.
- TOO_MANY_ROWS: Raised when a SELECT INTO statement returns more than one row.
- ZERO_DIVIDE: Raised when an attempt is made to divide a number by zero.
- INVALID_NUMBER: Raised when a conversion from a character string to a number fails.

Here is an example demonstrating the handling of a predefined exception:

```
DECLARE
    v_employee_id NUMBER := 1001;
    v_employee_name VARCHAR2(50);
BEGIN
    SELECT first_name INTO v_employee_name FROM employees WHERE
        employee_id = v_employee_id;
    DBMS_OUTPUT.PUT_LINE('Employee Name: ' || v_employee_name);
EXCEPTION
    WHEN NO_DATA_FOUND THEN
        DBMS_OUTPUT.PUT_LINE('No data found for employee ID ' ||
            v_employee_id);
    WHEN TOO_MANY_ROWS THEN
        DBMS_OUTPUT.PUT_LINE('More than one row found for employee ID ' ||
            v_employee_id);
    WHEN OTHERS THEN
        DBMS_OUTPUT.PUT_LINE('An unexpected error occurred.');
END;
```

The above code snippet attempts to retrieve the name of an employee based on the given employee ID. If no such employee exists, the NO_DATA_FOUND exception is handled by printing an appropriate message. If multiple rows are retrieved, the TOO_MANY_ROWS exception is managed. Any other unexpected error is caught by the WHEN OTHERS clause, which acts as a catch-all mechanism.

User-defined Exceptions

In addition to predefined exceptions, PL/SQL allows the creation and handling of user-defined exceptions. These exceptions are declared in the *DECLARE* section and can be raised explicitly using the RAISE statement.

```
DECLARE
    e_custom_exception EXCEPTION;
    v_value NUMBER := 10;
BEGIN
    IF v_value < 0 THEN
        RAISE e_custom_exception;
    ELSE
        DBMS_OUTPUT.PUT_LINE('Value is positive.');
    END IF;
EXCEPTION
    WHEN e_custom_exception THEN
        DBMS_OUTPUT.PUT_LINE('A custom exception has been raised.');
END;
```

In this example, an exception named e_custom_exception is declared. If the variable *v_value* is less than zero, the custom exception is raised using the RAISE statement, and the corresponding handler prints a specific message.

Propagation of Exceptions

When an exception is raised within a PL/SQL block, it propagates outwardly to enclosing blocks until it finds a handler or terminates the program if no handler is found.

Exception Propagation Example

```
DECLARE
    v_outer_value NUMBER := 5;
    e_inner_exception EXCEPTION;
BEGIN
    BEGIN
```

```
        v_outer_value := v_outer_value * 0;
        IF v_outer_value = 0 THEN
            RAISE e_inner_exception;
        END IF;
    EXCEPTION
        WHEN e_inner_exception THEN
            DBMS_OUTPUT.PUT_LINE('Inner block: Division by zero.');
            RAISE;
    END;

EXCEPTION
    WHEN OTHERS THEN
        DBMS_OUTPUT.PUT_LINE('Outer block: Exception caught.');
END;
```

Here, the inner block raises and catches the e_inner_exception, then propagates it using the RAISE statement. The outer block catches the propagated exception and prints a message.

Exception handling mechanisms in PL/SQL are indispensable for creating robust, fault-tolerant Oracle database applications. By leveraging predefined and user-defined exceptions, developers can anticipate and manage errors effectively, ensuring smooth program execution.

5.8 Packages and Modular PL/SQL

Packages in PL/SQL are schema objects that group logically related PL/SQL types, items, and subprograms. The use of packages facilitates modular programming, encouraging reusability, maintaining code organization, and enhancing functionality with ease of maintenance and performance improvements.

A package typically encapsulates a unit of related functionalities, providing a clear, modular structure to the code. Packages consist of two inherently linked parts: the package specification and the package body. The specification declares the types, constants, variables, exceptions, cursors, and subprograms that can be referenced from outside the package. The body fully defines these objects and implements the subprograms.

Package Specification

The package specification acts as the interface to the package. It declares public constructs, which are accessible and callable by other PL/SQL blocks, subprograms, or packages. Here is an example illustrating the creation of a package specification:

```
CREATE OR REPLACE PACKAGE emp_package IS
```

```
  -- Type declarations
  TYPE t_emp_rec IS RECORD (
    emp_id NUMBER,
    emp_name VARCHAR2(50),
    emp_salary NUMBER);

  -- Variable declarations
  g_bonus_rate CONSTANT NUMBER := 0.10;

  -- Procedure and function declarations
  PROCEDURE add_employee(
    p_emp_id IN NUMBER,
    p_emp_name IN VARCHAR2,
    p_emp_salary IN NUMBER);

  FUNCTION get_employee_salary(p_emp_id IN NUMBER) RETURN NUMBER;

END emp_package;
```

In the above code snippet, the package emp_package includes a type definition t_emp_rec, a constant g_bonus_rate, and declarations for a procedure add_employee and a function get_employee_salary. These elements are public and can be accessed by other PL/SQL blocks.

Package Body

The package body implements the specifications declared in the package. It includes the actual code for procedures and functions. The package body can also declare private elements that are not exposed via the package specification, hence encapsulating the internal workings.

```
CREATE OR REPLACE PACKAGE BODY emp_package IS

  PROCEDURE add_employee(
    p_emp_id IN NUMBER,
    p_emp_name IN VARCHAR2,
    p_emp_salary IN NUMBER) IS
  BEGIN
    INSERT INTO employees (emp_id, emp_name, emp_salary)
    VALUES (p_emp_id, p_emp_name, p_emp_salary);
  END add_employee;

  FUNCTION get_employee_salary(p_emp_id IN NUMBER) RETURN NUMBER IS
    v_emp_salary NUMBER;
  BEGIN
    SELECT emp_salary INTO v_emp_salary
    FROM employees
    WHERE emp_id = p_emp_id;
    RETURN v_emp_salary;
  END get_employee_salary;

END emp_package;
```

In this implementation, we provide the full definition of the add_employee procedure and the get_employee_salary function. The package body can also contain private constructs that are not exposed outside the package. For instance:

```
CREATE OR REPLACE PACKAGE BODY emp_package IS

  -- Private variable
  v_bonus CONSTANT NUMBER := 500;

  PROCEDURE add_employee(
    p_emp_id IN NUMBER,
    p_emp_name IN VARCHAR2,
    p_emp_salary IN NUMBER) IS
  BEGIN
    INSERT INTO employees (emp_id, emp_name, emp_salary)
    VALUES (p_emp_id, p_emp_name, p_emp_salary);
  END add_employee;

  FUNCTION get_employee_salary(p_emp_id IN NUMBER) RETURN NUMBER IS
    v_emp_salary NUMBER;
  BEGIN
    SELECT emp_salary INTO v_emp_salary
    FROM employees
    WHERE emp_id = p_emp_id;
    RETURN v_emp_salary;
  END get_employee_salary;

END emp_package;
```

Here, a private variable v_bonus is declared within the package body. This variable can be used by subprograms within the package body but is not visible to external PL/SQL blocks.

Benefits of Using PL/SQL Packages

- **Encapsulation of Related Constructs**: Packages group logically related constructs, providing a logical structure to your PL/SQL code.
- **Modularity**: By breaking the PL/SQL code into smaller modules, packages make it easier to manage, understand, and maintain the codebase.
- **Reusability**: Once a package is developed, its subprograms can be reused by different applications, reducing code redundancy.
- **Easier Change Management**: Changes in the implementation of a package can be confined to the package body without affecting the package specification or the applications that use the package.
- **Performance Improvements**: Packages are precompiled, leading to better performance and reduced memory usage.

Initialization Section

A package body can include an initialization section, which contains statements that are executed only once, the first time the package is referenced. This is useful for one-time variable initializations or for setting up the state that will be shared by all subprograms of the package.

```
CREATE OR REPLACE PACKAGE BODY emp_package IS

  -- Private variable
  v_bonus CONSTANT NUMBER := 500;

  PROCEDURE add_employee(
    p_emp_id IN NUMBER,
    p_emp_name IN VARCHAR2,
    p_emp_salary IN NUMBER) IS
  BEGIN
    INSERT INTO employees (emp_id, emp_name, emp_salary)
    VALUES (p_emp_id, p_emp_name, p_emp_salary);
  END add_employee;

  FUNCTION get_employee_salary(p_emp_id IN NUMBER) RETURN NUMBER IS
    v_emp_salary NUMBER;
  BEGIN
    SELECT emp_salary INTO v_emp_salary
    FROM employees
    WHERE emp_id = p_emp_id;
    RETURN v_emp_salary;
  END get_employee_salary;

BEGIN
  -- Initialization section
  DBMS_OUTPUT.PUT_LINE('Package emp_package initialized.');
END emp_package;
```

This initialization block will execute when the package is first invoked, outputting the message "Package emp_package initialized." via the DBMS_OUTPUT.PUT_LINE procedure.

Through the collective use of package specifications and package bodies, modular PL/SQL development is effectively realized, promoting a clear and organized approach to PL/SQL programming.

5.9 Triggers in PL/SQL

Triggers are specialized stored programs that automatically execute or fire when a specific event occurs in the database. This can include events related to both data manipulation and the data definition language. Triggers enable the enforcement of complex business rules, auditing, and extending the functionality of the database.

A trigger is associated with a table, view, or event and is composed of three main parts:

- The **triggering event or statement**: The condition that determines when the trigger should be fired, such as an INSERT, UPDATE, or DELETE operation.
- The **triggering restriction**: An optional condition that specifies additional criteria that must be met for the trigger to execute. This is commonly done with a WHEN clause.
- The **triggering action**: The PL/SQL block that contains the code to be executed when the trigger fires.

Syntax for Creating a Trigger

The basic syntax to create a trigger in PL/SQL is as follows:

```
CREATE [ OR REPLACE ] TRIGGER trigger_name
{ BEFORE | AFTER | INSTEAD OF }
{ INSERT | UPDATE | DELETE }
    [ OF column_name ]
    ON table_name
    [ REFERENCING OLD AS old_identifier NEW AS new_identifier ]
    [ FOR EACH ROW ]
    [ WHEN ( condition ) ]
DECLARE
    -- variable declarations
BEGIN
    -- PL/SQL block with statements to be executed
EXCEPTION
    -- exception handling statements
END;
```

Trigger Firing Sequence

Triggers can be fired before or after the specified event. The BEFORE option allows executing the trigger action before the event that triggered it, such as before inserting, updating, or deleting. Alternatively, the AFTER option executes the trigger action after the event.

Triggers can be further refined to handle row-level or statement-level events:

- **Row-level triggers** execute once for each row affected by the query. They use the FOR EACH ROW clause.
- **Statement-level triggers** execute once for the entire SQL statement, independent of the number of rows affected. They do not use the FOR EACH ROW clause.

To ensure detailed control over the event conditions, the WHEN clause can be used to specify an additional condition that the trigger must fulfill to be executed.

Examples of Triggers

Example 1: Auditing Changes with a Row-Level Trigger

An auditing trigger to log every insert operation on a certain table:

```
CREATE OR REPLACE TRIGGER audit_employee_inserts
AFTER INSERT ON employees
FOR EACH ROW
BEGIN
    INSERT INTO employee_audit (
        employee_id,
        action,
        action_date
    ) VALUES (
        :NEW.id,
        'INSERT',
        SYSDATE
    );
END;
```

Example 2: Enforcing Business Rules with a Before Trigger

A trigger to enforce a constraint that the salary of an employee must not be decreased:

```
CREATE OR REPLACE TRIGGER prevent_salary_decrease
BEFORE UPDATE OF salary ON employees
FOR EACH ROW
WHEN ( NEW.salary < OLD.salary )
BEGIN
    RAISE_APPLICATION_ERROR(-20001, 'Salary cannot be decreased.');
END;
```

INSTEAD OF Triggers

INSTEAD OF triggers are used with views to provide an alternative method for modifying the data in complex views that cannot be directly updated. These triggers allow the specification of actions to take instead of performing the DML operation originally intended:

```
CREATE OR REPLACE TRIGGER update_view_instead
INSTEAD OF UPDATE ON employee_view
FOR EACH ROW
BEGIN
    UPDATE employees
    SET first_name = :NEW.first_name,
        last_name = :NEW.last_name,
        salary = :NEW.salary
    WHERE employee_id = :OLD.employee_id;
END;
```

Managing Triggers

Triggers, once created, are managed using similar commands to other database objects:

- To disable a trigger:

```
ALTER TRIGGER trigger_name DISABLE;
```

- To enable a trigger:

```
ALTER TRIGGER trigger_name ENABLE;
```

- To drop a trigger:

```
DROP TRIGGER trigger_name;
```

Trigger Execution and Evaluation Order

When multiple triggers are defined for the same event, Oracle guarantees that the triggers execute in a particular order. However, it does not define a specific order of execution for triggers that fire at the same timing point. To manage dependencies, developers should avoid having multiple triggers on the same table for the same event if the execution order is critical.

Trigger Restrictions

Oracle has certain restrictions on the use of triggers:

- A trigger cannot change the NEW and OLD values if the trigger is not a BEFORE row trigger.
- Trigger body cannot contain transaction control statements like COMMIT, ROLLBACK, or SAVEPOINT.
- Triggers should be designed carefully to avoid recursive loops, where a trigger firing results in actions that cause the trigger to fire again.

Understanding and implementing triggers as part of an overall PL/SQL programming strategy enables robust, responsive, and rule-based processing within Oracle Database, catering to complex business algorithms and ensuring data integrity.

5.10 Dynamic SQL in PL/SQL

Dynamic SQL refers to SQL statements that are constructed and executed at runtime, allowing for more flexible and adaptable code. Unlike static SQL, where the SQL code is compiled into the PL/SQL blocks, dynamic SQL provides the ability to construct SQL statements dynamically based on variable inputs, conditions, or other runtime factors. This section addresses the principles and techniques of employing dynamic SQL in PL/SQL, outlining its syntax, use cases, advantages, and potential pitfalls.

Dynamic SQL in PL/SQL is typically managed through the EXECUTE IMMEDIATE statement or the DBMS_SQL package. Each method offers distinct functionalities and is appropriate for different scenarios.

Using EXECUTE IMMEDIATE

The EXECUTE IMMEDIATE statement is the simpler and more concise method for executing dynamic SQL. It supports both single-row and multiple-row operations, DDL statements, and PL/SQL blocks. Below is an example of constructing and executing a dynamic SQL statement using EXECUTE IMMEDIATE:

```
DECLARE
   sql_stmt VARCHAR2(200);
   table_name VARCHAR2(30) := 'employees';
BEGIN
   sql_stmt := 'SELECT COUNT(*) FROM ' || table_name;
   EXECUTE IMMEDIATE sql_stmt INTO var_count;
END;
/
```

This fragment demonstrates how to dynamically construct a SELECT statement using a table name stored in a variable. Note that EXECUTE IMMEDIATE can accommodate parameters by binding variables to the SQL string. Below is an example that includes both bind variables and using RETURNING INTO clause for DML operations:

```
DECLARE
   sql_stmt VARCHAR2(200);
   emp_id NUMBER := 100;
   new_salary NUMBER := 5000;
BEGIN
   sql_stmt := 'UPDATE employees SET salary = :1 WHERE employee_id = :2
         RETURNING salary INTO :3';
   EXECUTE IMMEDIATE sql_stmt USING new_salary, emp_id, OUT old_salary;
END;
/
```

Using DBMS_SQL Package

The DBMS_SQL package provides a more intricate method for executing dynamic SQL, offering fine-grained control over the execution context and supporting operations that are not straightforward with EXECUTE IMMEDIATE. This package is beneficial for executing SQL statements with an unknown number of columns or complex data types.

Here is an example of using the DBMS_SQL package:

```
DECLARE
   cursor_handle INTEGER;
   rows_processed INTEGER;
   sql_stmt VARCHAR2(1000);
BEGIN
   sql_stmt := 'UPDATE employees SET salary = salary * 1.10';
   cursor_handle := DBMS_SQL.OPEN_CURSOR;
   DBMS_SQL.PARSE(cursor_handle, sql_stmt, DBMS_SQL.NATIVE);
   rows_processed := DBMS_SQL.EXECUTE(cursor_handle);
   DBMS_SQL.CLOSE_CURSOR(cursor_handle);

   DBMS_OUTPUT.PUT_LINE('Number of rows updated: ' || rows_processed);
EXCEPTION
   WHEN OTHERS THEN
      IF DBMS_SQL.IS_OPEN(cursor_handle) THEN
         DBMS_SQL.CLOSE_CURSOR(cursor_handle);
      END IF;
      RAISE;
END;
/
```

This code snippet opens a dynamic cursor for the given SQL statement, parses it, executes it, and finally, retrieves the number of rows processed.

Advantages and Best Practices

Dynamic SQL provides a level of flexibility that static SQL cannot. It allows for: - Constructing SQL statements based on application logic. - Executing a variety of SQL commands dynamically. - Handling schema changes or heterogeneous database operations.

However, dynamic SQL can introduce risks, such as SQL injection attacks if not properly managed. Best practices to mitigate potential issues include: - Binding variables to avoid SQL injection. - Using the least privilege principle, ensuring the necessary grants are minimal. - Ensuring error handling is robust to manage runtime exceptions and resource deallocation. - Regular code reviews to detect potential security risks.

Potential Pitfalls

While dynamic SQL is powerful, it has inherent downsides: - Performance overhead due to runtime parsing and execution. - Increased complexity in debugging and maintenance. - Security vulnerabilities (e.g., SQL injection).

Effective use of dynamic SQL involves understanding its capabilities and incorporating defensive programming techniques to minimize risks while leveraging the flexibility it offers.

5.11 Error Handling and Debugging PL/SQL Code

Error handling and debugging are fundamental aspects of PL/SQL programming that ensure the robustness and reliability of database applications. Proper error handling allows developers to gracefully manage unexpected conditions, while effective debugging techniques facilitate the identification and resolution of issues in the code.

Oracle PL/SQL provides a robust framework for exception handling that enables developers to catch and manage errors. The primary mechanism for this is through the use of exceptions, which can be predefined by Oracle or user-defined.

Predefined Exceptions: Oracle provides several predefined exceptions that cover common error conditions. Some of the most frequently used predefined exceptions include:

- **NO_DATA_FOUND:** Raised when a SELECT INTO statement returns no rows.
- **TOO_MANY_ROWS:** Raised when a SELECT INTO statement returns more than one row.
- **ZERO_DIVIDE:** Raised when an attempt is made to divide a number by zero.
- **INVALID_CURSOR:** Raised when an illegal cursor operation is attempted.

User-Defined Exceptions: Developers can define their own exceptions when the predefined ones do not suffice. User-defined exceptions are declared in the declarative section of a PL/SQL block and must be explicitly raised using the RAISE statement.

```
DECLARE
   insufficient_funds EXCEPTION;
   account_balance NUMBER := 500;
BEGIN
   IF account_balance < 1000 THEN
      RAISE insufficient_funds;
   END IF;
EXCEPTION
   WHEN insufficient_funds THEN
      DBMS_OUTPUT.PUT_LINE('Insufficient funds for the transaction.');
END;
/
```

Exception Handling in PL/SQL Blocks: An exception-handling section in a PL/SQL block traps and manages raised exceptions. Each exception handler is written using the WHEN keyword followed by the exception name and an associated block of code.

```
DECLARE
   l_num NUMBER;
BEGIN
   l_num := 10 / 0;
EXCEPTION
   WHEN ZERO_DIVIDE THEN
      DBMS_OUTPUT.PUT_LINE('Division by zero is not allowed.');
   WHEN OTHERS THEN
      DBMS_OUTPUT.PUT_LINE('An unexpected error occurred.');
END;
/
```

The WHEN OTHERS clause is a catch-all exception handler that captures any exception not explicitly handled by other WHEN clauses. However, it should be used with caution as it can mask unexpected errors.

Debugging PL/SQL code involves systematically identifying and fixing defects within the logic of the PL/SQL block. Oracle PL/SQL provides several tools and techniques for effective debugging:

1. DBMS_OUTPUT Package: The DBMS_OUTPUT package is commonly used for simple debugging by displaying output messages and variable values during code execution.

```
DECLARE
   l_value NUMBER := 10;
BEGIN
   DBMS_OUTPUT.PUT_LINE('The value of l_value is: ' || l_value);
END;
/
```

2. DBMS_DEBUG Package: The DBMS_DEBUG package provides more advanced debugging capabilities, allowing developers to set breakpoints, examine variable values, and step through the execution of PL/SQL code.

3. Oracle SQL Developer: Oracle SQL Developer includes a PL/SQL debugger that enables interactive debugging, such as setting breakpoints, stepping into code, and inspecting variable values in real-time.

4. Exception Propagation: Exceptions can be propagated to calling programs or higher-level blocks using the RAISE statement. This allows exceptions to be managed at a higher level in the application's architecture.

```
CREATE OR REPLACE PROCEDURE proc_with_error AS
BEGIN
   RAISE_APPLICATION_ERROR(-20001, 'Custom error occurred');
END;
/
BEGIN
   proc_with_error;
EXCEPTION
   WHEN OTHERS THEN
      DBMS_OUTPUT.PUT_LINE(SQLERRM);
END;
/
```

5. Logging Error Information: Logging error details to a database table or external log can be invaluable for debugging and tracking application issues. This involves creating a logging mechanism that captures error messages, stack traces, and other diagnostic information.

```
CREATE TABLE error_log (
   log_id NUMBER PRIMARY KEY,
   error_message VARCHAR2(4000),
   log_date TIMESTAMP
);

CREATE OR REPLACE PROCEDURE log_error(p_message IN VARCHAR2) AS
BEGIN
   INSERT INTO error_log (log_id, error_message, log_date)
   VALUES (error_log_seq.NEXTVAL, p_message, SYSTIMESTAMP);
   COMMIT;
END;
/

DECLARE
   l_value NUMBER;
BEGIN
   l_value := 10 / 0;
EXCEPTION
   WHEN OTHERS THEN
      log_error('Error: ' || SQLERRM);
END;
/
```

Careful planning and implementation of error handling and debugging strategies enhance the maintainability and reliability of PL/SQL applications. Error handling and debugging are not just tools for fixing problems but are integral to producing high-quality, robust PL/SQL code.

5.12 Best Practices and Optimization in PL/SQL

Optimizing PL/SQL code ensures effective resource usage, improved performance, and maintainability of Oracle database applications. This section delves into various strategies for optimizing PL/SQL, focusing on best practices and techniques to achieve efficient code execution.

1. Use SQL Efficiently Efficient usage of SQL is paramount in writing performant PL/SQL code. Direct SQL operations are usually faster than equivalent PL/SQL loops and iterations.

Avoid executing overly complex SQL within loops:

```
FOR employee_rec IN (SELECT * FROM employees)
LOOP
    -- Complex SQL inside the loop
    SELECT department_name INTO dept_name
    FROM departments
    WHERE department_id = employee_rec.department_id;
END LOOP;
```

Instead, try to fetch all relevant data with a single SQL statement:

```
FOR employee_rec IN (SELECT e.*, d.department_name
                     FROM employees e
                     JOIN departments d ON e.department_id = d.department_id)
LOOP
    -- Use the joined result directly
    dept_name := employee_rec.department_name;
END LOOP;
```

2. Bulk Processing with BULK COLLECT and FORALL For operations involving multiple rows, leveraging BULK COLLECT and FORALL can significantly reduce context switches between SQL and PL/SQL, leading to performance gains.

Fetching multiple rows into a collection:

```
DECLARE
    TYPE employee_table_type IS TABLE OF employees%ROWTYPE;
    employee_table employee_table_type;
BEGIN
    -- Bulk collect rows from the employees table
    SELECT * BULK COLLECT INTO employee_table FROM employees WHERE
        department_id = 10;
    FOR indx IN 1..employee_table.COUNT LOOP
```

```
        -- Process each row
        DBMS_OUTPUT.PUT_LINE(employee_table(indx).employee_name);
    END LOOP;
END;
```

Performing bulk inserts:

```
DECLARE
    TYPE emp_array_type IS TABLE OF employees.employee_id%TYPE;
    emp_id_tab emp_array_type;
BEGIN
    -- Assuming emp_id_tab is already populated
    FORALL indx IN 1..emp_id_tab.COUNT
        INSERT INTO employees (employee_id, first_name, last_name)
        VALUES (emp_id_tab(indx), 'John', 'Doe');
END;
```

3. Minimize Context Switching Context switching between the PL/SQL engine and the SQL engine is resource-intensive. To minimize context switches, reduce the frequency of SQL executions within PL/SQL loops.

Inefficient context switching:

```
FOR i IN 1..1000 LOOP
    UPDATE employees SET salary = salary * 1.1 WHERE employee_id = i;
END LOOP;
```

Bulk updating to avoid frequent context switches:

```
EXECUTE IMMEDIATE 'UPDATE employees SET salary = salary * 1.1';
```

4. Avoid Hard Parses Frequently executed identical queries with different parameters can cause repeated hard parsing, which is computationally expensive. Use bind variables to reduce parse times.

Without bind variables (causing hard parses):

```
EXECUTE IMMEDIATE 'SELECT * FROM employees WHERE employee_id = ' ||
    v_employee_id;
```

Using bind variables:

```
EXECUTE IMMEDIATE 'SELECT * FROM employees WHERE employee_id = :1'
    INTO rec USING v_employee_id;
```

5. Leverage PL/SQL Native Compilation Enable PL/SQL native compilation to convert PL/SQL code into native compiled code, reducing execution times.

To enable native compilation:

```
ALTER SESSION SET plsql_code_type='NATIVE';
```

Compile the PL/SQL unit:

```
CREATE OR REPLACE FUNCTION calculate_bonus (employee_id NUMBER)
    RETURN NUMBER AS
  v_bonus NUMBER;
BEGIN
  -- Calculation logic here
  RETURN v_bonus;
END calculate_bonus;
```

6. Use Pipelined Table Functions Pipelined table functions allow row-by-row processing without requiring complete collection formation, reducing memory overhead and enhancing performance.

Example of a pipelined table function:

```
CREATE OR REPLACE FUNCTION get_employees (dept_id NUMBER)
RETURN emp_tab_type PIPELINED IS
BEGIN
  FOR rec IN (SELECT employee_id, first_name, last_name FROM employees
      WHERE department_id = dept_id) LOOP
    PIPE ROW (emp_rec_type(rec.employee_id, rec.first_name, rec.last_name));
  END LOOP;
  RETURN;
END get_employees;
```

7. Optimize Function Calls Reduce the overhead of function calls within SQL statements by using deterministic functions, which helps the optimizer understand that the function will always return the same result for the same input.

Defining a deterministic function:

```
CREATE OR REPLACE FUNCTION calculate_tax (salary NUMBER) RETURN
    NUMBER DETERMINISTIC AS
BEGIN
  -- Tax calculation logic here
  RETURN salary * 0.2;
END calculate_tax;
```

8. Efficient Exception Handling While robust exception handling is essential, it should be used judiciously to avoid masking performance issues or causing unnecessary overhead. Utilize predefined exceptions and bulk exception handling where appropriate.

Capturing bulk exceptions:

```
DECLARE
  TYPE emp_ids IS TABLE OF employees.employee_id%TYPE;
  v_emp_ids emp_ids := emp_ids();
BEGIN
  FORALL i IN v_emp_ids.FIRST..v_emp_ids.LAST SAVE EXCEPTIONS
    DELETE FROM employees WHERE employee_id = v_emp_ids(i);
EXCEPTION
  WHEN OTHERS THEN
```

```
    FOR i IN 1..SQL%BULK_EXCEPTIONS.COUNT LOOP
        DBMS_OUTPUT.PUT_LINE('Error at index: ' || SQL%
            BULK_EXCEPTIONS(i).ERROR_INDEX);
        DBMS_OUTPUT.PUT_LINE('Error code: ' || SQL%BULK_EXCEPTIONS
            (i).ERROR_CODE);
    END LOOP;
END;
```

9. Use PL/SQL Profiler Leverage the PL/SQL Profiler to analyze and identify performance bottlenecks. The profiler assists in pinpointing slow-running code segments and optimizing them accordingly.

Profiling PL/SQL code:

```
BEGIN
    DBMS_HPROF.start_profiling (location => 'tmp', filename => 'plsql_profiler.trc'
        );
    -- Execute code to be profiled
    DBMS_HPROF.stop_profiling;
END;
```

Analyzing the profiling data provides insights into the most time-consuming operations, allowing targeted optimization.

Efficient and careful application of these best practices significantly enhances PL/SQL code performance, providing a strong foundation for robust and scalable database applications.

Chapter 6

Oracle Database Administration

This chapter focuses on the critical aspects of Oracle Database administration. It covers installing and configuring the database, managing instances, storage, users, schemas, and tablespaces. Topics also include configuring network connections, monitoring performance, automating tasks, troubleshooting, upgrading, and migrating databases. The chapter provides essential knowledge and practical skills for effective database administration and maintenance.

6.1 Introduction to Oracle Database Administration

Oracle Database Administration encompasses a wide array of tasks and responsibilities essential for managing and maintaining the Oracle Database environment efficiently. The primary goal of a Database Administrator (DBA) is to ensure the seamless operation, optimal performance, security, and availability of the database. This section provides an in-depth exploration of the fundamental concepts and terminologies required to grasp the core duties and principles of Oracle Database Administration.

At the heart of Oracle Database Administration lies the management of database instances, which are the memory structures and background processes that interact with the database. An Oracle database instance includes memory structures such as System Global Area (SGA) and Program Global Area (PGA) and background processes like DBWn (Database Writer), LGWR (Log Writer), CKPT (Checkpoint), and SMON (System Monitor). The fundamental responsibility of a DBA involves starting, stopping, and monitoring these instances to ensure they run smoothly.

Another central aspect of database administration is storage management. This involves managing physical storage (datafiles) and logical storage constructs like tablespaces. The DBA ensures that datafiles are adequately sized to accommodate database growth while maintaining optimal performance. Logical storage areas, or tablespaces, are used to allocate space within the datafiles and must be monitored and adjusted as needed. The knowledge of redo log files, control files, and archive log files is also imperative as they play crucial roles in maintaining data integrity and enabling data recovery.

User and schema management is another critical function for a DBA. Users are database accounts that have the privilege to connect to the database, while schemas represent the collection of objects (tables, indexes, views, etc.) owned by a user. Managing database users involves creating, modifying, and deleting user accounts. It also entails assigning appropriate privileges and roles to ensure database security and compliance with organizational policies. Schema management involves ensuring the integrity, performance, and efficiency of schema objects.

Managing tablespaces involves creating, modifying, and deleting tablespaces to optimize storage allocation and performance. Proper tablespace management ensures that database objects are stored logically, promotes efficient data retrieval, and helps distribute I/O load effectively. The DBA must closely monitor tablespaces for any signs of saturation and take necessary actions such as resizing or adding new datafiles.

Oracle Database Administration also necessitates configuring and managing network connections. This includes setting up Oracle Net Services to allow clients to communicate with the database over a network. The DBA configures listeners, which wait for incoming client connection requests and handle connection establishment. Additionally, the DBA must manage network configurations, such as resolving network connection issues, ensuring secure connections, and optimizing network performance.

Monitoring and managing database performance is an ongoing responsibility that involves identifying and resolving performance bottlenecks. Tools and techniques such as Automatic Workload Repository (AWR) reports, Active Session History (ASH) reports, and SQL tuning can help a DBA analyze performance metrics and take appropriate actions to enhance database performance. The DBA must also use performance monitoring tools to track memory usage, I/O statistics, and CPU utilization.

Automating administrative tasks is an essential function for improving operational efficiency and reducing the time spent on routine activities. Oracle provides several tools and features for automation, such as scheduling jobs using Oracle Scheduler, automating backups, and leveraging Oracle Enterprise Manager (OEM) for comprehensive database management. Automation helps in maintaining consistency, reduces the potential for human error, and frees up the DBA to focus on more strategic and complex tasks.

Troubleshooting and problem resolution are critical skills for a DBA. Whenever issues arise—be it related to performance, connectivity, corruption, or any other anomalies—the DBA must quickly diagnose and resolve them. Familiarity with diagnostic tools, understanding Oracle error messages, and employing systematic troubleshooting methodologies are vital for efficient problem resolution.

Upgrading Oracle Database is a periodic necessity to take advantage of new features, enhancements, and security patches provided by Oracle. The DBA must plan and execute upgrades carefully to minimize downtime and ensure a smooth transition. This involves preparing a detailed upgrade plan, testing the upgrade process, performing the actual upgrade, and conducting post-upgrade validation.

Migration and transformation tasks involve moving databases across different environments, such as from on-premises to cloud infrastructure or between different hardware platforms. DBAs need to evaluate migration tools and techniques, ensure data consistency during the migration process, and validate the results post-migration.

Understanding these foundational concepts and responsibilities is critical for any DBA. The subsequent sections of this chapter provide detailed guidelines and practical steps to perform these tasks efficiently, thus ensuring the robust and secure operation of Oracle Database systems. For example, the following code snippet demonstrates starting up an Oracle database instance using SQL*Plus:

```
-- Connect to the database as SYSDBA
sqlplus / as sysdba

-- Start the database instance
STARTUP;
```

The output of this command might appear as follows:

```
ORACLE instance started.

Total System Global Area  4275781632 bytes
Fixed Size                  8892552 bytes
Variable Size            2952790016 bytes
Database Buffers          1291845632 bytes
Redo Buffers                7872512 bytes
Database mounted.
Database opened.
```

Knowledge of these processes and the capability to execute administrative tasks effectively ensures that the Oracle Database is maintained at peak performance and securely managed.

6.2 Installing and Configuring Oracle Database

The process of installing and configuring the Oracle Database is a crucial step for database administrators as it lays the foundation for a robust and scalable database environment. This section delves into the specifics of preparing your system, the installation procedure, and the subsequent configuration necessary to ensure optimal database performance.

System Requirements and Preparation

Before installing Oracle Database, it is imperative to verify that your server meets the necessary system requirements. This includes hardware specifications, such as CPU, memory, and disk space, as well as software prerequisites, including operating system versions and required packages or patches. The following examples illustrate typical hardware and software prerequisites:

- **CPU**: Multi-core processors with a minimum of 2 GHz per core.
- **Memory**: At least 4 GB RAM, with 8 GB or more recommended for production systems.

- **Disk Space**: A minimum of 10 GB of available disk space for installation files and additional space for database storage.
- **Operating System**: Oracle Linux 7, Red Hat Enterprise Linux 7, or compatible enterprise distributions.
- **Required Packages**: Ensure installation of specific OS packages such as binutils, gcc, glibc, libaio, and make.

Downloading Oracle Database Software

The Oracle Database software can be downloaded from the Oracle Technology Network (OTN) or the Oracle Software Delivery Cloud. It is essential to choose the correct version that aligns with your operating system and architecture. Follow these steps to download the software:

1. Visit the Oracle Technology Network (OTN) download page.
2. Select the appropriate Oracle Database version and platform.
3. Click Download and agree to the Oracle License Agreement.
4. Save the downloaded archive file to a desired directory on your server.

Oracle Installation Prerequisite Checks

Ensuring that all system prerequisites are met is crucial before starting the installation. Oracle provides a tool, runcluvfy, to perform these checks:

```
$ ./runcluvfy.sh stage -pre crsinst -n <node_list>
```

Ensure all checks pass. Address any reported issues before proceeding.

Starting the Oracle Universal Installer (OUI)

The Oracle Universal Installer (OUI) is a graphical tool used to install Oracle Database. To initiate the installation, you can execute the following command:

```
$ ./runInstaller
```

Choosing Installation Options

During the installation, you will be prompted to select various installation options:

- **Installation Type**: Choose between a Desktop Class or Server Class installation.
- **Oracle Base and Software Location**: Specify directories for Oracle Base (e.g., /u01/app/oracle) and Oracle Home (e.g., /u01/app/oracle/product/19.3.0/dbhome_1).
- **Configuration Options**: Define the database edition, feature set, and optionally create a database as part of the installation.

Setting Up Environment Variables

After the installation completes, configure the environment variables in your shell profile file (.bashrc or .profile):

```
export ORACLE_BASE=/u01/app/oracle
export ORACLE_HOME=$ORACLE_BASE/product/19.3.0/dbhome_1
export PATH=$PATH:$ORACLE_HOME/bin
export ORACLE_SID=orcl
```

Apply the changes using:

```
$ source ~/.bashrc
```

Running Post-Installation Tasks

Complete any remaining tasks such as setting up the listener, creating a database, and configuring essential network parameters.

Database Configuration Assistant (DBCA)

For database creation, Oracle provides the Database Configuration Assistant (DBCA). This tool simplifies the process of creating, configuring, and managing databases. Launch the DBCA using:

```
$ dbca
```

Follow the on-screen instructions to choose database templates, set database identifiers, specify storage options, and configure network settings. An example of DBCA configuration steps:

- **Database Identification**: Assign a Global Database Name (e.g., orcl.mydomain) and Oracle SID (e.g., orcl).
- **Storage Configuration**: Define database file locations (e.g., /u01/app/oracle/oradata).
- **Management Options**: Enable Oracle Enterprise Manager (OEM) for database monitoring and management.

Executing DBCA will create the necessary database files, configure initialization parameters, and initialize the database instance.

Validating Installation and Configuration

Upon completing the installation and configuration, validate the setup through various sanity checks:

```
$ sqlplus / as sysdba

SQL> SELECT status FROM v$instance;
```

```
STATUS
-------
OPEN
```

Ensure the instance status is OPEN.

This comprehensive process of installing and configuring Oracle Database ensures that the database environment is robust, secure, and ready for subsequent administrative tasks. Proper initial setup lays the groundwork for efficient database management and optimal performance.

6.3 Managing Oracle Database Instances

Managing Oracle Database Instances involves overseeing the operational environment of an Oracle database, which encompasses essential tasks like starting and stopping instances, monitoring their status, and configuring their parameters to ensure performance, reliability, and security.

An Oracle Database Instance consists of the system global area (SGA) and the background processes. The SGA is a shared memory structure that contains data and control information for the instance. Background processes handle many tasks, such as writing data to disk, managing memory structures, and logging information.

```
STARTUP;
```

The STARTUP command activates the Oracle instance, mounting and opening the database. It is essential to understand the different modes in which an instance can be started. These modes include NOMOUNT, MOUNT, and OPEN:

- **NOMOUNT:** The instance is started without mounting the

database. This mode is typically used for database creation or recovery scenarios.

- **MOUNT:** The instance is started and the database is mounted but not opened. This mode is used for performing specific maintenance tasks such as renaming datafiles, enabling archiving, or performing full database recovery.
- **OPEN:** The instance is fully started, the database is mounted and opened for use. Users can connect and perform operations on the database.

To start an instance in a specific mode, use the appropriate syntax:

```
STARTUP NOMOUNT;
STARTUP MOUNT;
STARTUP OPEN;
```

Shutting down an Oracle instance also has different modes, each serving a different purpose. The options include NORMAL, IMMEDIATE, TRANSACTIONAL, and ABORT:

- **NORMAL:** Waits for all users to disconnect before shutting down. It disallows new connections.
- **IMMEDIATE:** Rolls back active transactions and disconnects all users immediately without waiting for user sessions to end.
- **TRANSACTIONAL:** Waits for current transactions to complete and then shuts down.
- **ABORT:** Causes an immediate shutdown of the instance without preventing connected users from continuing their transactions. This is often used in emergency situations when the database must be taken offline quickly.

The syntax for each shutdown mode is as follows:

```
SHUTDOWN NORMAL;
SHUTDOWN IMMEDIATE;
SHUTDOWN TRANSACTIONAL;
SHUTDOWN ABORT;
```

Instance parameter configuration plays a crucial role in performance optimization and resource management. The initialization parameter file, init.ora, or the server parameter file, spfile, contains instance-specific parameters. To view current parameter settings:

```
SHOW PARAMETERS;
```

SHOW PARAMETERS lists all current parameter settings. Specific parameters can be modified dynamically using the ALTER SYSTEM command for instance-wide changes or the ALTER SESSION command for session-specific changes.

```
ALTER SYSTEM SET parameter_name = value SCOPE = {SPFILE|BOTH|
    MEMORY};
ALTER SESSION SET parameter_name = value;
```

The SCOPE clause specifies where the change occurs. SPFILE indicates that the parameter change is persistent across instance restarts, BOTH applies the change both in current memory and SPFILE, and MEMORY implies the change will only affect the current instance and will not persist after a restart.

Monitoring the status of an Oracle instance is essential for ensuring its operational integrity. This can be performed using several views available in the data dictionary, including V$INSTANCE, V$SESSION, and V$SYSTEM_EVENT.

```
SELECT INSTANCE_NAME, STATUS FROM V$INSTANCE;
```

The V$INSTANCE view provides the instance name and its current status. Understanding the state and workload of sessions connected to the database is necessary for diagnosing and resolving performance issues.

```
SELECT SID, SERIAL#, STATUS, SCHEMANAME, OSUSER, MACHINE
FROM V$SESSION;
```

V$SESSION can give detailed insights into each session, such as session ID (SID), serial number, status, schema name, operating system user, and the client machine name. Monitoring system events helps detect contention, resource bottlenecks, and transaction throughput issues.

```
SELECT EVENT, TOTAL_WAITS, TIME_WAITED
FROM V$SYSTEM_EVENT;
```

Efficient Oracle Database Instance management combines the knowledge of starting and shutting down instances, configuring parameters, and monitoring system status with practical analytical skills to ensure robust and effective database operation.

6.4 Storage Management

Storage management is a critical aspect of Oracle Database administration, providing the foundation for data availability, performance, and scalability. Efficient storage management ensures that the database can store, retrieve, and manage data in an optimized and organized manner. This section elaborates on key concepts and tasks including tablespace management, datafile handling, and storage optimization techniques.

Tablespaces and Datafiles

In Oracle Database, a tablespace is a logical storage unit that groups related data files for easier database management. Each tablespace consists of one or more datafiles, which physically store the database data on disk.

To create a new tablespace, the following SQL command is used:

```
CREATE TABLESPACE example_tbs
DATAFILE 'example_tbs01.dbf'
SIZE 100M
AUTOEXTEND ON
NEXT 10M
MAXSIZE 500M
EXTENT MANAGEMENT LOCAL
SEGMENT SPACE MANAGEMENT AUTO;
```

This command creates a tablespace named example_tbs with an initial datafile size of 100MB that can automatically extend in increments of 10MB up to a maximum size of 500MB. The CREATED TABLESPACE command includes options for extent management and segment space management policies.

Monitoring Tablespaces

Monitoring tablespaces is essential to ensure they have sufficient free space and are functioning optimally. The following query retrieves information about tablespace utilization:

```
SELECT tablespace_name,
       total_space,
       used_space,
       (total_space - used_space) AS free_space,
       ROUND((used_space / total_space) * 100, 2) AS pct_used
FROM (SELECT tablespace_name,
             SUM(bytes) / (1024 * 1024) AS total_space,
             SUM((bytes - free_space)) / (1024 * 1024) AS used_space
      FROM (SELECT tablespace_name,
                   bytes,
                   NVL(free_space.bytes, 0) AS free_space
            FROM dba_data_files
```

```
                LEFT JOIN (SELECT tablespace_name,
                                  file_id,
                                  SUM(bytes) AS bytes
                           FROM dba_free_space
                           GROUP BY tablespace_name, file_id) free_space
                ON dba_data_files.file_id = free_space.file_id)
    GROUP BY tablespace_name);
```

This query joins the DBA_DATA_FILES view with the DBA_FREE_-SPACE view to calculate total space, used space, free space, and the percentage of used space for each tablespace.

```
TABLESPACE_NAME  TOTAL_SPACE  USED_SPACE  FREE_SPACE  PCT_USED
---------------  -----------  ----------  ----------  --------
SYSTEM           700          500         200         71.43
USERS            150          50          100         33.33
EXAMPLE_TBS      100          20          80          20.00
```

Resizing Datafiles

When tablespaces are running out of space, datafiles can be resized to allocate additional storage. The resizing can be done manually using the ALTER DATABASE statement:

```
ALTER DATABASE DATAFILE 'example_tbs01.dbf' RESIZE 200M;
```

This command increases the size of the specified datafile to 200MB.

Automatic Storage Management (ASM)

Automatic Storage Management (ASM) is an integrated Oracle Database feature that simplifies storage management. By using disk groups, ASM dynamically distributes the database files across all available storage, optimizing performance and redundancy. To leverage ASM, one must create disk groups and configure the database to use them.

Creating an ASM disk group:

```
CREATE DISKGROUP example_dg EXTERNAL REDUNDANCY
DISK 'ORCL:DISK1', 'ORCL:DISK2';
```

In this command, example_dg is the name of the disk group, and ORCL:DISK1 and ORCL:DISK2 are the disk names.

Storage Optimization Techniques

Oracle Database provides several techniques to optimize storage usage and performance:

1. **Compression:** Data compression reduces the storage footprint by compressing table and index data. Creating a compressed table involves the following SQL command:

```
CREATE TABLE compressed_table (id NUMBER, data VARCHAR2(100))
COMPRESS FOR OLTP;
```

2. **Partitioning:** Partitioning allows large tables and indexes to be divided into smaller, more manageable pieces, improving performance and manageability. A partitioned table creation example is shown below:

```
CREATE TABLE partitioned_table (dept_id NUMBER, emp_name VARCHAR2(50))
PARTITION BY RANGE (dept_id) (
 PARTITION part1 VALUES LESS THAN (10),
 PARTITION part2 VALUES LESS THAN (20),
 PARTITION part3 VALUES LESS THAN (MAXVALUE));
```

3. **Data Archiving:** Archiving historical data reduces the size of active tables and improves query performance. Oracle provides the DBMS_ILM package to manage the lifecycle of database data.

These techniques collectively enhance storage efficiency, reduce costs, and improve overall database performance. Effective storage management is crucial for maintaining database health, scaling efficiently, and ensuring data integrity.

6.5 User and Schema Management

Oracle Database imposes a hierarchical structure on data storage and access, primarily governed through users and schemas. Proper management of these elements is crucial for maintaining security, integrity, and performance of the database system. This section explores the vital strategies and practices involved in user and schema management within Oracle Database.

User accounts in Oracle are essential for controlling access privileges and ensuring security. Each user is associated with a unique authentication method, default roles, and specific privileges that define their capabilities within the database. Oracle DBAs frequently create, modify, and manage these user accounts to align with organizational policies and user requirements.

The following SQL command illustrates the creation of a new user in Oracle Database:

```
CREATE USER john_doe IDENTIFIED BY securePassword
DEFAULT TABLESPACE users
TEMPORARY TABLESPACE temp
QUOTA 10M ON users;
```

In this command:

- john_doe is the username.
- securePassword is the password for the user.
- DEFAULT TABLESPACE users sets the default tablespace to which user's objects will belong.
- TEMPORARY TABLESPACE temp assigns a temporary tablespace for query operations.
- QUOTA 10M ON users limits the user's tablespace quota to 10 megabytes.

Executing this SQL command creates the user and establishes their initial properties. DBAs can subsequently manage the user's roles and privileges. The following example grants the CONNECT and RESOURCE roles to the user:

```
GRANT CONNECT, RESOURCE TO john_doe;
```

Roles in Oracle amalgamate multiple privileges, which may cover system and object privileges. DBAs can create custom roles and grant them to users, simplifying the management of user privileges:

```
CREATE ROLE custom_role;
GRANT SELECT, INSERT, UPDATE, DELETE ON employees TO custom_role;
GRANT custom_role TO john_doe;
```

Schemas are the logical containers within databases that group users' objects, such as tables, views, and procedures. Effectively, the term schema is synonymous with the user who owns the related database objects. When a user is created, a schema with the same name is automatically generated. Schemas allow for the logical organization of database objects and help manage object privileges seamlessly.

Another critical aspect of schema management is ensuring objects within the schema are organized and optimized for performance. For instance, proper indexing and partitioning of tables can significantly impact query performance. An example of creating an index within a schema for performance optimization is:

```
CREATE INDEX emp_name_idx ON employees (last_name, first_name);
```

Routine schema management tasks include monitoring storage quotas, reorganizing fragmented tables, and ensuring data is backed up. One of the ways to check user's tablespace quota usage is by querying the DBA_USAGE view:

```
SELECT * FROM DBA_TS_QUOTAS WHERE USERNAME = 'JOHN_DOE';
```

DBAs must also drop users and their associated schemas when they are no longer required. This step must be executed cautiously to prevent unintentional data loss. The command to drop a user and all their objects is:

```
DROP USER john_doe CASCADE;
```

The CASCADE option ensures that all objects owned by the user are removed alongside the user account.

Overall, efficient user and schema management ensure robust security, data integrity, and optimal performance of the Oracle Database. The aforementioned operations and best practices form the foundation upon which more advanced administrative tasks build, enabling a scalable and resilient database environment.

6.6 Managing Tablespaces and Datafiles

Proper management of tablespaces and datafiles is fundamental to the proficient administration of an Oracle Database. Tablespaces are logical structures that collectively store data in database files called datafiles. Understanding the mechanism of tablespaces and datafiles will facilitate efficient database organization, space management, and optimization.

Tablespaces are essential for various reasons: they allow the segregation of data, aid in performance tuning, provide backup and recovery flexibility, and assist in managing user quotas. Each tablespace comprises one or more datafiles, physically representing the stored data.

Creating Tablespaces is a critical activity. To create a tablespace, execute the CREATE TABLESPACE command. The syntax allows customization of numerous parameters:

```
CREATE TABLESPACE example_tbs
DATAFILE '/u01/oradata/example/example_tbs_01.dbf' SIZE 100M
AUTOEXTEND ON
NEXT 10M MAXSIZE UNLIMITED
LOGGING;
```

In the above command, example_tbs is the tablespace name. The

DATAFILE clause specifies the file path and size. The AUTOEXTEND clause ensures the file auto-extends by 10MB until the system storage capacity is reached (MAXSIZE UNLIMITED). LOGGING enables the generation of redo logs, essential for data recovery.

Managing Datafiles is another primary aspect. After creating tablespaces, one might need to alter them, especially the contained datafiles. A common operation is resizing datafiles:

```
ALTER DATABASE DATAFILE '/u01/oradata/example/example_tbs_01.dbf'
    RESIZE 200M;
```

This command resizes the specified datafile to 200MB. Another frequent task is adding datafiles to a tablespace:

```
ALTER TABLESPACE example_tbs
ADD DATAFILE '/u01/oradata/example/example_tbs_02.dbf' SIZE 200M;
```

Adding datafiles can help when tablespace utilization nears its capacity. Monitoring tablespace usage with the DBA_TABLESPACE_USAGE_METRICS view is prudent for proactive management.

Tablespace Types and their specific use cases are noteworthy:

- **Permanent Tablespaces**: Hold persistent user data and objects.
- **Temporary Tablespaces**: Store transient data, such as sort operations. Defined by the CREATE TEMPORARY TABLESPACE command:

  ```
  CREATE TEMPORARY TABLESPACE temp_tbs
  TEMPFILE '/u01/oradata/example/temp_tbs_01.dbf' SIZE 500M;
  ```

- **Undo Tablespaces**: Manage undo data for transaction rollbacks:

  ```
  CREATE UNDO TABLESPACE undo_tbs
  DATAFILE '/u01/oradata/example/undo_tbs_01.dbf' SIZE 200M;
  ```

Managing Tablespace Storage Parameters: Crucial parameters include AUTOEXTEND, storage quotas, and block sizes. Proper configuration ensures optimal performance and space utilization:

```
ALTER DATABASE DATAFILE '/u01/oradata/example/example_tbs_02.dbf'
AUTOEXTEND ON NEXT 20M MAXSIZE 1G;
```

Use the above command to adjust the auto-extend increment and maximum size settings of the datafile.

Tablespace and Datafile Status: Status states such as read-only, offline, online, and temporary updates facilitate maintenance operations:

```
ALTER TABLESPACE example_tbs READ ONLY;
ALTER TABLESPACE example_tbs READ WRITE;
ALTER TABLESPACE example_tbs OFFLINE;
ALTER TABLESPACE example_tbs ONLINE;
```

Monitoring tablespace and datafile health using views such as DBA_TABLESPACES, DBA_DATA_FILES, and DBA_TEMP_FILES is paramount for maintaining a healthy database.

```
SELECT TABLESPACE_NAME, FILE_NAME, BYTES, STATUS
FROM DBA_DATA_FILES
WHERE TABLESPACE_NAME = 'EXAMPLE_TBS';
```

This query retrieves essential datafile information, helping administrators monitor and manage the infrastructure.

By mastering the creation, modification, and monitoring of tablespaces and datafiles, Oracle Database administrators can ensure the efficient organization, utilization, and performance of the database environment. The flexibility in tablespace management enhances database scalability, reliability, and maintainability.

6.7 Configuring and Managing Network Connections

Oracle Database network configuration involves establishing communication between the Oracle Database and client applications, other databases, or remote users. Effective network configuration ensures seamless access, reliable performance, and secure data transfer. This section elaborates on configuring essential network components, managing network connectivity, and troubleshooting network issues.

Oracle Net Services, a suite of network components, simplifies and manages complex network environments. Key components include the *Listener*, *TNSNames.ora*, and *SQLNet.ora* files. The listener is a server process that handles client connection requests, while the *TNSNames.ora* file provides a directory matching service names to network addresses. The *SQLNet.ora* file configures various client and server network parameters.

Listener Configuration

To configure the listener, use Oracle Net Manager or manually edit the

Listener.ora file. This file defines the parameters for the database listener, including protocol addresses and service information.

An example of a *Listener.ora* file:

```
LISTENER =
  (DESCRIPTION_LIST =
    (DESCRIPTION =
      (ADDRESS = (PROTOCOL = TCP)(HOST = dbhost.example.com)(PORT =
          1521))
      (ADDRESS = (PROTOCOL = IPC)(KEY = EXTPROC1521))
    )
  )

SID_LIST_LISTENER =
  (SID_LIST =
    (SID_DESC =
      (SID_NAME = ORCL)
      (ORACLE_HOME = /u01/app/oracle/product/19.0.0/dbhome_1)
      (PROGRAM = extproc)
    )
    (SID_DESC =
      (GLOBAL_DBNAME = orcl.example.com)
      (SID_NAME = ORCL)
      (ORACLE_HOME = /u01/app/oracle/product/19.0.0/dbhome_1)
    )
  )
```

Invoke the listener control utility, lsnrctl, to start or manage the listener:

```
$ lsnrctl start
$ lsnrctl status
```

TNSNames.ora Configuration

The *TNSNames.ora* file maps net service names to connect descriptors. Each entry describes a service, including the protocol, host, and port.

Example *TNSNames.ora* file entry:

```
ORCL =
  (DESCRIPTION =
    (ADDRESS_LIST =
      (ADDRESS = (PROTOCOL = TCP)(HOST = dbhost.example.com)(PORT =
          1521))
    )
    (CONNECT_DATA =
      (SERVICE_NAME = ORCL)
    )
  )
```

This ensures that clients can connect to the service named *ORCL* by specifying only the net service name in their connection string:

```
CONNECT user/password@ORCL
```

SQLNet.ora Configuration

The *SQLNet.ora* file configures network parameters for client and server connections. Key parameters include NAMES.DIRECTORY_PATH to specify the naming methods (like TNSNAMES and LDAP), and SQLNET.EXPIRE_TIME to enable dead connection detection.

Example *SQLNet.ora* file:

```
NAMES.DIRECTORY_PATH = (TNSNAMES, ONAMES, HOSTNAME)
SQLNET.EXPIRE_TIME = 10
```

Configuring Oracle Net Service Names using Oracle Net Manager

Oracle Net Manager provides a graphical interface to configure Oracle Net Services. Start Oracle Net Manager from the Oracle Home directory's bin library:

```
$ $ORACLE_HOME/bin/netmgr
```

Use Oracle Net Manager to create or modify net service names, configure listeners, and set profile options for network parameters. Follow these steps:

- Navigate to the **Service Naming** section.
- Click on the **Create** button to add a new net service name.
- Specify the service name, select the appropriate protocol, and enter the host and port information.
- Test the connection using the **Test** button to ensure proper configuration.

Advanced Network Configuration

Oracle Database also supports advanced network configurations using features such as *Oracle Connection Manager*, *Oracle Advanced Security*, and *Oracle Multi-Threaded Server (MTS)*.

- **Oracle Connection Manager:** Acts as an intermediate server to multiplex or demultiplex connections, enabling load balancing, access control, and improved connection concentration.
- **Oracle Advanced Security:** Provides a robust framework for data encryption and integrity, ensuring secure data transmission over the network.

- **Oracle Multi-Threaded Server (MTS):** Supports efficient use of server resources by enabling shared server processes for multiple client sessions.

Network Troubleshooting

Network troubleshooting involves diagnosing and resolving issues that impede network communication. Common tools include tnsping, lsnrctl, and *Oracle Net Trace*.

- Use tnsping to test connectivity and resolve service names:

```
$ tnsping ORCL
```

- Use lsnrctl commands to check listener status and logs:

```
$ lsnrctl status
$ lsnrctl services
```

- Enable Oracle Net Trace to capture detailed information on network operations by setting tracing parameters in the *SQLNet.ora* file:

```
TRACE_LEVEL_CLIENT = SUPPORT
TRACE_DIRECTORY_CLIENT = /u01/app/oracle/diag/nettrace
```

6.8 Monitoring and Managing Database Performance

Effective monitoring and management of database performance are crucial to ensuring the optimal functioning of an Oracle Database. Performance tuning involves multiple aspects of the database environment, including the hardware platform, the operating system, and the Oracle Database itself. This section delves into various tools and techniques used to monitor and enhance database performance, laying particular emphasis on identifying performance bottlenecks, optimizing system parameters, and leveraging Oracle's performance-tuning features.

Database Performance Monitoring Tools

Oracle provides a suite of tools designed for monitoring and tuning database performance. Key tools include:

- **Automatic Workload Repository (AWR):** A repository that collects and maintains performance statistics to diagnose and resolve database performance issues. AWR performs snapshots of performance data at regular intervals.
- **Active Session History (ASH):** Part of the AWR infrastructure, ASH samples active database sessions to help identify transient performance problems.
- **Oracle Enterprise Manager (OEM):** A comprehensive management tool that provides a graphical interface for monitoring and managing the entire Oracle environment.
- **Statspack:** A diagnostic tool that collects and reports on database performance. Though it is now largely supplanted by AWR, Statspack remains useful for environments not licensed for Oracle Diagnostics Pack.

Understanding Key Performance Metrics

A variety of metrics can be monitored to assess the health and performance of an Oracle Database. The primary metrics include:

- **Database Wait Events:** Represents events that cause sessions to wait. Common wait events include I/O waits, lock contention, and network latency.
- **System Statistics:** Provides insights into CPU usage, memory utilization, and other server-related performance metrics.
- **SQL Execution Metrics:** Performance statistics on SQL execution, including execution time, buffer gets, and disk reads.
- **Instance Efficiency Metrics:** Measures like buffer cache hit ratio, library cache hit ratio, and shared pool free memory, which gauge the efficiency of various database operations.

Identifying Performance Bottlenecks

To identify performance bottlenecks, begin by examining the top waits and high-load SQL statements. This approach helps pinpoint areas of contention that may require optimization. SQL trace files and the tkprof utility can be valuable in detailing SQL execution and resource consumption:

```
ALTER SESSION SET sql_trace=true;
-- Execute the problematic SQL statements
ALTER SESSION SET sql_trace=false;
-- Use tkprof to format the trace output
tkprof tracefile.trc outputfile.prf
```

Optimizing System Parameters

System parameters significantly impact database performance. Adjustments should be made thoughtfully and based on empirical evidence from performance monitoring tools. Crucial parameters include:

- **Memory Allocation:** Parameters like SGA_TARGET and PGA_AGGREGATE_TARGET that dictate the amount of memory allocated to database operations.
- **I/O Configuration:** Managing datafile distribution and leveraging Automatic Storage Management (ASM) to optimize I/O performance.
- **Parallel Execution:** Configuring parallel execution parameters to enhance the performance of large-scale operations.

Using Automatic Database Diagnostic Monitor (ADDM)

ADDM analyzes AWR data to identify significant performance issues and recommends corrective actions. ADDM performs a top-down analysis, focusing on the root causes of performance problems. Run ADDM reports regularly to maintain optimal performance:

```
EXEC DBMS_ADDM.ANALYZE_DB(:begin_snap_id, :end_snap_id);
```

Leveraging SQL Tuning Advisor

The SQL Tuning Advisor helps optimize SQL statements by providing recommendations for SQL profile usage, indexing strategies, and rewriting queries. Access the advisor via Oracle Enterprise Manager or PL/SQL packages:

```
DECLARE
  l_sql_tune_task_id VARCHAR2(255);
BEGIN
  l_sql_tune_task_id := DBMS_SQLTUNE.create_tuning_task(
    sql_id => 'your_sql_id_here',
    scope => DBMS_SQLTUNE.scope_comprehensive
  );
  DBMS_SQLTUNE.execute_tuning_task(task_name => l_sql_tune_task_id);
  DBMS_OUTPUT.put_line('SQL Tuning Task ID: ' || l_sql_tune_task_id);
END;
```

Oracle Real Application Testing

Oracle's Real Application Testing (RAT) suite can capture production workloads and replay them in a test environment. This ensures that performance tuning or configuration changes do not inadvertently degrade performance under actual workload conditions.

For sustained database performance, constant monitoring and periodic tuning are indispensable. The tools and techniques covered, from AWR and ASH to ADDM and SQL Tuning Advisor, provide comprehensive means to diagnose and resolve performance issues, ensuring efficient and reliable Oracle Database operations.

6.9 Automating Administrative Tasks

Oracle Database administration involves numerous repetitive tasks, which, if performed manually, can be both time-consuming and prone to human error. Automating these tasks enhances efficiency, ensures consistency, and allows database administrators (DBAs) to focus on more strategic activities. This section will delve into various methods and tools for automating administrative tasks within Oracle Database environments, including the use of Oracle Scheduler, scripting with SQL*Plus, and leveraging Oracle Enterprise Manager.

Oracle Scheduler is a robust and feature-rich tool for automating database jobs. It allows for the efficient management and scheduling of tasks, supporting both time-based and event-based job execution. A basic job in Oracle Scheduler is defined by several components: job, program, schedule, and job class.

To create a simple job that runs a PL/SQL block, the following SQL*Plus script can be utilized:

```
BEGIN
   DBMS_SCHEDULER.create_job (
      job_name => 'my_simple_job',
      job_type => 'PLSQL_BLOCK',
      job_action => 'BEGIN DBMS_STATS.gather_schema_stats(''HR''); END;',
      start_date => SYSTIMESTAMP,
      repeat_interval => 'FREQ=DAILY; BYHOUR=2; BYMINUTE=0;
           BYSECOND=0',
      enabled => TRUE
   );
END;
/
```

In this example, the job my_simple_job executes a PL/SQL block that gathers schema statistics for the HR schema daily at 2:00 AM.

Programs and schedules can also be created separately and then associated with jobs. A program encapsulates the job action, and a schedule defines the frequency and timing:

```
BEGIN
    DBMS_SCHEDULER.create_program (
        program_name => 'my_program',
        program_type => 'PLSQL_BLOCK',
        program_action => 'BEGIN DBMS_STATS.gather_schema_stats(''HR'');
            END;',
        enabled => TRUE
    );

    DBMS_SCHEDULER.create_schedule (
        schedule_name => 'daily_2am_schedule',
        repeat_interval => 'FREQ=DAILY; BYHOUR=2; BYMINUTE=0;
            BYSECOND=0'
    );

    DBMS_SCHEDULER.create_job (
        job_name => 'my_complex_job',
        program_name => 'my_program',
        schedule_name => 'daily_2am_schedule',
        enabled => TRUE
    );
END;
/
```

By defining programs and schedules separately, you can reuse them across multiple jobs, enhancing maintainability and consistency.

Another essential aspect of automation in Oracle Database is scripting with SQL*Plus. SQL*Plus scripts can be utilized to automate routine tasks such as backups, user management, and performance monitoring. Consider the following script for backing up a database:

```
SET ECHO ON
SPOOL backup.log

CONNECT / AS SYSDBA

RUN {
    SHUTDOWN IMMEDIATE;
    STARTUP MOUNT;
    BACKUP DATABASE FORMAT '/u01/backups/full_%U.bkp';
    ALTER DATABASE OPEN;
}

SPOOL OFF
EXIT
```

Executing this script will shut down the database, mount it, perform a full backup, and then reopen it. The backup will be logged to backup.log for later review.

Oracle Enterprise Manager (OEM) provides a graphical interface that simplifies the automation of administrative tasks. It allows DBAs to define and manage jobs, monitor job execution, and analyze job logs. Through OEM, users can schedule backups, run SQL scripts, monitor system performance, and configure alerts.

To automate a SQL script execution using Oracle Enterprise Manager:

- Navigate to the *Job Activity* page.
- Click *Create Job* and select *SQL Script*.
- Provide a job name and select the target database.
- Enter the SQL script to be executed.
- Set the schedule for when the script should run.
- Review and submit the job.

OEM also supports the creation of complex workflows that involve conditional logic and multiple steps, providing a comprehensive solution for sophisticated automation requirements.

In summary, automating administrative tasks in Oracle Database is achieved through various tools and scripting techniques, each tailored to specific needs and preferences. By leveraging Oracle Scheduler, SQL*Plus scripting, and Oracle Enterprise Manager, DBAs can ensure the efficient, consistent, and error-free execution of routine tasks.

6.10 Troubleshooting and Problem Resolution

Effective troubleshooting and problem resolution are key competencies for an Oracle Database Administrator (DBA). This section delves into various techniques and tools that facilitate diagnosing and resolving issues in Oracle databases. Understanding the architecture, common problems, and available diagnostic tools are essential.

Oracle's diagnostic infrastructure provides numerous utilities and logs to investigate issues. Each type of problem requires a specific approach to troubleshooting. Common problems include connection errors, performance degradation, and data corruption, among others.

Identifying Connection Problems

Connection issues are frequently encountered in Oracle databases. These can stem from various sources, such as network configurations, database listener problems, or misconfigured client settings. To effectively diagnose connection issues, begin by checking the status of the listener and network components.

The tnsping utility can be used to test connectivity to Oracle services. The following command checks the connectivity:

```
tnsping <service_name>
```

If the tnsping command fails, it indicates a problem with the network or TNS configuration. In addition, examine the listener.log located in the $ORACLE_BASE/diag/tnslsnr/$HOST/$LISTENER/log/ directory for detailed listener diagnostics.

Checking Database Listener Status

Ensure the listener is running using the following commands:

```
lsnrctl status
lsnrctl start
```

If issues are found in the listener configuration, confirm that listener.ora is properly configured. Typical problems are incorrect hostname or port assignments.

Diagnosing Performance Issues

Performance bottlenecks are another critical concern. Oracle provides numerous tools, such as Automatic Workload Repository (AWR) reports, Active Session History (ASH) reports, and the SQL*Plus utility, to monitor and diagnose performance problems.

To generate an AWR report, execute:

```
@$ORACLE_HOME/rdbms/admin/awrrpt.sql
```

The AWR report highlights problem areas and provides insights into problematic SQL queries, wait events, and system statistics.

SQL Tuning

Poorly optimized SQL statements are common culprits of performance degradation. The EXPLAIN PLAN command is essential for understanding the execution plan of a query. Use the following command to generate an execution plan:

```
EXPLAIN PLAN FOR <sql_statement>;
SELECT * FROM TABLE(DBMS_XPLAN.DISPLAY);
```

This output shows the path taken by the query, helping to identify inefficiencies such as full table scans instead of index scans.

Memory and CPU Utilization

To diagnose memory and CPU bottlenecks, the Dynamic Performance Views (v$ views) are invaluable. For instance, to check the system's CPU usage:

```
SELECT * FROM v$sysstat WHERE name LIKE 'CPU used by this session';
```

Similarly, the v$memory_dynamic_component_s view provides insights into memory usage:

```
SELECT component, current_size, user_specified_size
FROM v$memory_dynamic_components;
```

Diagnosing and Resolving Data Corruption

Data corruption is less common but highly critical. Oracle's DBVERIFY utility helps detect potential physical corruption in datafiles. Use it as follows:

```
dbv FILE=<datafile> BLOCKSIZE=<block_size>
```

Whenever corruption is detected, determine whether it is physical or logical corruption. Traditional recovery techniques involve restoring from backups or utilizing Oracle's RMAN recovery features. The following command restores the corrupted block using RMAN:

```
BLOCKRECOVER CORRUPTION LIST;
```

Inline Diagnostic and Error Logs

Oracle allows capturing diagnostic data directly through inline diagnostics, using the Alert Log and Trace Files. The Alert Log is the primary source of diagnostic information and is located typically in the $ORACLE_BASE/diag/rdbms/{DB_NAME}/{DB_ID}/trace directory. Reviewing this log can highlight significant errors and events, including administrative operations and errors.

Trace files give granular level details regarding specific processes and sessions. Regularly monitoring these logs can preempt major issues by identifying patterns or recurring errors.

Proactive Monitoring and Alerts

Oracle Enterprise Manager (OEM) provides comprehensive monitoring capabilities. Utilize OEM to configure alerts for critical events such as tablespace usage, database response times, and session waits. Setting up these alerts ensures preemptive actions before issues escalate into outages.

- Thresholds define specific metrics for alert generation.
- Advice and Recommendations section offers automated tuning suggestions.
- Data Collection can be tailored to gather specific performance metrics.

Utilizing Oracle Support

Oracle Support Services, accessible through the My Oracle Support portal, offers extensive documentation and troubleshooting resources. When encountering persistent or unidentified problems, creating a Service Request (SR) enables contacting Oracle Support Engineers directly.

For efficient problem resolution, provide comprehensive diagnostic data, including logs, AWR reports, and error details when submitting an SR. Use the Oracle Diagnostic Methodology, comprising the following:

- Problem Definition - Clearly articulate the issue.
- Data Collection - Gather and present all relevant diagnostics.
- Root Cause Analysis - Identify underlying causes through systematic analysis.

Seamless operation of Oracle databases is predicated on a DBA's ability to effectively diagnose and resolve problems. Employing standard diagnostic tools, analyzing logs and reports, and maintaining proactive monitoring are crucial practices. With systematic problem resolution strategies, administrators can ensure optimal performance and reliability of Oracle Database systems.

6.11 Upgrading Oracle Database

Oracle Database upgrades are necessary to take advantage of new features, performance improvements, and security enhancements. This section delves into the methods, preparations, and steps required to upgrade an Oracle Database effectively, ensuring minimal downtime and data integrity.

Upgrading an Oracle Database involves moving from an older version to a newer one. This process can be complex, involving several pre-upgrade tasks, the actual upgrade operation, and post-upgrade tasks. The primary methods for upgrading Oracle Database include the Direct Upgrade method, the Export/Import method, and the Data Pump method. Each method has its specific use cases and requirements.

Before initiating an upgrade, it is imperative to perform a thorough assessment and preparation. Ensuring a successful upgrade requires attention to the following areas:

- **Compatibility and Interoperability:** Verify that the new Oracle Database version is compatible with existing applications and that any third-party software or custom applications are tested for interoperability.
- **Hardware and OS Requirements:** Confirm that the server hardware and operating system meet the requirements of the new Oracle Database version.
- **Backup Strategy:** Establish a reliable backup strategy to ensure data can be recovered in case of an upgrade failure. Take a full backup of the database before starting the upgrade process.
- **Pre-Upgrade Information Tool (DBUA in pre-upgrade mode):** Use Oracle's Database Upgrade Assistant (DBUA) in pre-upgrade mode to assess the readiness of the database for the upgrade. This tool checks database components for compatibility issues that need resolution before upgrading.
- **Testing:** Perform extensive testing on a cloned database environment to identify and mitigate potential issues during the upgrade.

To execute a Direct Upgrade from Oracle Database 11g to Oracle Database 19c, follow these detailed steps:

```
-- Step 1: Install the new Oracle Database 19c software
-- Ensure the new Oracle home is installed and ready to accept the upgraded database

-- Step 2: Run pre-upgrade checks using the preupgrade.jar tool provided by Oracle
java -jar $ORACLE_HOME/rdbms/admin/preupgrade.jar TERMINAL TEXT

-- This outputs checks and recommendations in the upg_summary.log file
```

```
-- Step 3: Perform any recommended pre-upgrade tasks based on the pre-upgrade tool's
    output

-- Step 4: Shut down the Oracle Database 11g instance
shutdown immediate;

-- Step 5: Start the database in upgrade mode using the 19c Oracle home
sqlplus / as sysdba
startup upgrade;

-- Step 6: Execute the "dbupgrade" command to start the upgrade process
$ORACLE_HOME/rdbms/admin/dbupgrade

-- Step 7: Execute any mandatory post-upgrade scripts as per the upgrade guide
@$ORACLE_HOME/rdbms/admin/utluptab.sql
```

While this example demonstrates a Direct Upgrade, it's crucial to consider other methods in scenarios where direct upgrading is not feasible. For example, if the database version gap is significant or if cross-platform migration is required, the Export/Import or Data Pump methods may be appropriate.

Export/Import Method: The Export/Import method involves creating an export dump file of the existing database and importing it into the new Oracle Database version. This method provides more control over the upgrade process and can help address compatibility issues.

```
-- Step 1: Export the schema(s) from the old database
expdp username/password@old_db schemas=schema_name directory=export_dir
    dumpfile=schema.dmp logfile=schema_exp.log;

-- Step 2: Pre-create the tablespaces and necessary schemas on the new database if
    required

-- Step 3: Import the dump file into the new database version
impdp username/password@new_db schemas=schema_name directory=import_dir
    dumpfile=schema.dmp logfile=schema_imp.log;
```

Data Pump Method: The Data Pump Export/Import method is a high-performance data movement utility provided by Oracle. This method can be used for large-scale database migrations and upgrades with parallelization and fine-grained control.

```
-- Step 1: Use Data Pump to export the database
-- Full Database Export
expdp system/password full=Y directory=data_pump_dir dumpfile=full_db.dmp
    logfile=full_db_exp.log

-- Step 2: Import the dump file into the new Oracle Database version
impdp system/password full=Y directory=data_pump_dir dumpfile=full_db.dmp
    logfile=full_db_imp.log
```

Post-upgrade tasks are essential to ensure the database operates optimally with the new version. These tasks include:

- **Upgrade Dictionary Statistics:** Gather dictionary statistics to improve the performance of the database dictionary queries.
- **Recompile Invalid Objects:** Recompile all invalid PL/SQL objects to ensure they are valid post-upgrade.

```
-- Example: Recompiling invalid objects
@$ORACLE_HOME/rdbms/admin/utlrp.sql
```

- **Testing Applications:** Conduct thorough testing of critical applications to verify their functionality post-upgrade.
- **Optimize Configurations:** Review and optimize initialization parameters and other database configurations.
- **Enable New Features:** Assess and enable new features or enhancements available in the upgraded version that can benefit business needs.

One must perform regular maintenance tasks and monitor the upgraded database closely for any issues that might arise.

6.12 Migration and Transformation

Migration and transformation of databases are critical tasks performed by database administrators to ensure data integrity, availability, and optimal performance as systems evolve. This section delves into the methodologies and tools used to migrate and transform Oracle databases efficiently. We will explore the planning, execution, and validation phases, focusing on the use of Oracle's native utilities and best practices.

Migration in the context of Oracle databases typically involves moving databases across different versions, platforms, or environments. Transformation often refers to modifying the database schema or structure to better meet changing business requirements. These processes must be carried out with minimal disruption to services, ensuring that data remains consistent and secure.

- **Migration Planning**

The initial phase involves thorough planning. A feasibility study determines the target database requirements, assesses compatibility issues, and evaluates potential risks. Creating a detailed migration plan is essential, encompassing timelines, resource allocations, and rollback strategies. Key activities include:

- Identification of source and target database versions.
- Evaluation of hardware and software compatibility.
- Estimation of downtime required for migration.
- Development of a comprehensive backup strategy.

- **Migration Execution**

Execution of database migration can be achieved using various Oracle tools and utilities. The choice of tool depends on factors such as the size and complexity of the database, downtime tolerance, and specific requirements of the target environment. Key tools include:

Oracle Data Pump: A high-performance utility for exporting and importing data and metadata. Data Pump provides parallel execution and fine-grained control for large-scale migrations. Example commands:

```
-- Exporting the schema
expdp system/password@source_db schemas=schema_name directory=
      data_pump_dir dumpfile=expfile.dmp logfile=explog.log

-- Importing the schema into target database
impdp system/password@target_db schemas=schema_name directory=
      data_pump_dir dumpfile=expfile.dmp logfile=implog.log
```

Oracle SQL Developer: An integrated development environment that provides database migration utilities, including the Migration Workbench. SQL Developer supports heterogeneous migrations, such as from non-Oracle databases.

Transportable Tablespaces: A method to move tablespaces between Oracle databases, enabling quick migration of large data sets. This method is efficient for cross-platform migrations when source and target platforms share compatible character sets and endian formats. Commands include:

```
-- Making the tablespace read-only
ALTER TABLESPACE tablespace_name READ ONLY;

-- Exporting the tablespace metadata
```

```
expdp system/password@source_db transport_tablespaces=tablespace_name directory
     =data_pump_dir dumpfile=expfile.dmp logfile=explog.log;

-- Copying the data files to target
-- Importing the tablespace metadata into the target database
impdp system/password@target_db transport_tablespaces=tablespace_name directory
     =data_pump_dir dumpfile=expfile.dmp logfile=implog.log;

-- Making the tablespace read-write in the target database
ALTER TABLESPACE tablespace_name READ WRITE;
```

Oracle GoldenGate: A real-time data integration and replication solution offering continuous availability and zero downtime for migrations. GoldenGate is particularly effective for large-scale environments requiring minimal impact on production.

- **Migration Validation**

Post-migration, it is critical to validate the success of the migration process. Validation strategies include:

- Checking data integrity and consistency between source and target databases.
- Performing application testing to ensure functionality is intact.
- Monitoring the performance of the target database to identify and resolve any issues.

Tools such as Oracle Real Application Testing (RAT) help simulate production workloads to test and tune the database post-migration, ensuring it meets performance and reliability expectations.

- **Transformation Processes**

Transformation involves altering the database structure, which might include normalization or denormalization of tables, changes in data types, or implementation of new indexing strategies. These changes aim to improve performance, support new applications, or facilitate compliance with new business rules.

Schema Conversion: Tools like Oracle SQL Developer and Oracle SQL*Plus can be used to script and apply schema changes. Example scripting:

```
-- Adding a new column with default value
ALTER TABLE table_name ADD column_name VARCHAR2(50) DEFAULT '
    default_value';

-- Modifying data type of a column
ALTER TABLE table_name MODIFY column_name NUMBER(10,2);
```

Data Transformation: Data transformation processes might involve ETL (Extract, Transform, Load) operations. Oracle Data Integrator (ODI) provides a robust platform for designing such transformations, ensuring data quality and consistency.

```
-- Example ETL task using PL/SQL
DECLARE
    CURSOR c1 IS SELECT old_column FROM old_table;
    BEGIN
        FOR record IN c1 LOOP
            -- Transformation logic here
            INSERT INTO new_table (new_column) VALUES (transformed_value);
        END LOOP;
    END;
```

Efficient execution of migration and transformation tasks demands thorough planning, effective utilization of Oracle tools, and rigorous validation to safeguard data integrity and performance. Adhering to best practices and leveraging Oracle's advanced utilities ensures successful outcomes and minimal disruption to business operations.

Chapter 7

Backup and Recovery

This chapter addresses the vital practices of backup and recovery in Oracle Database. It explains the concepts of using Oracle Recovery Manager (RMAN), performing backups, and executing database recovery. The chapter covers RMAN backup options, user-managed backup methods, and utilizing flashback technology. It also details managing archived redo logs, point-in-time recovery, cloning databases, and best practices to ensure data protection and disaster recovery.

7.1 Introduction to Backup and Recovery

Oracle databases are integral to the operations of many organizations, securing vital data that underpins business processes. Protecting this data from loss, corruption, or accidental deletion is essential to maintain operational continuity. This section delves into the fundamental principles of backup and recovery within the Oracle database environment, addressing the reasons and methodologies for safeguarding data.

Data loss can occur due to hardware failures, software bugs, user errors, or malicious attacks. Consequently, a robust backup and recovery strategy ensures that data can be restored to a consistent state, minimizing operational downtime and data loss risk.

Backup refers to creating a copy of data so that it can be restored in case of data loss. This process can be executed while the database is online (hot backup) or offline (cold backup). Each method has its own advantages and considerations:

- **Hot Backup:** Hot backups are performed while the database is running and accessible to users. This is critical for 24/7 operations as it allows continuous data protection without downtime. Oracle's Recovery Manager (RMAN) is proficient in handling such backups by ensuring data consistency even when the database is active.

- **Cold Backup:** Cold backups necessitate taking the database offline, ensuring a static data state during backup. This method significantly reduces complexity and ensures a high degree of data integrity since no transactions are in progress. However, it might not be suitable for non-stop operational environments due to the required downtime.

Recovery is the process of restoring and managing the database to its normal operational state after a failure. Recovery can be categorized primarily into:

- **Instance Recovery:** Performed automatically by the Oracle instance upon startup after a crash. It uses the redo logs to apply any committed transactions and remove uncommitted ones, ensuring database consistency.

- **Media Recovery:** Involves restoring physical files from backup in the event of disk failure or data corruption. Media recovery is typically executed by RMAN, which can automate many of the otherwise manual tasks associated with this process.

In the context of Oracle databases, RMAN emerges as a pivotal tool. RMAN simplifies the backup and recovery process, providing a comprehensive solution for managing backup strategies. It supports both offline and online backups and includes features like incremental backups, which only store changes made since the last backup, thus optimizing storage and performance.

Below is an example of an RMAN command for performing an incremental level 0 backup:

```
RMAN> BACKUP INCREMENTAL LEVEL 0 DATABASE;
```

Incremental backups, such as level 1, save all blocks that have changed since the last level 0 or level 1 backup, making them efficient in terms of storage and time.

```
RMAN> BACKUP INCREMENTAL LEVEL 1 DATABASE;
```

In case of a failure, RMAN facilitates recovery through commands that restore the database and apply necessary redo logs to bring the database to the consistent state just before the failure event.

```
RMAN> RESTORE DATABASE;
RMAN> RECOVER DATABASE;
```

RMAN's robust capabilities extend beyond conventional backups. Using RMAN, administrators can manage archived redo logs, perform point-in-time recovery, and clone databases efficiently. Archived redo logs, which store all changes made to the database, are crucial for media recovery. They enable point-in-time recovery, allowing administrators to restore the database to a specific moment, typically just before a failure or data corruption event occurred.

Flashback technology is another significant advancement in Oracle database recovery strategies. Flashback features provide a rich set of tools designed to view past states of database objects and to revert to a previous state without the need for media recovery.

Flashback Query lets you see the database content as of a previous time, using the AS OF clause in a SELECT statement. This is particularly useful for recovering from user errors at the object level.

```
SELECT * FROM employees AS OF TIMESTAMP (SYSTIMESTAMP - INTERVAL '
    10' MINUTE);
```

Flashback Table allows tables to be restored to a previous point in time, which is done through the FLASHBACK TABLE command.

```
FLASHBACK TABLE employees TO TIMESTAMP (SYSTIMESTAMP - INTERVAL '
    10' MINUTE);
```

Flashback Database, used to rewind the entire database to a past point in time, functions as a sophisticated alternative to point-in-time recovery while the database remains open.

```
RMAN> FLASHBACK DATABASE TO TIMESTAMP (SYSTIMESTAMP -
    INTERVAL '1' DAY);
```

Understanding and implementing robust backup and recovery strategies in Oracle Database is not just a safeguard but a necessity. Through consistent and reliable backup practices coupled with powerful recovery tools, organizations can ensure business continuity and protect against data loss incidents.

7.2 Oracle Backup and Recovery Concepts

Oracle Database backup and recovery strategies aim to preserve data integrity and ensure business continuity. This section delves into key concepts that underlie Oracle's robust backup and recovery mechanisms. Understanding these foundational principles is crucial for database administrators who need to protect data against loss and ensure that databases can be restored to a consistent state after an unexpected failure.

Oracle's backup and recovery environment supports two primary types of backups: physical and logical. Physical backups consist of copies of the physical files used to store and retrieve data, whereas logical backups involve extracting data using Oracle's Data Pump utility.

1. Physical Backups: Physical backups involve duplicating the physical database files:

- **Datafiles:** These files store user and system data.
- **Control Files:** These files contain metadata about the structure of the database.
- **Redo Log Files:** These files contain a record of changes made to the database, vital for recovery and ensuring data integrity.

2. Logical Backups: Logical backups utilize Oracle Data Pump Export/Import utilities to back up the logical database components:

- **Tables and Indexes:** These foundational objects are exported and imported at the logical level.
- **Schemas and Users:** Full schemas, including user definitions and associated objects, can be logically backed up.
- **Full Database:** A comprehensive logical backup encompassing all schemas and tables.

Oracle Recovery Manager (RMAN) serves as the primary tool for performing intricate backup and recovery operations. RMAN manages the database's backup, restore, and recovery functionalities, integrating seamlessly with Oracle Database and its features. Key RMAN components include:

- **Backup Sets:** RMAN can group backups into backup sets, which can potentially contain multiple datafile or archive log backups.
- **Image Copies:** Unlike backup sets, image copies are exact byte-for-byte copies of database files.

Consistency in Backups: RMAN ensures consistency in backups through various mechanisms:

- **Checkpointing:** By leveraging Oracle's checkpoint process, RMAN ensures data consistency during backup.
- **Archived Redo Logs:** RMAN utilizes these logs to handle point-in-time recovery or to synchronize backup sets with the cut-off time.

Types of RMAN Backups: RMAN supports different types of backup strategies:

- **Full Backups:** These include the entirety of the selected database or file.
- **Incremental Backups:** These backups capture only the changes since the previous backup, thus optimizing storage and reducing backup times.

Backup Modes: Two prominent backup modes in Oracle are:

- **Offline (Cold) Backups:** Backups taken while the database is shut down. This guarantees consistency but requires downtime.
- **Online (Hot) Backups:** Backups performed while the database is online and operational, using Oracle's ARCHIVELOG mode to ensure all changes are captured.

Backup Retention: Retention policies govern the period during which backups are kept. Prospective backups must comply with predefined retention parameters to manage storage effectively and ensure availability of historical data for recovery purposes.

Recovery Scenarios: Oracle supports various recovery scenarios to restore a database to its desired state:

- **Complete Recovery:** Restores the database to the most recent consistent state by applying all redo logs.
- **Incomplete Recovery:** Uses backups and partial logs to restore the database to a specific point in time, SCN (System Change Number), or specific time.

```
-- Example: Executing a Point-In-Time Recovery
RUN {
   SET UNTIL TIME '2023-05-01:12:00:00';
   RESTORE DATABASE;
   RECOVER DATABASE;
}
```

Flashback Technology: Oracle's Flashback technology complements traditional backup and recovery by providing rapid recovery to correct certain human errors. Flashback capabilities include:

- **Flashback Database:** Rewinds the database to a previous point in time.
- **Flashback Table:** Restores a table to an earlier state without requiring a full database recovery.
- **Flashback Drop:** Recovers dropped tables using the Recycle Bin feature.

```
-- Example: Using Flashback to Restore a Table
FLASHBACK TABLE employees TO TIMESTAMP TO_TIMESTAMP('2023-05-01
      10:30:00', 'YYYY-MM-DD HH24:MI:SS');
```

Oracle Data Pump: This utility is integral for logical backups and facilitates high-speed movement of data and metadata between databases. Oracle Data Pump offers export and import functionalities, enhancing flexibility in backup strategy.

```
# Example: Exporting a Schema Using Data Pump
expdp system/password@DB schemas=sales directory=dpump_dir dumpfile=sales.dmp
      logfile=sales_exp.log
```

Effective utilization of Oracle's backup and recovery concepts ensures that data can be protected against accidental loss or failure, minimizes downtime, and maintains data consistency. Integrating these techniques and tools adapted to the organization's specific operational requirements establishes a reliable safeguard for critical database environments.

7.3 Configuring the Oracle Recovery Manager (RMAN)

To utilize RMAN for backup and recovery operations, proper configuration of the Oracle Recovery Manager (RMAN) environment is essential. Configuration ensures that backups are automated, efficient, and tailored to the specific needs of the database. The configuration involves setting various parameters, managing channels, and understanding the RMAN repository.

The configuration steps for RMAN are presented with a focus on practical execution and clear understanding of each element.

Starting RMAN

First, RMAN is typically started from the command line or the Oracle Database command prompt. To initiate RMAN:

```
$ rman
```

Connecting RMAN to the target database is crucial. For example, to connect to a database using the sysdba role:

```
RMAN> CONNECT TARGET sys/password@TARGET_DB
```

If using a recovery catalog, connect as follows:

```
RMAN> CONNECT CATALOG rman/catalog_pwd@CATALOG_DB
```

Configuring Persistent Settings

RMAN allows configuring settings that persist across sessions through the CONFIGURE command. These configurations include backup destinations, retention policies, and channel allocation. To check the current configuration, use:

```
RMAN> SHOW ALL;
```

To set a specific configuration, such as the default device type to disk:

```
RMAN> CONFIGURE DEFAULT DEVICE TYPE TO DISK;
```

Similarly, to set the retention policy, which determines how long backups should be retained:

```
RMAN> CONFIGURE RETENTION POLICY TO REDUNDANCY 3;
```

This command retains the three most recent backups. Alternatively, to specify a time-based retention policy:

```
RMAN> CONFIGURE RETENTION POLICY TO RECOVERY WINDOW OF 7
    DAYS;
```

Backup Sets and Image Copies

Configure RMAN to create backup sets or image copies. Backup sets are RMAN-specific binary files, while image copies are exact replicas of datafiles:

```
RMAN> CONFIGURE DEVICE TYPE DISK BACKUP TYPE TO BACKUPSET;
```

To use image copies, modify the command:

```
RMAN> CONFIGURE DEVICE TYPE DISK BACKUP TYPE TO COPY;
```

Configuring Channels

Channels represent the connections that RMAN uses to perform backup and recovery operations. Configuring channels allows for parallelization, enhancing performance.

To configure an automatic channel for disk drives:

```
RMAN> CONFIGURE CHANNEL DEVICE TYPE DISK FORMAT '/u01/backup/%
    U';
```

For tape drives, adjust accordingly:

```
RMAN> CONFIGURE CHANNEL DEVICE TYPE sbt PARMS 'SBT_LIBRARY=/
    usr/lib/libobk.so';
```

To configure multiple channels, enhancing parallelism:

```
RMAN> CONFIGURE DEVICE TYPE DISK PARALLELISM 2;
RMAN> CONFIGURE CHANNEL 1 DEVICE TYPE DISK FORMAT '/u01/backup/
    ch1_%U';
RMAN> CONFIGURE CHANNEL 2 DEVICE TYPE DISK FORMAT '/u01/backup/
    ch2_%U';
```

Control File Autobackup

The control file stores critical metadata, hence configuring automatic control file backups is recommended:

```
RMAN> CONFIGURE CONTROLFILE AUTOBACKUP ON;
```

To specify the format for these autobackups:

```
RMAN> CONFIGURE CONTROLFILE AUTOBACKUP FORMAT FOR DEVICE
    TYPE DISK TO '/u01/backup/%F';
```

Snapshot Control File

For consistent image copies, RMAN uses a snapshot control file. Configure its location:

```
RMAN> CONFIGURE SNAPSHOT CONTROLFILE NAME TO '/u01/backup/
    snapcf_TARGET_DB.f';
```

Maintenance and Validation Commands

Regularly validate and maintain the RMAN environment. For example, crosscheck backups to ensure RMAN's repository matches the physical backup data:

```
RMAN> CROSSCHECK BACKUP;
```

To delete expired backups:

```
RMAN> DELETE EXPIRED BACKUP;
```

Validation is also key to detect corrupted or missing data files:

```
RMAN> VALIDATE BACKUPSET;
```

These configuration tasks ensure RMAN's operations are optimized and reliable. Understanding and implementing these commands will provide a solid foundation in managing Oracle Database backups using RMAN effectively.

7.4 Backing Up an Oracle Database

Oracle Database backup is a critical operation to protect data from loss due to hardware failures, software issues, or other unforeseen circumstances. This section will explore various methods of backing up an Oracle Database, focusing on the use of Oracle Recovery Manager (RMAN), an essential tool for performing efficient and consistent backups.

Backing up an Oracle Database involves creating copies of datafiles, control files, and archived redo logs, capturing the state of the database at a specific point in time. There are two principal types of backups: physical backups and logical backups. This section will primarily deal with physical backups, as logical backups, which involve exporting data using Oracle Data Pump, are outside the primary scope of RMAN-based strategies.

Full Database Backup Using RMAN

A full database backup captures all database files, enabling a comprehensive restoration in the event of a failure. To perform a full backup using RMAN, initiate an RMAN session and issue the *BACKUP DATABASE* command:

```
rman TARGET /
RUN {
  BACKUP DATABASE;
}
```

This command creates a backup of the entire database, including all datafiles and the control file. The backups are stored based on the configuration defined in RMAN, typically at the default location or a specified backup destination.

Incremental Backups Using RMAN

Incremental backups are more efficient than full backups as they only capture changes made since the last backup. RMAN supports two types of incremental backups: *Level 0* and *Level 1*. A Level 0 incremental backup is akin to a full backup, establishing a baseline. Subsequent Level 1 backups only capture blocks changed since the last Level 0 or Level 1 backup.

To perform a Level 0 incremental backup, use the following RMAN command:

```
rman TARGET /
RUN {
  BACKUP INCREMENTAL LEVEL 0 DATABASE;
}
```

For a Level 1 incremental backup, which can be a differential or cumulative backup, use the respective RMAN command:

Differential Level 1:

```
rman TARGET /
RUN {
  BACKUP INCREMENTAL LEVEL 1 DATABASE;
}
```

Cumulative Level 1:

```
rman TARGET /
RUN {
  BACKUP INCREMENTAL LEVEL 1 CUMULATIVE DATABASE;
```

```
}
```

The choice between differential and cumulative backups depends on recovery requirements and available backup storage. Differential backups are smaller and faster but may require more time during recovery. Conversely, cumulative backups simplify recovery at the expense of potentially larger backup sizes.

Archived Redo Log Backup

Backing up archived redo logs is crucial for ensuring no committed transaction is lost. After performing a database backup, it is a best practice to back up all archived redo logs generated since the last backup. Use the following RMAN command to back up archived logs:

```
rman TARGET /
RUN {
  BACKUP ARCHIVELOG ALL;
}
```

This command ensures that all archived logs are included in the backup, safeguarding transactional data that allows for point-in-time recovery.

Control File and SPFILE Backup

The control file and server parameter file (SPFILE) contain essential metadata and configuration information necessary for database restoration. Backing them up separately allows for their quick recovery in case of corruption or loss. RMAN provides commands to back up the control file and the SPFILE:

```
rman TARGET /
RUN {
  BACKUP CURRENT CONTROLFILE;
  BACKUP SPFILE;
}
```

Alternatively, these backups can be included in the database backup process by using the *INCLUDE CURRENT CONTROLFILE* option:

```
rman TARGET /
RUN {
  BACKUP DATABASE INCLUDE CURRENT CONTROLFILE;
}
```

Creating and Managing Backup Sets

RMAN organizes backups into logical containers called *backup sets*, which consist of one or more backup pieces. Each piece is a physical file containing backed-up data. RMAN allows for the efficient creation and management of these sets, with options for compression and parallelization to optimize performance.

To create a compressed backup set:

```
rman TARGET /
RUN {
 BACKUP AS COMPRESSED BACKUPSET DATABASE;
}
```

Compression reduces the storage space required for backups and is particularly useful for larger databases or limited storage environments.

Validating Backups

Ensuring the integrity and usability of backups is imperative. RMAN provides the *VALIDATE* command to verify that backups can be successfully restored. This command reads the data without performing any actual backup or restoration, detecting any errors in the process:

```
rman TARGET /
RUN {
  BACKUP DATABASE VALIDATE;
  VALIDATE BACKUPSET 'primary-key';
}
```

Execute the validation periodically to ensure the ongoing reliability of the backup strategy.

Properly configured backup retention policies and regular testing are key components of a holistic backup strategy. By following best practices and leveraging RMAN's capabilities, database administrators can achieve effective data protection, minimizing the risks associated with data loss.

7.5 RMAN Backup Options and Strategies

Oracle Recovery Manager (RMAN) provides a plethora of backup options and strategies to create a comprehensive and efficient backup and recovery plan tailored to the specific needs of an Oracle Database environment. Understanding these options is crucial for maximizing data protection and ensuring quick recovery in case of data loss scenarios.

The core RMAN backup operations can be broadly classified into full backups and incremental backups. Each type serves specific needs depending on the business requirements and data change rate.

Full Backups involve backing up every data block within the database, regardless of whether it has been modified since the last backup. This approach provides a complete snapshot of the database at a specific point in time. Full backups are particularly useful for initial backups or periodic consistency checks.

In contrast, **Incremental Backups** only involve backing up data blocks that have changed since the last backup, reducing the backup's size and increasing efficiency. Incremental backups are categorized into:

- **Level 0:** Backs up the entire database, similar to a full backup, and serves as a base for subsequent incremental backups.
- **Level 1:** Backs up only the data blocks that have changed since the last level 0 or level 1 backup. Level 1 backups can be cumulative, where all changes since the last level 0 backup are captured, or differential, where only changes since the last level 1 backup are included.

Backup Destination Options include various storage configurations that determine where the backup files will reside. These options cater to different storage architectures and redundancy requirements:

- **Disk-Based Backups:** Direct backups to disk storage, which can offer high performance due to faster access times. RMAN can leverage file systems, ASM Disk Groups, or NFS-mounted storage as disk backup destinations.
- **Tape-Based Backups:** Utilize tape devices for backups, usually managed by Media Management Software (MMS). This approach is common in environments with extensive archival requirements due to the cost-effectiveness of tape storage for long-term data retention.
- **SBT (System Backup to Tape):** RMAN integrates with third-party media management software to interact with tape backup systems seamlessly. The CONFIGURE CHANNEL DEVICE TYPE 'SBT_TAPE' command is vital for setting up SBT channels.

Backup Techniques and Options provide additional control and flexibility during RMAN operations:

- **Backup Sets vs. Image Copies:** Backup sets are logical backup units created by RMAN, supporting compression and multiplexing of data files into backup pieces. Image copies are uncompressed, exact byte-for-byte copies of database files, often used for quick restoration tasks.

- **Compression:** RMAN can compress backup sets to save storage space, using either Basic, ZLIB (default), or higher compression algorithms such as BZIP2. This can be configured using the CONFIGURE COMPRESSION ALGORITHM command.
- **Encryption:** Protecting backups through encryption ensures data security during storage. RMAN supports transparent encryption with Oracle Advanced Security or wallet-based encryption techniques.
- **Multisection Backups:** Large data files can be backed up in parallel sections to optimize performance. Use the BACKUP... SECTION SIZE syntax to specify the section size.
- **Incremental Merge:** With Oracle Managed Files (OMF), RMAN supports the creation of an incrementally updated backup, whereby level 1 incremental backup changes are merged into an image copy of the database, effectively making it up-to-date with every incremental operation.

Backup Strategies are tailored plans that incorporate various RMAN functionalities to meet specific Recovery Point Objectives (RPO) and Recovery Time Objectives (RTO):

- **Full Weekly and Incremental Daily:** A common strategy is to take a full backup once a week with daily level 1 incremental backups. This reduces the time taken to perform daily backups while ensuring data can be restored accurately.
- **Disk-to-Disk-to-Tape (D2D2T):** This hybrid approach involves initially backing up to disk for fast backup and recovery times, followed by transferring these backups to tape for long-term storage.
- **Real-Time Backups:** Configuring RMAN to perform real-time backups of the redo log files ensures that transactions are continually protected. This can be achieved using the ARCHIVELOG mode and the CONFIGURE ARCHIVELOG DELETION POLICY command.

Below is an example script that illustrates a comprehensive RMAN backup strategy:

```
RUN {
  ALLOCATE CHANNEL disk1 DEVICE TYPE DISK;
  ALLOCATE CHANNEL disk2 DEVICE TYPE DISK;
  BACKUP INCREMENTAL LEVEL 0
    DATABASE FORMAT '/backups/full_%d_L0_%U' TAG 'WEEKLY_FULL';

  BACKUP INCREMENTAL LEVEL 1 CUMULATIVE
    DATABASE FORMAT '/backups/inc_%d_L1_%U' TAG 'DAILY_INC'
    KEEP UNTIL TIME 'SYSDATE + 7' RESTORE POINT 'STRATEGIC_RP';

  BACKUP AS BACKUPSET ARCHIVELOG ALL
    FORMAT '/backups/arch_%d_%U' DELETE INPUT;

  RELEASE CHANNEL disk1;
  RELEASE CHANNEL disk2;
}
```

The execution result of the above script, illustrating the RMAN operations success messages, would look like this:

```
RMAN-03090: Starting backup at 01-OCT-2023 10:00:00
RMAN-08030: channel disk1: starting full datafile backup set
RMAN-08500: channel disk1: specifying datafile(s) in backup set
 ...

file backup finished successfully
...
```

Adopting an effective RMAN backup strategy involves periodic review and adjustments based on the evolving database workload, data growth patterns, and recovery requirements. Automated monitoring and alert systems should be in place to ensure backup operations are completed successfully, and any failures are promptly addressed to maintain robust database protection.

7.6 Performing Database Recovery with RMAN

Database recovery is an essential capability within Oracle databases for maintaining data integrity and availability. Oracle Recovery Manager (RMAN) facilitates this process with a suite of commands and methodologies to efficiently restore and recover the database to a consistent state. This section delves into the practical aspect of performing database recovery using RMAN.

RMAN enables multiple recovery scenarios, including complete database recovery, point-in-time recovery, and tablespace recovery. The specific recovery approach depends on the type and extent of data loss or corruption encountered. This section will elaborate on common scenarios and provide RMAN commands to accomplish these tasks effectively.

To perform database recovery, the database must be in the appropriate state: in the case of complete database recovery, the database is generally started in the MOUNT state, whereas for point-in-time recovery, the database must be started but not open.

1. Complete Database Recovery

Complete recovery uses available backups and archived redo logs to restore the database to the time of the last consistent backup. The following steps outline this process:

1. Start RMAN and connect to the target database.

```
$ rman target /
```

2. Shutdown the database if it is running, and then start the database in MOUNT mode.

```
RMAN> SHUTDOWN IMMEDIATE;
RMAN> STARTUP MOUNT;
```

3. Restore the database files from the backup using the RESTORE DATABASE command.

```
RMAN> RESTORE DATABASE;
```

4. Perform the media recovery using the RECOVER DATABASE command.

```
RMAN> RECOVER DATABASE;
```

5. Open the database in resetlogs mode.

```
RMAN> ALTER DATABASE OPEN RESETLOGS;
```

2. Point-in-Time Recovery

Point-in-time recovery (PITR) restores the database to a specific timestamp or system change number (SCN), which is useful in scenarios of logical corruption or user error. The following steps are used for point-in-time recovery:

1. Connect to RMAN.

```
$ rman target /
```

2. Shutdown and then start the database in the MOUNT state.

```
RMAN> SHUTDOWN IMMEDIATE;
RMAN> STARTUP MOUNT;
```

3. Perform the incomplete recovery. Specify the time or SCN to which the database should be restored.

```
RMAN> RUN {
    SET UNTIL TIME 'YYYY-MM-DD:HH24:MI:SS';
    RESTORE DATABASE;
    RECOVER DATABASE;
}
```

Alternatively, you can set an SCN:

```
RMAN> RUN {
    SET UNTIL SCN scn_number;
    RESTORE DATABASE;
    RECOVER DATABASE;
}
```

4. Open the database with the RESETLOGS option.

```
RMAN> ALTER DATABASE OPEN RESETLOGS;
```

3. Tablespace Recovery

Recovering individual tablespaces can be accomplished without affecting the entire database. This is useful for localized failures restricted to specific tablespaces. Utilize the following procedure:

1. Connect to RMAN.

```
$ rman target /
```

2. Take the affected tablespace offline.

```
RMAN> SQL 'ALTER TABLESPACE tablespace_name OFFLINE
    IMMEDIATE';
```

3. Restore and recover the tablespace.

```
RMAN> RESTORE TABLESPACE tablespace_name;
RMAN> RECOVER TABLESPACE tablespace_name;
```

4. Bring the tablespace back online.

```
RMAN> SQL 'ALTER TABLESPACE tablespace_name ONLINE';
```

4. Block Media Recovery

For cases where corruption is isolated to specific data blocks, block media recovery can be performed to avoid the impact on other parts of the database. The following steps detail the process:

1. Detect and identify the corrupted blocks using the DBMS_REPAIR package or querying V$DATABASE_BLOCK_CORRUPTION view.

```
SQL> SELECT * FROM V$DATABASE_BLOCK_CORRUPTION;
```

2. Connect to RMAN and start block recovery for the identified blocks.

```
$ rman target /
RMAN> BLOCKRECOVER DATAFILE datafile_number BLOCK
      block_number;
```

3. Verify that the blocks have been recovered and there are no lingering corruption issues.

```
SQL> SELECT * FROM V$DATABASE_BLOCK_CORRUPTION;
```

Each of the above recovery scenarios underscores the importance of maintaining consistent and up-to-date backups, as well as archived redo logs, to ensure data can be accurately recovered. RMAN's powerful command line and scripting capabilities provide robust measures to tackle various data recovery challenges efficiently.

Thus, understanding and implementing these RMAN recovery procedures are crucial for any database administrator tasked with ensuring high availability and data integrity of Oracle databases. The granularity of RMAN operations allows tailored recovery solutions to meet specific organizational needs, minimizing downtime and data loss.

7.7 User-Managed Backup and Recovery

User-managed backup and recovery methods involve the manual copying and restoration of database files. This approach requires a comprehensive understanding of the Oracle database architecture, file systems, and the necessary database commands. Despite the prevalence of Oracle Recovery Manager (RMAN) for most modern backup and recovery tasks, understanding user-managed techniques remains crucial for scenarios where RMAN may not be feasible.

Components of User-Managed Backup and Recovery:

- **Datafiles**: These contain the user's actual data. Each Oracle database consists of one or more datafiles.
- **Control Files**: These are crucial for the database's operation, storing metadata about the database's structure.
- **Online Redo Log Files**: These log files record all changes made to the database's data. They are essential for data integrity and recovery.
- **Archived Redo Log Files**: These are archived copies of online redo logs, used during recovery to capture changes that occurred after the last backup.
- **Parameter File (PFILE) or Server Parameter File (SPFILE)**: These files store configuration parameters for starting instances of the Oracle database.

Performing a User-Managed Backup:

1. *Backup of Datafiles*: Use the OS copy command to back up datafiles.

```
$ cp /u01/oradata/orcl/system01.dbf /u02/backup/system01.dbf
```

Ensure the database is in ARCHIVELOG mode to facilitate hot backups (online backups).

2. *Placing Tablespaces in Backup Mode*:

```
SQL> ALTER TABLESPACE users BEGIN BACKUP;
-- Copy the datafiles to the backup location
$ cp /u01/oradata/orcl/users01.dbf /u02/backup/users01.dbf
SQL> ALTER TABLESPACE users END BACKUP;
```

3. *Backing Up Control Files*:

```
SQL> ALTER DATABASE BACKUP CONTROLFILE TO '/u02/backup/control01.ctl
    ';
```

4. *Backing Up Redo Logs*: Ensure redo logs are archived before backup.

```
SQL> ALTER SYSTEM ARCHIVE LOG CURRENT;
$ cp /u01/oradata/arch/*.arc /u02/backup/
```

Recovering an Oracle Database Manually: In the event of a failure, manual recovery steps depend on the specific files affected (i.e., datafiles, control files, or redo logs).

1. *Restoring Datafiles*:

```
$ cp /u02/backup/users01.dbf /u01/oradata/orcl/users01.dbf
```

2. *Recovering the Database*:

```
SQL> RECOVER DATABASE;
\begin{FittedVerbatim}
ORA-00279: Change 12345 generated at 02/12/2023 10:12:36 needed for thread 1
ORA-00289: Suggestion: /u01/archive/1_23.\#\#\#.dbf
ORA-00280: Change 12345 for thread 1 is in sequence #23
\end{FittedVerbatim}

SQL> ALTER DATABASE RECOVER AUTOMATIC;
\begin{FittedVerbatim}
Media recovery complete.
\end{FittedVerbatim}
```

3. *Opening the Database*: After successful recovery, open the database.

```
SQL> ALTER DATABASE OPEN;
```

Database Modes and Implications: The approach to user-managed backup and recovery varies depending on whether the database is in NOARCHIVELOG or ARCHIVELOG mode. In NOARCHIVELOG mode, only cold backups (offline backups) are possible since changes are not retained beyond the current redo log files. Conversely, ARCHIVELOG mode allows for both online and offline backups, facilitating continuous availability and point-in-time recovery.

1. *Switching to ARCHIVELOG Mode*:

```
$ sqlplus / as sysdba
SQL> SHUTDOWN IMMEDIATE;
SQL> STARTUP MOUNT;
SQL> ALTER DATABASE ARCHIVELOG;
SQL> ALTER DATABASE OPEN;
```

Adhering to user-managed techniques is fundamental when RMAN is not an option or for educational purposes to appreciate the Oracle architecture's underlying mechanics. This level of understanding enables DBAs to implement robust backup and recovery strategies when relying solely on OS-level commands and SQL*Plus. Additionally, user-managed backups can complement automated solutions, offering a diversified approach to data protection.

7.8 Configuring and Utilizing Flashback Technology

Flashback technology is a suite of Oracle Database features that allow you to view past states of database objects or return database objects to a previous state without the need for complex recovery operations. This technology can be vital when managing and resolving human errors, such as unintended data modifications or deletions.

The primary components of Flashback technology include Flashback Query, Flashback Table, Flashback Drop, Flashback Database, and Flashback Transaction Query. Before using these features, it is necessary to configure the database environment properly.

The following steps outline the configuration process for Flashback Technology:

- Enable Archive Log Mode
- Configure the Flash Recovery Area
- Set the appropriate database initialization parameters
- Ensure appropriate privileges are granted to users

Step 1: Enable Archive Log Mode

Flashback Technology relies on the availability of redo logs. Ensure the database operates in Archivelog mode as follows:

```
SHUTDOWN IMMEDIATE;
STARTUP MOUNT;
ALTER DATABASE ARCHIVELOG;
ALTER DATABASE OPEN;
```

Step 2: Configure the Flash Recovery Area

The Flash Recovery Area (FRA) is a unified location to store all recovery-related files. Configure it using the following commands:

```
ALTER SYSTEM SET DB_RECOVERY_FILE_DEST='/u01/app/oracle/
    flash_recovery_area';
ALTER SYSTEM SET DB_RECOVERY_FILE_DEST_SIZE=10G;
```

Step 3: Set Initialization Parameters

Certain initialization parameters must be set to use Flashback Technology:

- DB_RECOVERY_FILE_DEST: Defines the location of the FRA
- DB_RECOVERY_FILE_DEST_SIZE: Specifies the size of the FRA
- DB_FLASHBACK_RETENTION_TARGET: Determines retention period for flashback logs (in minutes)

For instance:

```
ALTER SYSTEM SET DB_FLASHBACK_RETENTION_TARGET=1440; -- 1 day
    retention
ALTER SYSTEM SET DB_RECOVERY_FILE_DEST_SIZE=20G;
```

Step 4: Grant Appropriate Privileges

Ensure that users have the necessary privileges to use Flashback features. Typical privileges include:

```
GRANT FLASHBACK ANY TABLE TO [username];
GRANT EXECUTE ON DBMS_FLASHBACK TO [username];
```

Following this setup, various Flashback features can be utilized effectively.

Flashback Query

Allows querying data as it existed at an earlier point in time:

```
SELECT * FROM employees AS OF TIMESTAMP TO_TIMESTAMP('2023-04-05
    10:00:00', 'YYYY-MM-DD HH24:MI:SS');
```

Flashback Table

Restores a table to an earlier state without restoring data files:

```
FLASHBACK TABLE employees TO TIMESTAMP TO_TIMESTAMP('2023-04-05
    10:00:00', 'YYYY-MM-DD HH24:MI:SS');
```

Flashback Drop

Recovers dropped tables using the Recycle Bin:

```
FLASHBACK TABLE employees TO BEFORE DROP;
```

Flashback Database

Enables rolling back the entire database to a previous time, often used when significant changes are made erroneously:

```
FLASHBACK DATABASE TO TIMESTAMP TO_TIMESTAMP('2023-04-05 10:00:00',
        'YYYY-MM-DD HH24:MI:SS');
```

Verifying Flashback Operations

After performing flashback operations, verification is essential to ensure data integrity. For example, after a Flashback Table operation, validate the state of the table:

```
SELECT COUNT(*) FROM employees WHERE hire_date < TO_DATE('2023-04-05',
        'YYYY-MM-DD');
```

Managing Flashback Logs

Flashback logs, stored in the FRA, must be monitored to avoid space management issues. Queries to view flashback logs include:

```
SELECT * FROM V$FLASHBACK_DATABASE_LOG;
```

Regularly review FRA usage:

```
SELECT * FROM V$RECOVERY_FILE_DEST;
```

```
Example output:
NAME                                   SPACE_USED SPACE_RECLAIMABLE
/u01/app/oracle/flash_recovery_area       5000M       500M
```

By adhering to these configuration steps and guidelines, Flashback Technology can be leveraged to maintain data consistency, correctness, and recoverability, thereby enhancing the robustness of Oracle Database deployment.

7.9 Managing Archived Redo Logs

Archived redo logs are an integral component of Oracle Database backup and recovery strategies. They are crucial for recovering a database to a specific point in time and are particularly useful in situations where the database is in ARCHIVELOG mode. Detailed understanding and effective management of these logs can significantly enhance the reliability and efficiency of the database recovery process.

Oracle Redo Logs and Archived Redo Logs
Redo logs are files that record all changes made to the database. They are essential for maintaining data integrity and consistency. Oracle

uses a group of redo log files to capture changes made to the database. When a redo log file is full, the instance begins writing to the next file in the group. Redo log groups allow the database to recover from an instance failure by reapplying the changes recorded in these files.

Archived redo logs are copies of redo log files that have been archived before being overwritten. This occurs when the database is running in ARCHIVELOG mode. The significance of archived redo logs lies in their role in media recovery situations, such as restoring a database after a disk failure.

Enabling ARCHIVELOG Mode

To utilize archived redo logs, the database must be in ARCHIVELOG mode. The following steps demonstrate how to switch the database to ARCHIVELOG mode:

```
SHUTDOWN IMMEDIATE;
STARTUP MOUNT;
ALTER DATABASE ARCHIVELOG;
ALTER DATABASE OPEN;
```

The SHUTDOWN IMMEDIATE command shuts down the database, ensuring that all users are disconnected and the database is closed cleanly. Next, the STARTUP MOUNT command starts the instance and mounts the database but leaves it in a closed state. The ALTER DATABASE ARCHIVELOG command sets the database into ARCHIVELOG mode. Lastly, the ALTER DATABASE OPEN command opens the database for normal operations.

Configuring the Archive Destination

After enabling ARCHIVELOG mode, it is essential to configure the destination where the archived redo logs will be stored. This can be accomplished using the LOG_ARCHIVE_DEST initialization parameter:

```
ALTER SYSTEM SET LOG_ARCHIVE_DEST='/u01/app/oracle/archivelogs';
```

The above command sets the archive destination to the specified directory. It is critical to ensure that the destination directory has sufficient space to store the archived logs, as running out of space can halt the database operations.

Managing Archived Redo Logs Using RMAN

Oracle Recovery Manager (RMAN) provides robust functionality for managing archived redo logs. Through RMAN, users can back up, delete, and catalog archived redo logs conveniently. Below is an example of how to back up archived redo logs using RMAN:

```
RMAN> BACKUP ARCHIVELOG ALL;
```

This command instructs RMAN to back up all existing archived redo logs. It is advisable to automate this process by scheduling backups regularly to avoid accumulation of logs and potential data loss.

Deleting Archived Redo Logs

Over time, the archived redo logs can consume significant disk space and require efficient management. RMAN can be used to delete logs that are no longer needed. For instance:

```
RMAN> DELETE ARCHIVELOG ALL COMPLETED BEFORE 'SYSDATE-7';
```

This command deletes all archived redo logs older than seven days. Adjusting the retention policy according to the backup strategy is essential for optimal use of storage resources.

Cataloging Archived Redo Logs

In certain situations, especially during recovery operations, RMAN might need to catalog archived redo logs that were manually copied to the archive directory and not recorded in the RMAN repository. Use the following command to catalog such logs:

```
RMAN> CATALOG ARCHIVELOG '/u01/app/oracle/archivelogs/log1_1.arc';
```

This enables RMAN to recognize and utilize the archived redo logs when performing recovery operations.

Monitoring Archived Redo Logs

Effective management of archived redo logs also involves continuous monitoring. Oracle provides views such as V$ARCHIVED_LOG and V$LOG_HISTORY which provide detailed information about the archived logs:

```
SELECT SEQUENCE#, FIRST_TIME, NEXT_TIME FROM V$ARCHIVED_LOG
    ORDER BY SEQUENCE#;
SELECT SEQUENCE#, FIRST_CHANGE#, NEXT_CHANGE# FROM
    V$LOG_HISTORY ORDER BY SEQUENCE#;
```

These queries help in tracking the archived redo logs by showing their sequence numbers and timestamps. Monitoring these views helps database administrators in auditing and managing the archived logs effectively.

Managing archived redo logs involves enabling ARCHIVELOG mode, configuring the archive destination, utilizing RMAN functionalities, and monitoring the Oracle database's archived redo logs for efficient and effective backup and recovery operations.

7.10 Performing Point-in-Time Recovery

Point-in-Time Recovery (PITR) is a critical operation in Oracle Database, allowing database administrators (DBAs) to restore the database to a specific moment in time. PITR is essential when data corruption, application errors, or user mistakes occur. This technique uses backups in conjunction with archived redo logs to bring the database to a state before the problem occurred without losing recent data modifications.

PITR involves several steps: identifying the exact point in time for recovery, configuring the necessary settings, placing the database in the correct state for recovery, and executing the recovery process with Oracle Recovery Manager (RMAN).

First, identify the precise SCN (System Change Number) or the exact time to which the database should be recovered. This point should be chosen meticulously based on the nature of the error and logging information.

The database must be in ARCHIVELOG mode to perform PITR. Ensure that the database is currently in this mode by executing the following command:

```
SQL> ARCHIVE LOG LIST;
```

This command will display the archiving mode status. If the database is not in ARCHIVELOG mode, change it by shutting down the database and restarting it after setting the archive log mode:

```
SQL> SHUTDOWN IMMEDIATE;
SQL> STARTUP MOUNT;
SQL> ALTER DATABASE ARCHIVELOG;
SQL> ALTER DATABASE OPEN;
```

Next, configure RMAN with the appropriate channel settings if they are not already set, as these are required to read backup pieces and archived redo logs:

```
RMAN> CONFIGURE CHANNEL DEVICE TYPE DISK FORMAT '/path/to/backup
    /%U';
```

The following RMAN command will execute the actual Point-in-Time Recovery based on a specified target time. Replace the timestamp TO_DATE('YYYY-MM-DD:HH24:MI:SS', 'YYYY-MM-DD:HH24:MI:SS') with the desired recovery time:

```
RUN {
  SET UNTIL TIME "TO_DATE('2023-06-24:15:30:00', 'YYYY-MM-DD:HH24:MI:SS')
      ";
  RESTORE DATABASE;
  RECOVER DATABASE;
}
```

Alternatively, if recovering to an SCN, use:

```
RUN {
  SET UNTIL SCN 123456;
  RESTORE DATABASE;
  RECOVER DATABASE;
}
```

After ensuring the successful application of archived redo logs up to the target time or SCN, open the database with the RESETLOGS option to complete the recovery and create a new incarnation of the database:

```
RMAN> ALTER DATABASE OPEN RESETLOGS;
```

Verifying the recovery is paramount. Query the database to check any specific tables or data structures that might have been affected by the recovery procedure:

```
SQL> SELECT * FROM specific_table WHERE timestamp_column > TO_DATE('
     2023-06-24:15:30:00', 'YYYY-MM-DD:HH24:MI:SS');
```

If any anomalies or missed recoveries are found, additional recovery steps might be necessary. Ensure no data discrepancies exist post-recovery.

During the entire PITR process, proper log management and monitoring are crucial. Maintain precise logs of every action taken, which will be helpful for auditing and troubleshooting. PITR should be followed by a full database backup to capture the new state post-recovery, facilitating future recoveries if needed.

Here is a summarized example of a typical RUN block for performing Point-in-Time Recovery:

```
RUN {
  ALLOCATE CHANNEL c1 DEVICE TYPE DISK;
  SET UNTIL TIME "TO_DATE('2023-06-24:15:30:00', 'YYYY-MM-DD:HH24:MI:SS')
      ";
  RESTORE DATABASE;
  RECOVER DATABASE;
  RELEASE CHANNEL c1;
}
```

This RUN block allocates a disk channel, sets the recovery time, restores the database, applies the necessary archived redo logs, and finally releases the allocated channel.

Executing Point-in-Time Recovery should be practiced in a controlled environment to fine-tune the process and minimize downtime during actual recovery scenarios. Using RMAN scripts simplifies the automation and reduces the risk of manual errors. Continuous monitoring and validation ensure the database's integrity and availability post-recovery. This process is crucial for maintaining data reliability and consistency in an enterprise environment.

7.11 Cloning and Duplicating Databases

Database cloning and duplication involves creating an exact copy of an Oracle Database, which can be used for various purposes such as testing, development, or as a standby database for disaster recovery. Oracle Recovery Manager (RMAN) provides robust tools to facilitate the cloning and duplicating of databases efficiently.

A crucial prerequisite for cloning or duplicating databases is ensuring that the source database is in a consistent state. Before proceeding, it is essential to identify whether the duplication will be performed on the same host or a different host, as the approach slightly differs based on this factor.

Using RMAN for Cloning

RMAN simplifies the cloning process with the DUPLICATE command. When using RMAN, it is essential to configure the necessary auxiliary instance on the target server, where the duplicate database will reside.

```
RUN {
  ALLOCATE AUXILIARY CHANNEL aux1 DEVICE TYPE DISK;
  DUPLICATE TARGET DATABASE TO dupdb FROM ACTIVE DATABASE;
}
```

The snippet above illustrates a basic RMAN script to duplicate a database. The ALLOCATE AUXILIARY CHANNEL command assigns a channel for the auxiliary instance, while the DUPLICATE TARGET DATABASE TO dupdb FROM ACTIVE DATABASE command duplicates the active database to a new database named dupdb.

Duplication from Backup

RMAN also supports duplication from an existing backup, which can be advantageous if the source database cannot be down or if transferring data over the network is not feasible. This method uses an existing backup to create the duplicate database.

```
RUN {
  ALLOCATE AUXILIARY CHANNEL aux1 DEVICE TYPE DISK;
  DUPLICATE TARGET DATABASE TO dupdb BACKUP LOCATION '/
       backup_path';
}
```

In this case, the command BACKUP LOCATION specifies the directory where the backup pieces reside. RMAN will use this backup to create the duplicate database, reducing the impact on the source database's performance.

Configuring the Auxiliary Instance

Regardless of the duplication method, configuring the auxiliary instance is vital. This involves setting various Oracle initialization parameters to ensure a smooth duplication process.

```
DB_NAME=dupdb
DB_FILE_NAME_CONVERT=('source_datafile_path','auxiliary_datafile_path')
LOG_FILE_NAME_CONVERT=('source_logfile_path','auxiliary_logfile_path')
```

The DB_NAME parameter defines the name of the duplicate database. The DB_FILE_NAME_CONVERT and LOG_FILE_NAME_CONVERT parameters specify the conversion paths for the data files and log files, ensuring that Oracle correctly maps the files from the source to the auxiliary locations.

Post-Duplication Steps

After successfully cloning or duplicating a database, there are several post-duplication steps to validate and configure the new database instance.

1. **Verify the Database:** Perform a series of checks to ensure the duplicate database is consistent and functional. This includes checking data file integrity, log file status, and overall database health.

```
SQL> SELECT * FROM V$DATAFILE_HEADER;
SQL> SELECT * FROM V$LOGFILE;
```

2. **Adjust Configuration:** Update any configuration settings unique to the duplicated environment, such as network settings, parameter files, and user privileges.

```
SQL> ALTER SYSTEM SET LOCAL_LISTENER='(ADDRESS=(PROTOCOL=TCP)(HOST=aux_host)(PORT=1521))';
SQL> ALTER SYSTEM SET INSTANCE_NAME='aux_instance';
```

3. **Cleanup:** Remove any temporary files or auxiliary configurations

used during the duplication process.

```
$ rm -rf /path/to/temporary/files/*
```

Automating the Duplication Process

For environments requiring frequent duplication, automating the process through shell scripts or Oracle Scheduler can enhance efficiency and consistency.

```
#!/bin/bash
export ORACLE_SID=source_db
export ORACLE_HOME=/u01/app/oracle/product/19.0.0/dbhome_1

rman target / <<EOF
RUN {
  ALLOCATE AUXILIARY CHANNEL aux1 DEVICE TYPE DISK;
  DUPLICATE TARGET DATABASE TO dupdb FROM ACTIVE DATABASE;
}
EOF
```

This Bash script leverages RMAN to perform duplication. By scheduling this script, administrators can ensure regular and automated database duplications.

Studying and practicing database cloning and duplication using RMAN equips database administrators with the skills required to manage efficient database development and backup strategies. This knowledge ensures minimized downtime and optimal database performance during critical operations.

7.12 Best Practices for Backup and Recovery

Effective backup and recovery strategies are pivotal in ensuring data integrity, availability, and minimal downtime in an Oracle Database environment. The following best practices provide a comprehensive guide designed for database administrators to optimize their backup and recovery processes:

Regular Backup Schedule:

- **Frequency:** Establish a regular backup schedule, taking into account the criticality of your data and the acceptable recovery time objective (RTO) and recovery point objective (RPO). Daily backups are commonly recommended for high-transaction databases.

- **Types of Backups:** Implement a combination of full, incremental, and differential backups to balance the trade-off between backup duration and storage requirements. Full backups capture the entire database, while incremental backups capture only the changes since the last backup, and differential backups capture changes since the last full backup.

Retention and Archival Policies:

- **Retention Period:** Define retention policies based on organizational requirements and regulatory compliance. Retain backups long enough to recover from accidental data loss or corruption, while avoiding excessive storage costs.

- **Archived Logs:** Store archived redo logs for sufficient time to facilitate point-in-time recovery. Ensure that these logs are included in the backup procedure and not stored solely on disk.

Storage Strategies:

- **Offsite Storage:** To protect against data center disasters, use offsite or cloud storage for a second copy of your backups. Offsite backups should be stored in environments with suitable security measures.

- **Redundancy:** Maintain multiple copies of backups in different physical locations to prevent data loss due to localized failures.

Testing Backup and Recovery Procedures:

- **Regular Testing:** Periodically test backup and recovery processes in a controlled environment to ensure that backup files are usable and recovery procedures are effective. Testing should include scenarios such as full database recovery, tablespace recovery, and point-in-time recovery.

- **Documented Procedures:** Maintain detailed, documented recovery procedures that are easily accessible to the DBA team. This documentation should cover various recovery scenarios, including worst-case situations.

Utilizing RMAN Effectively:

- **Catalog Usage:** Use the RMAN recovery catalog to store metadata about backups, improving manageability and providing an additional layer of protection for your backup information.
- **Backup Optimization:** Enable RMAN features like compression and block change tracking to optimize backup performance and storage utilization. Compression reduces the size of backup files, while block change tracking helps to speed up incremental backups.

Monitoring and Alerting:

- **Automated Monitoring:** Implement automated monitoring tools to track the status of backup jobs, ensuring that they complete successfully and within the expected timeframe.
- **Alert Configuration:** Configure alerts and notifications for backup-related failures or issues, enabling prompt corrective action.

Security Considerations:

- **Encryption:** Utilize encryption for backup data to ensure it is secure both in transit and at rest. Oracle RMAN supports backup encryption, providing robust data protection.
- **Access Control:** Restrict access to backup storage locations and RMAN configurations to authorized personnel only. Implement strong authentication and authorization mechanisms to minimize security risks.

Retention and Purging of Backups:

- **Data Purging:** Implement automated purging policies to remove obsolete backups and archived logs that are no longer required. This helps in managing storage resources efficiently.

```
-- Example of configuring an RMAN backup schedule
CONNECT TARGET /
RMAN> CONFIGURE RETENTION POLICY TO REDUNDANCY 2;
RMAN> CONFIGURE BACKUP OPTIMIZATION ON;
RMAN> CONFIGURE DEFAULT DEVICE TYPE TO DISK;
RMAN> RUN {
   ALLOCATE CHANNEL ch1 DEVICE TYPE DISK;
   BACKUP DATABASE PLUS ARCHIVELOG;
   SQL 'ALTER SYSTEM ARCHIVE LOG CURRENT';
}
```

```
-- Expected Output from RMAN execution log
Starting backup at 15-MAR-2023
allocated channel: ch1
channel ch1: SID=237 device type=DISK
channel ch1: starting full datafile backup set
channel ch1: specifying datafile(s) in backup set
...
channel ch1: backup set complete, elapsed time: 00:04:32
Finished backup at 15-MAR-2023
```

Executing these practices will reinforce the robustness and reliability of your backup and recovery plans. Configurations should align with your database environment, operation needs, and organizational policies. Advocating for continuous evaluation and improvement of these strategies ensures the resilience of your Oracle Database infrastructure.

Chapter 8

Performance Tuning and Optimization

This chapter focuses on strategies for performance tuning and optimization in Oracle Database. It covers methods for monitoring and analyzing database performance, using Oracle Enterprise Manager, and optimizing SQL queries. Topics include indexing strategies, memory management, disk I/O optimization, and managing sessions and processes. Additionally, the chapter explores the use of Automatic Workload Repository (AWR), Active Session History (ASH), and other performance tuning tools and best practices.

8.1 Introduction to Performance Tuning

Performance tuning in Oracle Database involves a careful and systematic approach to optimizing the database's efficiency and effectiveness. The main goal is to ensure that database operations are executing in the most efficient manner possible, thereby providing users with rapid and reliable access to data. Effective performance tuning is critical for maintaining a responsive and scalable database environment, particularly as the size and complexity of the database grow over time.

Performance tuning can be broadly categorized into various key areas: SQL query optimization, indexing strategies, memory management, disk I/O optimization, and session and process management. Each of these areas can significantly impact the performance of an Oracle Database, and thus must be carefully monitored and tuned.

SQL query optimization involves improving the efficiency of SQL statements. Poorly written SQL can cause significant performance bottlenecks. Techniques such as rewriting queries, using appropriate join methods, and leveraging SQL hints can greatly enhance SQL performance.

Indexing strategies include the creation and maintenance of appropriate indexes. Indexes improve the speed of data retrieval operations at the cost of additional storage and maintenance overhead. Proper indexing requires an understanding of query patterns and the underlying data distribution.

Memory management focuses on allocating and utilizing memory resources efficiently. Oracle Database provides various memory structures such as the System Global Area (SGA) and the Program Global Area (PGA) to store data that supports database operations. Proper configuration and tuning of these memory areas are essential for optimal database performance.

Disk I/O optimization targets the efficient use of disk resources. Disk I/O is often one of the most significant factors affecting database performance. Techniques such as proper data file placement, storage configuration, and RAID level selection can improve disk I/O performance.

Session and process management involves controlling the number of concurrent users and processes to ensure they do not overwhelm the system resources. Configuring parameters such as the maximum number of sessions, processes, and transactions can prevent excessive resource contention and ensure smooth database operation.

Monitoring is an integral part of performance tuning. The use of tools such as Oracle Enterprise Manager (OEM), Automatic Workload Repository (AWR), and Active Session History (ASH) allows for the continuous monitoring and analysis of database performance. These tools provide valuable insights into potential performance issues and help guide the tuning process.

To illustrate a practical aspect of performance tuning, consider the example of SQL query optimization. Assume you have a table EMPLOYEES with a large number of rows and a query that retrieves employee names based on their department. The initial query is shown below:

```
SELECT NAME FROM EMPLOYEES WHERE DEPARTMENT_ID = 10;
```

If an index is not present on the DEPARTMENT_ID column, this query may result in a full table scan, leading to significant performance degradation. Creating an index on the DEPARTMENT_ID column can optimize the query performance:

```
CREATE INDEX idx_department_id ON EMPLOYEES(DEPARTMENT_ID);
```

After the index is created, the query can execute more efficiently by using the index to quickly locate the relevant rows.

Another aspect of performance tuning involves memory management. For instance, if the size of the Oracle SGA is inadequately configured, the database might experience excessive disk I/O due to frequent reads and writes. Properly setting the SGA and PGA parameters ensures that the database can cache frequently accessed data and reduce the need for physical I/O operations.

Configuration of SGA and PGA can be done through the initialization parameters such as:

```
ALTER SYSTEM SET sga_target = 4G SCOPE=BOTH;
ALTER SYSTEM SET pga_aggregate_target = 2G SCOPE=BOTH;
```

These commands will adjust the sizes of the SGA and PGA, potentially improving the overall performance of the database by optimizing memory utilization.

Disk I/O optimization might involve moving frequently accessed data files to faster disks or configuring the database storage to use more efficient RAID levels. For example, placing the redo log files on high-speed SSDs could significantly reduce write latencies.

Lastly, managing sessions and processes involves configuring database parameters to control the load on the system. Oracle's initialization parameters, such as PROCESSES and SESSIONS, dictate the maximum number of operating system processes and database sessions, respectively.

```
ALTER SYSTEM SET processes = 200 SCOPE=SPFILE;
ALTER SYSTEM SET sessions = 300 SCOPE=SPFILE;
```

Adjusting these parameters helps ensure that the database can handle the required workload without becoming overloaded.

Understanding these fundamental concepts is crucial for effective performance tuning in Oracle Database. Each tuning operation should be carefully planned and tested to avoid unintended consequences that might arise from improper adjustments. By continuously monitoring the database performance and making informed adjustments, significant improvements in efficiency and responsiveness can be achieved.

8.2 Understanding Database Performance

Understanding the performance of an Oracle Database requires a comprehensive grasp of the factors influencing its operation, such as system architecture, workload characteristics, and resource utilization. Performance tuning aims to ensure the database operates efficiently, minimizing resource contention and maximizing throughput.

At the core of database performance lies the balance between CPU, memory, disk, and network resources. A performance issue often reflects an imbalance among these resources or constraints in one or more subsystems.

A conceptual model to grasp performance involves:

- **Response Time:** The elapsed time a user experiences while executing a task in the database. This includes the time taken by the Oracle server to process the request and the time spent transferring results back to the user.
- **Throughput:** The number of units of work the database can process in a given time frame. This metric is generally concerned with the volume of transactions and queries executed.
- **Utilization:** Reflects how much of the system's total capacity is being used. Metrics of utilization consider CPU, memory, disk I/O, and network bandwidth.

Factors Affecting Database Performance

Several key factors affect Oracle Database performance, and understanding these is pivotal to identifying and resolving performance issues.

1. Workload Characteristics: The type of workload (OLTP vs. OLAP), the complexity of queries, and the transaction volume significantly determine performance profiles. OLTP workloads typically involve numerous short, atomic transactions, stressing concurrency and quick response. In contrast, OLAP workloads are read-intensive, involving complex queries processing large data volumes.

2. *Schema Design:* Efficient database design minimizes access paths and optimizes data retrieval. Denormalization and data partitioning strategies often enhance performance by reducing join complexities and improving parallelism.

3. *Query Execution Plans:* The execution plan of a SQL query dictates how the database will access data (e.g., full table scans, index scans). Poor execution plans, often resulting from suboptimal SQL statements or outdated statistics, can severely degrade performance.

```
EXPLAIN PLAN FOR
SELECT employee_id, first_name, last_name
FROM employees
WHERE department_id = 10;
SELECT * FROM TABLE(DBMS_XPLAN.DISPLAY());
```

4. *Indexing:* Appropriate index usage can drastically improve query performance, reducing logical and physical I/O. Over-indexing or incorrect index types, however, may lead to worsened performance due to increased maintenance overhead.

5. *Hardware Resources:* The availability and configuration of CPU, memory, disk subsystems, and network interfaces are integral to database performance. Bottlenecks in any of these resources can limit overall system efficiency.

Performance Metrics and Diagnostic Tools

Oracle provides extensive tools and metrics to diagnose performance issues. These tools offer insights into system operations and help pinpoint bottlenecks. Key among these tools are:

1. *Automatic Workload Repository (AWR):* AWR collects, processes, and maintains performance statistics for problem detection and resolution. Its snapshots provide a historical view of database performance, revealing trends and anomalies.

2. *Active Session History (ASH):* ASH samples active database sessions, providing real-time and historical data about query execution, wait events, and session activity. This helps in identifying transient performance issues.

3. *Oracle Enterprise Manager (OEM):* OEM offers a graphical interface for monitoring and managing the Oracle environment. It provides real-time diagnostics, performance metrics, and tuning recommendations.

4. *SQL Trace and TKPROF:* SQL Trace generates trace files that provide detailed information on SQL execution, including waits and resource usage. TKPROF formats this raw trace data for easier analysis.

```
ALTER SESSION SET sql_trace = TRUE;
-- Run the SQL statements to trace
ALTER SESSION SET sql_trace = FALSE;
```

5. *Statspack:* Statspack, an older but still useful tool, collects and displays performance data. It enables performance comparisons over time and across different workload periods.

Key Performance Indicators (KPIs)

Effective performance monitoring hinges on a set of KPIs:

- **Buffer Cache Hit Ratio:** Measures the percentage of logical reads found in memory, indicating effective use of the buffer cache.
- **Library Cache Hit Ratio:** Reflects the efficiency of shared SQL execution plans, with high hit ratios suggesting minimal parsing and recompilation.
- **Disk I/O Throughput:** Monitors read/write operations frequency and latency, identifying potential disk subsystem bottlenecks.
- **Latch Hit Ratio:** Suggests concurrency control efficiency. High miss ratios might signal contention and a need to adjust initialization parameters.
- **Wait Events:** Categorizes and measures wait times, helping to identify why CPU is not being effectively utilized.

Performance tuning is an iterative and continuous effort, requiring regular monitoring, metrics analysis, and adjustments based on observed data. Understanding database performance involves not only modeling theoretical concepts but also effectively leveraging Oracle's diagnostic tools to achieve an optimized database environment.

8.3 Monitoring Oracle Database Performance

Effective monitoring of Oracle Database performance is critical to ensure that the system runs efficiently and meets the required Service

Level Agreements (SLAs). This section delves into various methods and tools available to monitor the performance of an Oracle Database.

Central to Oracle Database monitoring are the metrics and tools that provide insights into the health, efficiency, and capacity of the database system. Oracle provides several built-in tools and views to facilitate comprehensive performance monitoring.

Dynamic Performance Views (V$ Views): These views are frequently used to access real-time performance-related data. They are prefixed with 'V$', indicating that they contain dynamic performance data. Key V$ views include:

- V$SYSSTAT: Contains system-level statistics since the instance started.
- V$SESSTAT: Provides session-level statistics.
- V$SYSTEM_EVENT: Shows system-wide wait events.
- V$SESSION_EVENT: Displays wait events for each session.
- V$SQL: Lists statistics on SQL statements that are in the shared pool.

The V$ views provide a snapshot of the database's current performance metrics. For example, the following SQL query retrieves critical information from the V$SYSSTAT view:

```
SELECT name, value
FROM V$SYSSTAT
WHERE name LIKE '%parse%'
OR name LIKE '%execute count%';
```

Data Dictionary Views: These views store metadata about the database objects and provide persistent information. For performance monitoring, certain views of interest include:

- DBA_HIST_ACTIVE_SESS_HISTORY: Retrieves historical data about active sessions.
- DBA_HIST_SQLSTAT: Provides historical statistics for SQL statements.
- DBA_HIST_SNAPSHOT: Captures a snapshot of the system-level statistics at regular intervals.

With these views, database administrators can query historical data to analyze trends and performance over time. For example, to retrieve information about the most resource-intensive SQL statements over a period, one might use:

```
SELECT sql_id,
       SUM(executions_delta) AS executions,
       SUM(buffer_gets_delta) AS buffer_gets
FROM DBA_HIST_SQLSTAT
GROUP BY sql_id
ORDER BY buffer_gets DESC
FETCH FIRST 10 ROWS ONLY;
```

Automatic Workload Repository (AWR): AWR is a built-in repository that captures and stores statistical data related to database performance. This data is used by the Oracle Database to optimize workloads. AWR generates reports that provide deep insights into performance issues. An example of generating an AWR report is as follows:

```
BEGIN
  DBMS_WORKLOAD_REPOSITORY.create_snapshot ();
END;
/
@?/rdbms/admin/awrrpt.sql
```

The output of an AWR report includes important sections such as:

- **Load Profile**: Provides an overview of the workload in terms of transactions, reads, writes, and other metrics.
- **Instance Efficiency Percentages**: Shows key ratios and percentages that indicate the efficiency of instance operations.
- **Top SQL Statements**: Lists the SQL statements that are consuming the most resources.

Active Session History (ASH): ASH is a subsystem of AWR that provides a minute-by-minute sample of active session statistics. ASH data can be queried using:

```
SELECT sample_time,
       session_id,
       sql_id,
       event,
       state
FROM V$ACTIVE_SESSION_HISTORY
WHERE session_id = :session_id
AND sample_time > SYSDATE - 0.01;
```

This query would help in pinpointing periods of high activity or contention for a specific session.

Oracle Enterprise Manager (OEM): OEM provides a graphical interface for monitoring and managing Oracle Databases. It includes features for real-time performance monitoring, diagnostics, and resolution. OEM's Performance Page shows vital performance indicators such as:

- **Top Activity**: Displays the highest database activity by wait class and sessions.
- **DB Time**: Shows the time the database spends on user calls.
- **Resource Waits**: Highlights waits on various resources, aiding in bottleneck identification.

OEM's Automatic Database Diagnostic Monitor (ADDM) evaluates AWR data to provide analysis on performance issues. It can suggest recommendations for tuning and optimization.

Monitoring performance in Oracle Database involves a multifaceted approach using dynamic views, data dictionary views, AWR, ASH, and OEM. Each tool and view offers a unique perspective, enabling database administrators to comprehensively evaluate and enhance database performance.

8.4 Using Oracle Enterprise Manager for Performance Tuning

Oracle Enterprise Manager (OEM) serves as a comprehensive suite for managing Oracle databases and applications with a centralized, integrated interface. In the context of performance tuning, OEM offers extensive tools for real-time monitoring, diagnostics, and advanced analytics. The effectiveness of OEM in identifying and resolving performance issues hinges on its various components and features, including database monitoring, target discovery, performance pages, advisors, and robust reporting mechanisms.

One of the critical functionalities of Oracle Enterprise Manager for performance tuning is the **Performance Page**. This page provides a detailed overview of the database's current state by displaying real-time statistics on various performance metrics. These metrics include CPU usage, memory usage, I/O activity, and wait events. The Performance Page allows database administrators (DBAs) to quickly spot anomalies or trends indicating potential performance bottlenecks.

```
-- Open Oracle Enterprise Manager
-- Navigate to Targets > Databases
-- Select the target database name
-- Click on Performance tab
```

By examining the components of the Performance Page, such as the **Top Activity**, DBAs can view the most resource-intensive sessions, SQL statements, and PL/SQL blocks. Utilizing the filters, they can narrow down specific time windows or types of activity to diagnose issues effectively. For example, DBAs can filter by "Top SQLs by CPU" to identify which SQL queries are consuming the most CPU resources.

Performance analysis extends beyond real-time monitoring. Oracle Enterprise Manager also facilitates historical analysis through its **Active Session History (ASH)** reports. ASH provides granular details about active sessions, which include wait events, session IDs, SQL IDs, and module information. By mining ASH data, DBAs can detect historical trends and recurring performance issues.

```
SELECT sample_time, session_id, sql_id, wait_class, event
FROM dba_hist_active_sess_history
WHERE sample_time BETWEEN '01-Jan-2023' AND '31-Jan-2023'
ORDER BY sample_time;
```

In conjunction with ASH, the **Automatic Workload Repository (AWR)** reports provide a comprehensive view of the database's performance over regular intervals. AWR snapshots can be scheduled, and the repository data includes load profile, instance efficiency percentages, top SQL statements, and segment statistics. A typical AWR report offers insights into potential areas of optimization, such as resource-intensive queries or inefficient use of indexes.

To generate an AWR report, the following PL/SQL procedure can be executed:

```
BEGIN
  DBMS_WORKLOAD_REPOSITORY.create_snapshot ();
END;
/

BEGIN
  DBMS_WORKLOAD_REPOSITORY.awr_report_html (
    7692, -- DBID
    1, -- Instance ID
    100, -- Start Snapshot ID
    110, -- End Snapshot ID
    'awr_report_jan.html'
  );
END;
/
```

The **Advisors** available within Oracle Enterprise Manager are pivotal for proactive performance tuning. The SQL Tuning Advisor scrutinizes high-load SQL statements and recommends changes such as creating indexes, restructuring SQL queries, or gathering fresh statistics. The SQL Access Advisor, on the other hand, evaluates the physical storage structures, advising on indexes, materialized views, and partitioning schemes that can improve query performance.

```
DECLARE
  tuning_task_id VARCHAR2(100);
BEGIN
  tuning_task_id := DBMS_SQLTUNE.create_tuning_task(
    sql_id => 'abcdefg12345678',
    scope => DBMS_SQLTUNE.scope_comprehensive,
    time_limit => 3600,
    task_name => 'sql_tuning_task',
    description => 'Tuning task for high CPU SQL'
  );

  DBMS_SQLTUNE.execute_tuning_task(task_name => 'sql_tuning_task');
END;
/

SELECT DBMS_SQLTUNE.report_tuning_task ('sql_tuning_task') FROM dual;
```

Adopting performance baselines within Oracle Enterprise Manager can significantly enhance the ability to detect deviations from expected performance behaviors. Baselines capture the database's typical performance metrics over a specified period, serving as a benchmark. When deviations surpass a pre-defined threshold, alerts are triggered, allowing DBAs to respond promptly to potential performance degradation.

Furthermore, the **Real-time SQL Monitoring** feature provides instant access to the execution details of SQL statements currently running. This feature is particularly valuable for monitoring long-running queries or batch jobs. It displays execution plans, statistics on rows processed, and elapsed time, enabling immediate identification of problematic steps within SQL execution.

```
-- Navigate to Performance > SQL Monitoring in Oracle Enterprise Manager
-- Select the active SQL statement to view detailed metrics and execution plan
```

Effective use of Oracle Enterprise Manager for performance tuning necessitates a combination of real-time monitoring, historical trend analysis, advisory tools, and proactive alert mechanisms. DBAs must leverage these functionalities to maintain optimal database performance and swiftly address emerging issues.

8.5 Optimizing SQL Queries

Optimizing SQL queries is an essential aspect of database performance tuning. Efficient queries reduce the load on the database system and improve response times for applications. Key techniques include understanding and leveraging indexing, writing efficient SQL, using appropriate data types, and rewriting queries for better performance.

SQL query optimization begins with analyzing the SQL statements for potential inefficiencies. The SQL execution plan, obtained using the EXPLAIN PLAN command or tools like Oracle SQL Developer, provides insights into how Oracle Database executes a given query. The plan outlines the order of operations, join methods, and access paths used by the optimizer. Efficient queries often have specific characteristics: they minimize full table scans, utilize indexes effectively, and avoid unnecessary sorting and grouping.

```
EXPLAIN PLAN FOR
SELECT employee_id, last_name, first_name
FROM employees
WHERE department_id = 50;
```

The output of EXPLAIN PLAN can be viewed using the DBMS_XPLAN.DISPLAY function, which formats the execution plan into a readable structure.

```
SELECT * FROM TABLE(DBMS_XPLAN.DISPLAY);
```

Effective indexing is pivotal for query optimization. Indexes allow the database to locate rows faster than scanning an entire table. Oracle Database supports various types of indexes, including B-tree, bitmap, and function-based indexes. Choosing the correct type of index based on the query patterns greatly enhances performance. For example, B-tree indexes are suitable for high-cardinality columns often present in WHERE clauses, while bitmap indexes are efficient for low-cardinality columns used in analytic queries.

```
CREATE INDEX emp_dept_idx ON employees(department_id);
```

To ensure indexes are used effectively, the optimizer needs accurate and up-to-date statistics. Oracle Database includes the DBMS_STATS package to gather statistics for tables and indexes. Regular collection of statistics ensures the optimizer makes informed decisions.

```
EXEC DBMS_STATS.GATHER_TABLE_STATS('HR', 'EMPLOYEES');
```

Writing efficient SQL involves avoiding unnecessary columns in SELECT statements, using WHERE clauses to filter rows early, and eliminating subqueries when possible. Using set-based operations (joins) instead of row-by-row operations (nested loops) is another best practice. The Oracle optimizer can automatically rewrite queries if transformations like views or subqueries impact performance.

```
SELECT employee_id, last_name
FROM employees
WHERE department_id = 50
ORDER BY last_name;
```

Appropriate data types in table definitions also affect query performance. Using the ideal data type for columns, such as NUMBER instead of VARCHAR2 for numerical data, reduces storage and processing overhead. For dates, the DATE or TIMESTAMP types should be used instead of VARCHAR2.

Query rewriting can further optimize performance. Common techniques include eliminating redundant joins, using UNION ALL instead of UNION when duplicates are irrelevant, and breaking down complex queries into simpler ones. These methods can help maintain both query maintainability and execution speed.

```
SELECT employee_id FROM dept_10_employees
UNION ALL
SELECT employee_id FROM dept_20_employees;
```

Monitoring and profiling tools assist in identifying performance bottlenecks at the query level. Oracle SQL Trace and the TKPROF tool provide detailed tracing of SQL execution, allowing in-depth examination of query performance. Leveraging these tools helps detect and rectify inefficient SQL statements.

```
ALTER SESSION SET SQL_TRACE = TRUE;
```

Oracle's Automatic Database Diagnostic Monitor (ADDM) analyzes AWR data and provides recommendations, including SQL tuning advice, which can be acted upon to enhance query performance.

A repository of frequently used queries, well-designed with performance in mind, facilitates efficient execution patterns and minimizes overhead on the database. Consistent application of these optimization strategies delivers measurable improvements in both query response times and overall database performance.

8.6 Indexing Strategies and Management

Effective indexing is a cornerstone of database performance optimization. Indexes enable the database management system to quickly locate and access the data in a table without scanning the entire table, thereby significantly improving query performance. This section delves into various indexing strategies and their management to enhance Oracle Database performance.

Types of Indexes

Oracle Database supports several types of indexes, each suited for different kinds of queries and data distributions:

- **B-tree Indexes**: Standard and the most commonly used type of index. Suitable for high selectivity data.
- **Bitmap Indexes**: Best for columns with low cardinality (few distinct values).
- **Clustered Indexes**: Ensures that the physical order of rows in the table matches the order of the index; Oracle supports index-organized tables (IOT).
- **Function-based Indexes**: Facilitates indexing of expressions or functions to optimize queries with WHERE clause conditions on the computed results.
- **Partitioned Indexes**: Enhances manageability and performance in large tables by dividing the index into smaller, more manageable pieces.
- **Reverse Key Indexes**: Distributes insertion load more evenly across the index structure.

Creating Indexes

Creating an index involves defining the schema of the columns to be indexed. Below is an SQL command to create a B-tree index:

```
CREATE INDEX idx_employee_lastname
ON employees (last_name);
```

For a bitmap index, the syntax would differ slightly:

```
CREATE BITMAP INDEX idx_employee_dept
ON employees (department_id);
```

Function-based indexes are especially useful when queries involve mathematical calculations or string manipulations:

```
CREATE INDEX idx_employee_upper_lastname
ON employees (UPPER(last_name));
```

Maintaining Indexes

Index maintenance involves regular monitoring and rebuilding to maintain optimal performance. Over time, indexes can become fragmented due to DML (Data Manipulation Language) operations like INSERT, UPDATE, and DELETE. Fragmentation can lead to inefficient index scans.

Rebuilding indexes can help mitigate fragmentation. The command to rebuild an index is:

```
ALTER INDEX idx_employee_lastname REBUILD;
```

Oracle allows rebuilding indexes online, meaning that the index remains available for queries during the rebuild process:

```
ALTER INDEX idx_employee_lastname REBUILD ONLINE;
```

Index Usage and Analysis

Understanding whether and how indexes are being used is critical. Oracle provides various tools and views to analyze index usage:

- V$OBJECT_USAGE: This view tracks index usage. For a specific index, we can enable monitoring:

  ```
  ALTER INDEX idx_employee_lastname MONITORING USAGE;
  ```

  Later, we can query the V$OBJECT_USAGE view:

  ```
  SELECT * FROM V$OBJECT_USAGE
  WHERE INDEX_NAME = 'IDX_EMPLOYEE_LASTNAME';
  ```

- DBMS_STATS.GATHER_INDEX_STATS: Gathers index statistics, crucial for the optimizer to make informed decisions. Example for a specific index:

  ```
  EXEC DBMS_STATS.GATHER_INDEX_STATS('SCOTT', '
      IDX_EMPLOYEE_LASTNAME');
  ```

Index Design Principles

Index design is an iterative process necessitating consideration of the workload, query patterns, and data distribution. Design principles include:

- **Selectivity**: High selectivity indexes are more effective. Selectivity is defined as the ratio of the number of distinct values in the indexed column to the total number of records.
- **Index Columns Used in WHERE Clause**: Prioritize columns frequently utilized in WHERE clauses, join conditions, and filter criteria.
- **Composite Indexes**: Consider composite indexes (indexes on multiple columns) when queries often filter on multiple columns.
- **Avoid Over-indexing**: Too many indexes can degrade overall performance because every insert, update, or delete operation must also update all relevant indexes.
- **Analyze Workload Patterns**: Use tools like Oracle Enterprise Manager and the Automatic Workload Repository (AWR) reports to identify heavy query patterns that can benefit from indexing.

Monitoring and Tuning Indexes with Oracle Tools

Several Oracle tools can be used for monitoring and tuning indexes, such as Oracle Enterprise Manager (OEM):

- **Oracle Enterprise Manager (OEM)**: Allows visualization of index usage and performance metrics, supports performance and advisory reports.
- **SQL Access Advisor**: Provides recommendations for index creation, deletion, and restructuring based on workload analysis.
- **Automatic Workload Repository (AWR)**: AWR snapshots can reveal details about query performance issues possibly related to indexing.

Case Study: Optimizing Indexes

Consider a scenario where a table ORDERS with a large dataset is experiencing performance issues on queries filtering by order date and $\mathrm{customer\_id}$. Analysis with AWR and SQL Access Advisor suggests the creation of composite indexes.

Creating the suggested composite index:

```
CREATE INDEX idx_orders_date_customer
ON orders (order_date, customer_id);
```

Subsequent performance analysis reveals significant improvements in query execution times:

```
Execution Time Before Index: 15 seconds
Execution Time After Index: 2 seconds
```

This case exemplifies the impact of well-designed indexes on overall database performance.

Understanding and implementing indexing strategies and management within Oracle Database can drastically improve query performance while ensuring that resources are utilized efficiently. Always align indexing strategies with the specific workload patterns and query requirements for optimal results.

8.7 Memory Tuning and Management

Memory tuning and management are crucial components of Oracle Database performance optimization. Efficient use of memory can significantly enhance database performance, reducing disk I/O and increasing query execution speed. This section delves into various aspects of memory architecture in Oracle, outlining strategies for effectively managing and tuning these areas.

The System Global Area (SGA) and Program Global Area (PGA) are the two main memory structures within Oracle Database. The SGA is a shared memory area that holds data and control information for an Oracle instance. In contrast, the PGA is a non-shared memory region containing data and control information for server processes.

Configuring the System Global Area (SGA)

The SGA consists of several components, each playing a vital role in database operations:

- Buffer Cache
- Shared Pool
- Large Pool
- Java Pool

- Streams Pool

Buffer Cache stores copies of data blocks read from data files. When a query is executed, Oracle first searches the Buffer Cache for the required data before performing a read operation from disk. Tuning the size of the Buffer Cache can significantly reduce the amount of disk I/O.

To adjust the Buffer Cache size, the DB_CACHE_SIZE parameter can be set in the initialization parameter file:

```
ALTER SYSTEM SET DB_CACHE_SIZE = 1024M;
```

The **Shared Pool** is another critical component of the SGA. It stores SQL statements, PL/SQL code, and data dictionary cache information. Efficient management of the Shared Pool ensures high hit ratios, minimizing the need for parsing and re-loading:

```
ALTER SYSTEM SET SHARED_POOL_SIZE = 512M;
```

The **Large Pool** is an optional area used for large memory allocations in operations such as parallel query execution and RMAN backup and restore. By configuring the LARGE_POOL_SIZE parameter, one can optimize these operations:

```
ALTER SYSTEM SET LARGE_POOL_SIZE = 128M;
```

For Java-based applications, the **Java Pool** can be configured. It stores Java code and data in a specialized memory area, set by the JAVA_POOL_SIZE parameter:

```
ALTER SYSTEM SET JAVA_POOL_SIZE = 64M;
```

Similarly, Oracle Streams rely on the **Streams Pool** for memory allocation. Setting the STREAMS_POOL_SIZE parameter adjusts the size of this memory area:

```
ALTER SYSTEM SET STREAMS_POOL_SIZE = 32M;
```

Tuning the Program Global Area (PGA)

The PGA serves as private memory for each Oracle server process. PGA memory management can be automatic or manual. With automatic PGA memory management, Oracle dynamically adjusts the amount of memory dedicated to the PGA based on workload characteristics and available resources.

The PGA_AGGREGATE_TARGET parameter specifies the target

aggregate PGA memory available to all server processes:

```
ALTER SYSTEM SET PGA_AGGREGATE_TARGET = 1G;
```

In addition, the WORKAREA_SIZE_POLICY parameter dictates whether Oracle automatically manages the size of work areas used by memory-intensive operations like sorting and hashing. Setting this parameter to AUTO enables automatic management:

```
ALTER SYSTEM SET WORKAREA_SIZE_POLICY = AUTO;
```

By leveraging these parameters, Oracle can effectively balance memory usage, optimizing overall system performance.

Dynamic SGA and PGA Tuning

Oracle allows for dynamic adjustment of memory parameters without requiring an instance restart. This capability provides flexibility in adapting to changing workload demands.

To verify current SGA and PGA settings and their utilization, queries against the **V$SGA_TARGET_ADVICE** and **V$PGA_TARGET_ADVICE** views can provide valuable insights:

```
SELECT SIZE_FACTOR, ESTD_DB_TIME, ESTD_PHYSICAL_READS
FROM V$SGA_TARGET_ADVICE
WHERE SGA_SIZE = (SELECT value FROM V$PARAMETER WHERE name = '
    sga_max_size');

SELECT SIZE_FACTOR, ESTD_PGA_CACHE_HIT_PERCENTAGE,
    ESTD_OVERALLOC_COUNT
FROM V$PGA_TARGET_ADVICE;
```

```
Output Example for SGA Target Advice:
   SIZE_FACTOR | ESTD_DB_TIME | ESTD_PHYSICAL_READS
   ------------------------------------------------
       0.5     |    10036    |        1624
       1.0     |     5020    |         812
       1.5     |     3268    |         406

Output Example for PGA Target Advice:
   SIZE_FACTOR | ESTD_PGA_CACHE_HIT_PERCENTAGE | ESTD_OVERALLOC_COUNT
   ----------------------------------------------------------------
       0.5     |             75               |         10
       1.0     |             88               |          5
       1.5     |             93               |          3
```

Periodic monitoring and adjustments, tailored to the specific workload requirements, can maintain optimal performance levels.

Efficient memory management in Oracle Database involves a thorough understanding of its memory architecture and the careful application of tuning techniques. Through comprehensive configuration and continuous tuning of both SGA and PGA components, database performance can be enhanced, ensuring rapid query responses and efficient resource utilization.

8.8 Disk I/O and Storage Optimization

Disk I/O and storage optimization are critical to the overall performance of an Oracle database. Efficient management of these resources can significantly enhance database throughput and responsiveness. The optimization process involves a deep understanding of how Oracle interacts with the underlying storage system, the configuration of key parameters, and the effective use of tools and techniques designed to monitor and tune I/O operations.

Oracle databases rely heavily on disk I/O for reading and writing data, redo logs, undo segments, and performing backup and recovery operations. To optimize disk I/O, it is essential to consider several factors: disk layout, RAID configurations, file placement, and the use of solid-state drives (SSDs).

Disk Layout and RAID Configurations

The disk layout should be designed to minimize contention and maximize throughput. Data files can be spread across multiple disks to balance the I/O load and reduce bottlenecks. Implementing RAID (Redundant Array of Independent Disks) configurations can enhance performance and reliability. Among the various RAID levels, RAID 0 (striping) offers high performance but no redundancy, RAID 1 (mirroring) provides redundancy with moderate performance, and RAID 5 (striped with parity) balances performance and redundancy but may suffer from write performance penalties. RAID 10 (a combination of RAID 1 and RAID 0) is often recommended for databases as it provides both high performance and redundancy.

File Placement Strategy

Proper file placement is crucial for reducing I/O contention. Oracle recommends the following file placement strategies:

- **Data Files**: Spread data files across multiple disks or disk groups to balance the I/O load. Avoid placing all data files on a single disk.
- **Redo Log Files**: Place redo log files on high-performance storage to support high write throughput. Consider using SSDs for redo logs to ensure fast transaction logging.

- **Temp Files**: Temporary files should also be placed on high-performance storage to facilitate efficient sorting and other temporary operations.
- **Control Files**: Multiplex control files across different disks to provide redundancy and improve fault tolerance.

Solid-State Drives (SSDs)

The use of SSDs can significantly improve I/O performance due to their lower latency and higher throughput compared to traditional spinning disks (HDDs). SSDs are particularly beneficial for:

- Redo log files: Due to their write-intensive nature, placing redo logs on SSDs can enhance logging speed.
- Frequently accessed data: Tablespaces or data files with high read/write activity can benefit from the fast access times of SSDs.

Monitoring Disk I/O Performance

Monitoring disk I/O performance is essential to identify bottlenecks and ensure optimal performance. Oracle provides several tools and views to monitor I/O activity:

- **Automatic Workload Repository (AWR)**: AWR reports provide comprehensive information on I/O statistics, helping in the identification of I/O bottlenecks.
- **V$ views**: Views such as V$SYSTEM_EVENT, V$SESSTAT, V$FILESTAT, and V$SYSTEM_STATISTICS offer real-time I/O statistics.
- **Oracle Enterprise Manager (OEM)**: OEM provides graphical tools and dashboards to monitor and analyze I/O performance.

Tuning Database Parameters

Oracle Database provides several parameters that can be tuned to optimize I/O performance:

- **DB_BLOCK_SIZE**: The database block size should be set appropriately based on the type of application. OLTP applications typically benefit from smaller block sizes, whereas DSS environments may perform better with larger block sizes.

- **DB_FILE_MULTIBLOCK_READ_COUNT**: This parameter determines the number of blocks read in one I/O operation during table scans. Setting an appropriate value can help in balancing I/O performance.

- **DISK_ASYNC_IO**: Enables or disables asynchronous I/O. Asynchronous I/O can improve performance by allowing queries to continue processing while I/O operations are being completed.

Striping and Parallelism

Striping data across multiple disks can enhance performance by allowing multiple I/O operations to be performed concurrently. Oracle Database supports parallel query execution, which can be configured to use multiple processes for scanning, sorting, and joining data. Parallel execution can significantly reduce query response times for large data sets.

```
-- Example: Enabling Parallel Execution for a Table
ALTER TABLE employees PARALLEL (DEGREE 4);
```

```
-- Expected Output: Table altered.
```

Using Oracle Direct Path Reads

Direct Path Reads allow Oracle to bypass the buffer cache and read data blocks directly from disk into the PGA (Program Global Area). This can reduce buffer cache contention and enhance read performance for large table scans or bulk data load operations.

```
-- Example: Enabling Direct Path Reads for a Session
ALTER SESSION ENABLE PARALLEL DML;
```

```
-- Expected Output: Session altered.
```

Effective disk I/O and storage optimization require a comprehensive approach that includes proper disk layout, strategic file placement, the use of SSDs, continuous monitoring of I/O performance, tuning of database parameters, and leveraging parallelism and direct path reads. These efforts collectively ensure that the database operates efficiently, providing fast and reliable access to data.

8.9 Managing Sessions and Processes

In Oracle Database, effective management of sessions and processes is critical for maintaining optimal database performance. Proper handling of these elements ensures resource allocation is efficient and helps prevent bottlenecks. This section focuses on the management of sessions and processes, explaining their roles, interactions, and tools available for their administration.

Sessions in Oracle Database refer to individual connections made to the database by user applications. Each session can execute SQL statements, PL/SQL code, and carry out various transactions. Processes, on the other hand, are operating system-level entities that execute database application code and interact with system resources. Oracle manages both user and background processes to facilitate database operations.

User Sessions and Processes

Every time an application connects to the Oracle Database, a user session and a corresponding process are created. The user process is responsible for managing user applications and interacting with the Oracle server process. Each user session can be associated with multiple transactions, where each transaction represents a discrete unit of work.

To list all sessions currently active in the database, the following SQL query can be used:

```
SELECT SID, SERIAL#, USERNAME, STATUS
FROM V$SESSION
ORDER BY USERNAME;
```

The output of this query will display all session IDs (SID), serial numbers, usernames, and their respective statuses. This helps in identifying the active sessions and taking administrative actions if necessary.

```
SID SERIAL# USERNAME        STATUS
---- -------- --------------- --------
  12   1598 SCOTT           ACTIVE
  34   2231 HR              INACTIVE
 105   4456 SYS             ACTIVE
```

Session Management

Managing sessions involves various administrative actions such as altering session parameters, terminating inactive sessions, and monitoring session-level resource usage. The following PL/SQL code can be used to terminate a session:

```
ALTER SYSTEM KILL SESSION 'SID,SERIAL#';
```

For example, to terminate the session with SID 34 and serial number 2231:

```
ALTER SYSTEM KILL SESSION '34,2231';
```

Successful execution of this command ensures that a problematic or rogue session which may be consuming excessive resources or causing deadlocks is terminated.

Background Processes

Oracle Database relies on several background processes to manage its internal operations. Some of these processes include:

- **DBWn (Database Writer):** Responsible for writing modified data from the database buffer cache to the data files on disk.
- **LGWR (Log Writer):** Writes redo log entries from the redo log buffer in the SGA to the online redo log files on disk.
- **CKPT (Checkpoint):** Signals DBWn to write all necessary data to disk and updates the data file headers and control files.
- **SMON (System Monitor):** Performs instance recovery, if necessary, at instance startup and handles cleanup of temporary segments.
- **PMON (Process Monitor):** Responsible for cleaning up after failed processes by rolling back the transaction and releasing resources.

Understanding and managing these background processes is essential for ensuring Oracle Database operates smoothly. The DBA can utilize various tools to monitor the performance and health of these processes, such as Oracle Enterprise Manager and dynamic performance views like V$PROCESS.

Using V$PROCESS

The V$PROCESS view provides information about the processes running in the Oracle Database. To gather details about the current processes, execute:

```
SELECT PID, SPID, USERNAME, PROGRAM
FROM V$PROCESS
ORDER BY PID;
```

This query will reveal the process IDs (PID), system process IDs (SPID), usernames, and associated programs for all running processes.

```
PID  SPID   USERNAME      PROGRAM
---- ------- ------------- -------------------
  1  1234    ORACLE     ORACLE@host (DBW1)
  2  1235    ORACLE     ORACLE@host (LGWR)
  3  1236    ORACLE     ORACLE@host (PMON)
```

Such information is crucial when there is a need to diagnose performance issues or abnormal behavior related to database processes.

Resource Allocation and Limits

Careful monitoring and management of sessions and processes also involves setting appropriate resource and profile limits using Oracle Resource Manager and profiles.

Resource Manager allows for the setting of priorities and resource allocations among different sessions and processes. This ensures that high-priority applications receive the necessary resources to function efficiently, thereby optimizing overall database performance.

Profiles can be created and assigned to users to limit their resource consumption, effectively controlling how users interact with the database.

To create a profile that limits the number of concurrent sessions:

```
CREATE PROFILE limit_sessions
   LIMIT SESSIONS_PER_USER 5;
```

To assign this profile to a user:

```
ALTER USER hr PROFILE limit_sessions;
```

Implementing such profiles aids in preventing any single user from overloading the database by creating too many concurrent sessions, thus leading to more balanced resource distribution.

Dynamic Performance Views

Dynamic performance views, such as V$SESSION, V$PROCESS, and V$RESOURCE_LIMIT, are essential for obtaining real-time insights into session and process statistics. Regularly querying these views allows DBAs to proactively manage the database's operational health.

For example, to check the current resource usage limits:

```
SELECT RESOURCE_NAME, CURRENT_UTILIZATION, MAX_UTILIZATION,
    LIMIT_VALUE
FROM V$RESOURCE_LIMIT;
```

This information helps in understanding the load on the database and whether resource limits are being approached or exceeded.

```
RESOURCE_NAME          CURRENT_UTILIZATION  MAX_UTILIZATION  LIMIT_VALUE
---------------------- -------------------  ---------------  -----------
sessions                        45              50              100
processes                       30              30              200
enqueue_locks                   35              45              100
```

Effective session and process management in Oracle Database directly influences system performance. By vigilant monitoring, appropriate resource allocation, and proactive termination of problematic sessions and processes, a DBA ensures smooth and efficient database operations.

8.10 Automatic Workload Repository (AWR) and Active Session History (ASH)

The Automatic Workload Repository (AWR) and Active Session History (ASH) are essential components in Oracle Database for performance tuning and diagnostics. Both these tools provide valuable insights into system performance, helping database administrators (DBAs) identify and resolve potential issues. Understanding how to effectively utilize AWR and ASH is crucial for maintaining and optimizing database performance.

AWR is a repository of performance statistics that are automatically collected and maintained by Oracle Database. The statistics collected include information about database workloads, system configuration, and various performance metrics. AWR snapshots are taken at regular intervals, typically once every hour, and are stored for a configurable retention period, which by default is eight days.

- **AWR Snapshots**: Snapshots are periodic samples of database performance data. They capture a wealth of statistics related to system performance, including SQL execution times, wait events, and resource usage. Snapshots can be manually created or automatically generated at predefined intervals.
- **AWR Reports**: These reports provide a detailed analysis of database performance for a specified time period, typically between two snapshots. AWR reports summarize various metrics such as CPU usage, memory usage, IO statistics, and significant SQL statements.

- **Retention and Purging**: The retention period for AWR snapshots is customizable. DBAs can adjust retention settings according to the requirements of their environment. Older snapshots that exceed the retention period are purged automatically.

To generate an AWR report, one can use the following SQL*Plus commands:

```
SQL> @$ORACLE_HOME/rdbms/admin/awrrpt.sql
```

Upon executing this command, Oracle prompts for the report type (HTML or TEXT), the start and end snapshot IDs, and other optional details. The output will include comprehensive information that can be used for detailed performance analysis.

ASH, on the other hand, is a component of the AWR that captures session activity, providing insights into what active sessions are doing in real-time. ASH data is sampled every second and stored in a circular buffer in memory. This means the most recent session activity is always available without having to rely solely on the regular AWR snapshots.

- **ASH Data Collection**: It captures information about all active database sessions, including the SQL executing, the wait events encountered, and session states. This helps in identifying performance bottlenecks and understanding the workload characteristics in real-time.
- **ASH Reporting**: Through ASH reports, DBAs can analyze session activity over a specified period. These reports help pinpoint problematic SQL, contention issues, and other performance bottlenecks.
- **V$ACTIVE_SESSION_HISTORY**: This dynamic performance view allows queries against the ASH data. DBAs can filter and fetch real-time session activity data tailored to their needs. An example query to fetch the top SQL by wait time would look like:

```
SELECT sql_id,
       COUNT(*) AS wait_count
FROM v$active_session_history
WHERE sample_time BETWEEN :start_time AND :end_time
GROUP BY sql_id
ORDER BY wait_count DESC;
```

ASH is particularly useful for diagnosing transient performance issues that might be missed by the less frequent AWR snapshots. By providing granular, session-level data, ASH can uncover patterns and problems that impact user sessions.

A practical scenario where both AWR and ASH shine is in troubleshooting a performance issue reported by an end-user experiencing slow query performance. The steps might include:

- Fetching the relevant AWR report to identify any periods of high resource usage or unusual activity.
- Using ASH data to drill down into specific sessions and examine the SQL statements being executed, the wait events encountered, and any contention issues.
- Correlating the findings from AWR and ASH to pinpoint the root cause of the performance degradation.

The combined use of AWR and ASH thus provides a powerful framework for both proactive performance monitoring and reactive troubleshooting. These tools enable DBAs to maintain the database in an optimal state by making informed decisions backed by empirical data.

8.11 Using Oracle Performance Tuning Tools

Oracle Database provides a comprehensive set of tools to assist in performance tuning and optimization. These tools allow database administrators to diagnose and rectify inefficiencies, ensuring the database performs at an optimal level. This section delves into the use of key Oracle performance tuning tools, including Automatic Database Diagnostic Monitor (ADDM), SQL Tuning Advisor, SQL Access Advisor, and Oracle Trace.

Automatic Database Diagnostic Monitor (ADDM)

ADDM provides proactive monitoring and diagnostic capabilities for Oracle Databases. It automatically analyzes system performance data collected in AWR snapshots and identifies performance bottlenecks and potential issues.

The following example demonstrates how to generate an ADDM report:

```
-- Connect to the database as a privileged user
SQL> @?/rdbms/admin/addmrpt.sql
```

```
-- Specify the beginning and ending snapshot IDs
Enter value for begin_snap: 100
Enter value for end_snap: 101

-- Name the report
Enter value for report_name: addm_report.txt
```

The ADDM report provides a detailed analysis of the system's performance during the specified time interval. It includes findings, impacts, and recommendations to resolve performance issues.

SQL Tuning Advisor

The SQL Tuning Advisor helps optimize SQL queries by providing recommendations for SQL statements. Activated within Oracle Enterprise Manager or via DBMS_SQLTUNE package, it analyzes SQL statements and provides tuning suggestions to improve execution performance.

Example usage through the DBMS_SQLTUNE package:

```
-- Create a tuning task
DECLARE
  my_task VARCHAR2(30);
BEGIN
  my_task := DBMS_SQLTUNE.create_tuning_task(
               sql_id => 'd9mftz0anx5xd',
               scope => DBMS_SQLTUNE.scope_comprehensive,
               time_limit => 60,
               task_name => 'my_sql_tuning_task',
               description => 'Tuning task for specific SQL');
END;
/

-- Execute the tuning task
EXEC DBMS_SQLTUNE.execute_tuning_task(task_name => 'my_sql_tuning_task'
      );

-- Review the tuning recommendations
SELECT DBMS_SQLTUNE.report_tuning_task('my_sql_tuning_task') FROM dual;
```

The output is a detailed report, showing index recommendations, statistics collection suggestions, and other possible enhancement strategies.

SQL Access Advisor

SQL Access Advisor recommends changes to schema objects that can improve the efficiency of SQL operations. Recommendations include creating, dropping, and modifying indexes, materialized views, and partitioning of tables.

Example invocation through DBMS_ADVISOR package:

```
-- Create a tuning task for a SQL workload
```

```
DECLARE
  workload_name VARCHAR2(30);
  task_name VARCHAR2(30);
BEGIN
  workload_name := 'test_workload';
  task_name := DBMS_ADVISOR.CREATE_TASK('Access Advisor');

  -- Define a workload that includes SQL statements
  DBMS_ADVISOR.LOAD_SQLWKLD(
    task_name => task_name,
    workload_name => workload_name,
    sql_text => 'SELECT * FROM employees WHERE department_id = 10');

  -- Execute the advisor task
  DBMS_ADVISOR.EXECUTE_TASK(task_name);
END;
/

-- Review advisor recommendations
SELECT DBMS_ADVISOR.GET_TASK_REPORT('sql_access_adv_task') FROM
    dual;
```

The output indicates changes that can lead to improvements in SQL statement performance.

Oracle Trace

Oracle Trace is a powerful tool for tracking and diagnosing performance at a granular level. It can capture detailed information about SQL statement execution, allowing a deep dive into performance-related events.

To enable Oracle Trace:

```
-- Set up Trace file directory and enable tracing
ALTER SESSION SET tracefile_identifier = 'my_trace';
ALTER SESSION SET events '10046 trace name context forever, level 12';

-- After performing the queries of interest, disable tracing
ALTER SESSION SET events '10046 trace name context off';
```

The generated trace file can be found in the user dump destination directory, and conventional tools such as TKPROF can interpret its content:

```
-- Execute TKPROF to interpret trace file
$ tkprof my_trace.trc my_trace.txt explain=<username>/<password>
```

The resulting output provides detailed information such as parsing, execution, and fetch statistics for SQL statements.

By leveraging these tools, database administrators can ensure that Oracle databases operate efficiently and robustly, capable of meeting performance demands and maintaining optimal levels of service. The suite of diagnostic and tuning tools included with Oracle Database provides comprehensive capabilities to address and resolve performance issues in a systematic fashion.

8.12 Best Practices for Database Optimization

To achieve optimal performance in Oracle Database, employing a combination of best practices is crucial. These best practices are derived from extensive experience and empirical research in database administration. This section outlines these practices in a systematic manner, ensuring that database administrators (DBAs) and developers can implement them effectively.

Regularly Monitor and Analyze Performance Metrics

Maintaining high database performance requires continuous monitoring and analysis of various performance metrics. Utilizing tools such as Automatic Workload Repository (AWR) and Active Session History (ASH) allows for the collection and analysis of crucial performance data. With these tools, DBAs can identify performance bottlenecks and address them proactively.

Optimize SQL Queries

Efficient SQL queries play a pivotal role in database performance. Ensuring that queries are optimized to minimize resource consumption is essential. Utilize the Oracle SQL Tuning Advisor to analyze high-load SQL statements and receive recommendations for performance improvements. Additionally, use the EXPLAIN PLAN statement to understand query execution plans and make necessary adjustments.

```
EXPLAIN PLAN FOR
SELECT employee_name
FROM employees
WHERE department_id = 10;
SELECT * FROM TABLE(DBMS_XPLAN.DISPLAY);
```

Effective Indexing

Indexes are vital for accelerating data retrieval. Implement indexing strategies that align with the actual usage patterns of the database. Avoid over-indexing, which can degrade performance during data modifications (INSERT, UPDATE, DELETE). Utilize the Oracle Index Advisor to identify indexing opportunities and periodically review and maintain indexes to ensure they are optimal.

```
CREATE INDEX emp_dept_idx ON employees(department_id);
```

Optimize Memory Allocation

Proper memory management is critical for the efficient execution of database operations. Configure the System Global Area (SGA) and Program Global Area (PGA) according to the workload. Utilize Automatic Memory Management (AMM) for dynamic adjustment of memory allocation. Regularly monitor memory usage and adjust parameters such as DB_CACHE_SIZE, SHARED_POOL_SIZE, and PGA_AGGREGATE_TARGET.

Efficient Disk I/O Management

Efficient disk I/O management involves optimizing the physical storage layout and employing appropriate storage technologies. Use Oracle Automatic Storage Management (ASM) to simplify storage management and improve performance. Periodically analyze I/O performance using tools like iostat and AWR reports, and distribute I/O load evenly across available disks to prevent bottlenecks.

Manage Sessions and Processes

Efficient management of database sessions and processes ensures that resources are not excessively consumed. Use Oracle Resource Manager to allocate CPU and I/O resources among sessions based on predefined policies. Monitor sessions to identify and terminate long-running or idle sessions that could impact performance.

```
ALTER SYSTEM KILL SESSION 'sid,serial#';
```

Utilize Partitioning

Partitioning large tables improves performance by reducing the amount of data scanned during query execution. Implement partitioning strategies based on the data access patterns. Common partitioning methods include range, list, and hash partitioning. Regularly evaluate and adjust partitions as data volume and access patterns evolve.

```
CREATE TABLE sales (
    sales_id NUMBER,
    sales_date DATE,
    amount NUMBER
)
PARTITION BY RANGE (sales_date) (
    PARTITION sales_q1 VALUES LESS THAN (TO_DATE('01-APR-2021','DD-
        MON-YYYY')),
    PARTITION sales_q2 VALUES LESS THAN (TO_DATE('01-JUL-2021','DD-MON
        -YYYY'))
);
```

Implement Wait Event Tuning

Identifying and addressing wait events can significantly enhance database performance. Use AWR and ASH reports to analyze wait events, and implement solutions to minimize the impact of these events. This may involve optimizing queries, configuring instance parameters, or tuning the underlying hardware.

Leverage Parallel Processing

Enable parallel processing for resource-intensive queries to improve performance. Configure parallel execution parameters such as parallel_max_servers and parallel_min_percent according to the system's capabilities. Monitor the performance impact and adjust settings as necessary.

```
ALTER SESSION ENABLE PARALLEL DML;
ALTER TABLE employees PARALLEL 4;
```

Maintain Database Statistics

Accurate statistics are vital for the Oracle optimizer to generate efficient execution plans. Use DBMS_STATS to gather statistics regularly and ensure they reflect the current state of the database. Schedule statistics collection during low-usage periods to minimize impact on performance.

```
EXEC DBMS_STATS.GATHER_TABLE_STATS('HR', 'EMPLOYEES');
```

Adopt a Proactive Maintenance Strategy

Implement a proactive maintenance strategy to address potential issues before they impact performance. This includes regular database backups, patching, and applying recommended updates. Additionally, conduct periodic performance audits to ensure adherence to best practices and identify areas for improvement.

By systematically applying these best practices, databases can achieve sustainable high performance, improve resource utilization, and ensure optimal user experiences.

Chapter 9

Security and User Management

This chapter covers the critical aspects of security and user management in Oracle Database. It includes managing user accounts, roles, privileges, and implementing authentication and authorization mechanisms. Topics also encompass data encryption, network security, user profiles, auditing, compliance, Virtual Private Database (VPD), and row-level security. The chapter provides essential strategies for ensuring database security and handling security incidents effectively.

9.1 Introduction to Database Security

Database security is a critical aspect of database management systems, particularly for systems such as Oracle Database, which are deployed in environments with sensitive and mission-critical data. Ensuring the security of an Oracle Database involves protecting the data from unauthorized access, ensuring data integrity, and maintaining data availability. This section explores the foundational concepts of database security, discusses the potential threats and vulnerabilities, and elucidates the fundamental measures that can be employed to secure an Oracle Database.

Data Confidentiality: Data confidentiality ensures that sensitive information is only accessible to authorized users. In Oracle Database, data confidentiality is achieved through a combination of authentication mechanisms, access controls, and data encryption techniques. Proper implementation of these mechanisms helps prevent unauthorized data access and protects against data breaches.

Data Integrity: Data integrity refers to the accuracy and consistency of data over its lifecycle. In Oracle Database, enforcing data integrity involves implementing constraints, triggers, and consistent transaction management practices. Any unauthorized modifications, whether intentional or accidental, can compromise data integrity, leading to incorrect or misleading information which can impact decision-making processes.

Data Availability: Data availability ensures that authorized users have continuous access to the database when needed. High availability is achieved through redundancy, backup and recovery strategies, and robust infrastructure design. Protecting the database from Denial of Service (DoS) attacks and other disruptions is crucial for maintaining data availability.

Threats and Vulnerabilities: Understanding the potential threats and vulnerabilities is the first step in fortifying an Oracle Database. Common threats include SQL injection, unpatched vulnerabilities, insider threats, and network-based attacks. SQL injection exploits vulnerabilities in application code to execute arbitrary SQL commands. Unpatched software can be exploited by attackers to gain unauthorized access. Insider threats stem from disgruntled or careless employees, while network-based attacks can intercept data in transit.

Authentication: Authentication verifies the identity of users before they can access the database. Oracle Database supports multiple authentication methods, including password authentication, Kerberos, and Lightweight Directory Access Protocol (LDAP). Strong password policies and multi-factor authentication enhance the security of the authentication process.

Authorization: Authorization controls what authenticated users can do within the database. It involves granting and revoking permissions based on roles and privileges. Oracle Database utilizes Role-Based Access Control (RBAC) to efficiently manage user permissions. Fine-grained access control can be enforced using Virtual Private Database (VPD) and row-level security policies.

Encryption: Data encryption protects sensitive data at rest and in transit. Oracle Database offers Transparent Data Encryption (TDE) for encrypting data stored in tablespaces and Oracle Advanced Security for encrypting data transmitted over the network. Proper encryption key management is vital to ensure data confidentiality and integrity.

Auditing: Auditing involves tracking and recording database activities to monitor access and changes to data. Oracle Database provides comprehensive auditing capabilities to log user activities, schema changes, and security-relevant events. Configuring and analyzing audit trails help detect suspicious activities and support compliance with regulatory requirements.

Compliance: Compliance with legal and regulatory requirements is essential for many organizations. Regulations such as the General Data Protection Regulation (GDPR) and the Health Insurance Portability and Accountability Act (HIPAA) impose strict requirements on data protection. Oracle Database offers features to facilitate compliance, including data masking, audit trails, and detailed logging.

Implementing Security Measures: Securing an Oracle Database is an ongoing process that involves a combination of technical control measures, user education, and proactive monitoring. It starts with the proper configuration of the database and the operating system on which it runs. Regularly applying patches and updates is essential to address known vulnerabilities. Implementing principle of least privilege ensures users have only the permissions necessary for their job functions. Continuous monitoring and periodic security assessments help identify and remediate potential security issues.

Database Security Best Practices: Adopting best practices is crucial for maintaining the security posture of Oracle Database. These practices include using strong passwords, enabling encryption, regularly auditing database activities, and ensuring secure configurations. Establishing incident response procedures is vital for promptly addressing security breaches and minimizing their impact.

Examining Oracle Database security is essential for safeguarding sensitive information and maintaining the trust of stakeholders. By understanding the core principles, recognizing potential threats, and implementing robust security measures, database administrators can significantly enhance the security of their Oracle Database environments.

9.2 User Accounts and Privileges

Effective management of user accounts and privileges is essential for maintaining the security and integrity of an Oracle Database. This section delves into the creation, management, and enforcement of user accounts, as well as the assignment of privileges, which dictate what actions users can perform within the database.

User accounts provide each user with a distinct identity within the Oracle Database, facilitating access control, auditing, and security. Each user is associated with a schema, which is a collection of database objects such as tables, views, and procedures that the user owns.

The creation of a user account in Oracle Database is accomplished with the CREATE USER statement. Below is the basic syntax for creating a user:

```
CREATE USER username
IDENTIFIED BY password
DEFAULT TABLESPACE tablespace
TEMPORARY TABLESPACE temp_tablespace;
```

Example:

```
CREATE USER johndoe
IDENTIFIED BY securePassword123
DEFAULT TABLESPACE users
TEMPORARY TABLESPACE temp;
```

This statement creates a user account named johndoe with a specified password. The default tablespace is set to users, and the temporary tablespace is set to temp.

After creating user accounts, it is crucial to assign the appropriate privileges to allow users to perform necessary operations while restricting unauthorized actions. Privileges in Oracle Database are categorized into system privileges and object privileges.

System privileges authorize users to perform specific administrative tasks at the database level. Examples include the ability to create tables, create users, or execute system-wide operations. System privileges are granted using the GRANT statement. For instance:

```
GRANT CREATE SESSION TO johndoe;
GRANT CREATE TABLE TO johndoe;
```

The above statements grant johndoe the ability to create a session (log into the database) and create tables.

Object privileges allow users to perform actions on specific database objects, such as tables, views, sequences, and procedures. These privileges include actions like SELECT, INSERT, UPDATE, DELETE, and EXECUTE. The syntax for granting object privileges is also based on the GRANT statement. For example:

```
GRANT SELECT, INSERT ON employees TO johndoe;
```

In this example, johndoe is granted the ability to perform SELECT and INSERT operations on the employees table.

Revoking privileges from a user is equally important for maintaining security, especially when a user's role in the organization changes. The REVOKE statement is used to remove privileges:

```
REVOKE CREATE TABLE FROM johndoe;
REVOKE SELECT ON employees FROM johndoe;
```

In addition to granting and revoking individual privileges, roles can be used to simplify privilege management. Roles are named groups of privileges that can be granted to users. This abstraction layer allows for more efficient and hierarchical management of privileges. Creating a role and granting it to a user is illustrated below:

```
CREATE ROLE app_developer;
GRANT CREATE SESSION, CREATE TABLE, CREATE VIEW TO app_developer;
GRANT app_developer TO johndoe;
```

In this scenario, the role app_developer is first created and assigned several system privileges. This role is subsequently granted to johndoe, effectively bestowing all the associated privileges to that user.

Another critical element in user account management is account locking and expiration policies, which safeguard against unauthorized access. Accounts can be locked manually using the ALTER USER statement:

```
ALTER USER johndoe ACCOUNT LOCK;
```

To unlock an account, the following statement is used:

```
ALTER USER johndoe ACCOUNT UNLOCK;
```

Password expiration policies can be enforced by defining user profiles. A profile is a named set of resource limits and password parameters that can be assigned to a user as follows:

```
CREATE PROFILE default_profile LIMIT
PASSWORD_LIFE_TIME 90
```

```
PASSWORD_GRACE_TIME 7
FAILED_LOGIN_ATTEMPTS 5;
ALTER USER johndoe PROFILE default_profile;
```

In this example, the profile default_profile is created with specific password management parameters. The profile enforces a password lifetime of 90 days, a grace period of 7 days for password changes, and locks the account after 5 failed login attempts. The profile is then assigned to johndoe.

Effectively managing user accounts and privileges is essential for maintaining security, controlling access, and ensuring compliance within the Oracle Database. Robust policies and practices must be established to monitor and adjust these elements regularly.

9.3 Authentication and Authorization

Authentication and authorization are cornerstone concepts in database security, ensuring that only legitimate users gain access to the database and its resources. Authentication verifies the identity of a user, while authorization determines what established users are allowed to do within the database. This section elaborates on the methods of authentication and details the various facets of authorization within Oracle Database.

Authentication is the process of confirming that a user's claim to a certain identity is valid. Oracle Database supports multiple authentication methods:

- **Password-Based Authentication:** Users must provide a valid combination of username and password. This is managed internally by Oracle Database.
- **Kerberos Authentication:** A network authentication protocol designed to provide strong authentication for client/server applications by using secret-key cryptography. Oracle Database can be configured to use Kerberos for user authentication.
- **RADIUS Authentication:** Remote Authentication Dial-In User Service (RADIUS) is a protocol for providing centralized authentication, authorization, and accounting management. Database clients can connect using RADIUS.

- **Certificate Authentication:** Secure Sockets Layer (SSL) with X.509 certificates can be used to authenticate users or applications connecting to the Oracle Database.
- **Operating System Authentication:** Users can be authenticated by the operating system. In this method, the operating system's user accounts are mapped to the Oracle user accounts.

Oracle Database's password-based authentication remains the most commonly implemented method due to its simplicity and straightforward management. Password policies can be enforced to enhance security by defining password complexity, expiration, and lockout rules.

Authorization in Oracle Database is managed primarily through privileges and roles. A privilege allows a user to perform a specific action or to access certain data. There are two types of privileges in Oracle Database:

- **System Privileges:** These are administrative privileges that allow users to perform particular operations database-wide. Examples include CREATE TABLE, ALTER USER, and DROP DATABASE.
- **Object Privileges:** These apply to specific database objects such as tables, views, sequences, procedures, and more. Examples include SELECT, INSERT, UPDATE, and EXECUTE.

Roles are named groups of privileges that can be assigned to users or to other roles, simplifying the process of privilege management. Rather than assigning multiple specific privileges to users, a role can be created with the required privileges and then granted to users. This approach enhances maintainability and security by allowing administration at the role level.

To illustrate, consider the following example of creating a role and granting it to a user:

```
CREATE ROLE data_analyst;

GRANT SELECT, INSERT, UPDATE ON sales_data TO data_analyst;

GRANT data_analyst TO john_doe;
```

In this example, the role data_analyst is created with SELECT, INSERT, and UPDATE privileges on the sales_data table. This role is then granted to the user john_doe, allowing him to perform the specified actions on the sales_data table.

Oracle Database also supports Fine-Grained Access Control (FGAC) to implement row-level security. FGAC allows the creation of security policies that control database access at the row level based on user-specific criteria. These policies are enforced at runtime, ensuring security constraints are always adhered to.

An example of creating a FGAC policy can be demonstrated using the DBMS_RLS package:

```
BEGIN
  DBMS_RLS.ADD_POLICY(
    object_schema => 'hr',
    object_name => 'employees',
    policy_name => 'emp_policy',
    function_schema => 'hr',
    policy_function => 'emp_security_check',
    statement_types => 'SELECT, INSERT, UPDATE');
END;
/
```

In this example, a policy named emp_policy is applied to the employees table within the hr schema. The policy function emp_security_check defines the logic for access control and will be evaluated for the specified SQL statement types (SELECT, INSERT, and UPDATE), ensuring that only rows meeting the criteria specified in emp_security_check are accessible to users.

Finally, it is crucial to emphasize regular audits and reviews of the assigned privileges and roles to ensure that they align with the principle of least privilege (PoLP). Regularly performing such audits mitigates risks associated with overly broad permissions and helps in maintaining a robust security posture.

By meticulously implementing authentication and authorization measures, Oracle Database administrators can significantly enhance the security of their database environments, ensuring that only authenticated users can access data, and only authorized users can perform specific operations.

9.4 Role-Based Access Control

Role-Based Access Control (RBAC) is a critical feature in Oracle Database that facilitates the management of user permissions by associating them with roles rather than directly assigning them to individual users. This methodology simplifies the administrative overhead associated with managing a large number of users and permissions. In this section, we will explore the concepts, creation, and management of roles, as well as the assignment of privileges and roles to users.

Concepts and Principles

RBAC operates on the principle of grouping related privileges into roles. Roles act as intermediaries between users and the actual privileges required to perform database tasks. By assigning a role to a user, the user automatically acquires all the privileges associated with that role.

- **Privileges:** Privileges are specific rights to execute certain SQL statements or access certain objects. They are categorized into system privileges and object privileges.
- **Roles:** Roles are collections of privileges that can be granted to users or other roles.
- **User:** A user is any entity that can be authenticated by the Oracle database.

Benefits of Using Roles

The use of roles in Oracle Database offers several benefits:

- **Simplicity:** Roles simplify user management by allowing DBAs to grant and revoke privileges in bulk.
- **Security:** By grouping privileges into roles, the attack surface is minimized. Roles can be enabled or disabled as needed.
- **Scalability:** Roles facilitate the scaling of security policies as more users are added to the database.

Creating Roles

Roles can be created using the CREATE ROLE statement. The following example demonstrates how to create a role:

```
CREATE ROLE finance_manager;
```

Assigning Privileges to Roles

Once a role is created, system and object privileges can be assigned to it. The GRANT statement is used to assign these privileges. For example, to grant system privileges to the finance_manager role:

```
GRANT CREATE SESSION, CREATE TABLE TO finance_manager;
```

And to grant object privileges, such as the ability to select from a specific table:

```
GRANT SELECT ON hr.employees TO finance_manager;
```

Granting Roles to Users

After defining a role and assigning the necessary privileges, the role can be granted to users. The following SQL statement demonstrates how to grant the finance_manager role to a user:

```
GRANT finance_manager TO john_doe;
```

Enabling and Disabling Roles

Users can have multiple roles, and not all roles assigned to a user need to be enabled simultaneously. The SET ROLE statement enables specific roles for the user session. For example:

```
SET ROLE finance_manager;
```

To disable all roles except the specified one:

```
SET ROLE finance_manager IDENTIFIED BY <role_password>;
```

Revoking Roles and Privileges

Roles and privileges can be revoked using the REVOKE statement. To revoke a role from a user:

```
REVOKE finance_manager FROM john_doe;
```

To revoke a specific privilege from a role:

```
REVOKE CREATE TABLE FROM finance_manager;
```

Common Role Usage Scenarios

Roles in Oracle Database can be categorized based on their typical usage:

- **Application Roles:** These are roles created to serve specific application-related tasks and are usually tightly coupled with business logic.
- **Administrative Roles:** Roles such as DBA, which include a wide range of system privileges necessary for database maintenance

and operation.

- **Custom Roles:** These roles are tailor-made to fit specific organizational policies or requirements.

Security Considerations

When using roles, it is essential to ensure that:

- Roles are granted according to the principle of least privilege.
- Regular audits are conducted to review the assigned roles and privileges.
- Roles with high privileges are protected with passwords.

Example Scenario

Consider a scenario where a company has multiple departments, each needing specific database access. By creating roles tailored to each department's needs, database administrators can efficiently manage permissions. For example, we could have roles like sales_manager, hr_manager , and it_support, each with distinct privileges suited to the functions of their respective departments.

By implementing RBAC, the company ensures consistent and secure access control, simplifying routine management tasks and enhancing overall security.

```
> GRANT finance_manager TO department_head;
> GRANT hr_manager TO hr_lead;
> GRANT it_support TO tech_staff;
```

This structured approach to managing user access not only ensures that users have the appropriate level of access but also that the system remains secure and manageable as the organization grows.

9.5 Data Encryption

Data encryption is a fundamental aspect of database security, ensuring that sensitive information is protected from unauthorized access. Oracle Database provides robust encryption mechanisms to secure data both at rest and in transit. This section delves into several key encryption features and techniques provided by Oracle, including Transparent Data Encryption (TDE), column-level encryption, and tablespace encryption.

Transparent Data Encryption (TDE) is a widely used Oracle feature that encrypts data at the storage level. It protects data stored in data files to prevent unauthorized access to the data on the media at the operating system level.

To configure TDE, follow these steps:

1. Set up an Oracle Wallet, which securely stores the master encryption key:

```
-- Set up the location for the Oracle Wallet
ALTER SYSTEM SET ENCRYPTION KEY IDENTIFIED BY 'password';
```

2. Create the Wallet:

```
-- Create the Wallet
ADMINISTER KEY MANAGEMENT CREATE KEYSTORE '$ORACLE_BASE/
    admin/$ORACLE_SID/wallet' IDENTIFIED BY 'password';
```

3. Open the Wallet:

```
-- Open the Wallet
ADMINISTER KEY MANAGEMENT SET KEYSTORE OPEN IDENTIFIED BY '
    password';
```

4. Set the TDE master encryption key:

```
-- Set the TDE master encryption key
ADMINISTER KEY MANAGEMENT SET KEY IDENTIFIED BY 'password' WITH
    BACKUP USING 'backup_identifier';
```

5. Encrypt a tablespace:

```
-- Encrypt the tablespace
ALTER TABLESPACE example_tablespace ENCRYPTION ONLINE USING 'AES256'
    ENCRYPT;
```

Column-level encryption provides a more granular approach to encryption, allowing specific columns of a table to be encrypted:

```
-- Create a table with an encrypted column
CREATE TABLE sensitive_data (
  id NUMBER,
  sensitive_info VARCHAR2(100) ENCRYPT USING 'AES256'
);
```

Tablespace encryption is another powerful feature that allows entire tablespaces to be encrypted without requiring changes to the applications accessing the database. It is particularly useful for encrypting large amounts of data efficiently.

To encrypt a new tablespace:

```
-- Create and encrypt a new tablespace
CREATE TABLESPACE encrypted_ts DATAFILE 'encrypted_ts01.dbf' SIZE 100M
ENCRYPTION USING 'AES256' DEFAULT STORAGE(ENCRYPT);
```

To encrypt an existing tablespace:

```
-- Encrypt an existing tablespace
ALTER TABLESPACE existing_ts ENCRYPTION ONLINE USING 'AES256'
    ENCRYPT;
```

Oracle also supports **Data Redaction** as a means to mask sensitive data at runtime in query results. This feature can be configured to redact data selectively, based on user roles and policies.

For example, to redact a column except for the last four digits:

```
-- Configure data redaction on a column
BEGIN
  DBMS_REDACT.ADD_POLICY(
    object_schema => 'HR',
    object_name => 'EMPLOYEES',
    policy_name => 'EMPSSN_REDACT',
    column_name => 'SSN',
    expression => '1=1', -- Always redact this column
    action => DBMS_REDACT.PARTIAL,
    function_type => DBMS_REDACT.FULL,
    function_parameters => 'LAST_4_DIGITS', -- Only show last 4 digits
    policy_description => 'Redact SSNs except last 4 digits'
  );
END;
/
```

Network encryption protects data in transit between the client and the server. This ensures that data cannot be intercepted and read by unauthorized parties during transmission.

To configure Oracle Native Network Encryption:

```
-- Configure encryption on the server side
ALTER SYSTEM SET SQLNET.ENCRYPTION_SERVER='REQUIRED' SCOPE=
    BOTH;
ALTER SYSTEM SET SQLNET.ENCRYPTION_TYPES_SERVER='(AES256)'
    SCOPE=BOTH;
```

To configure encryption on the client side:

```
-- Configure encryption on the client side
ALTER SYSTEM SET SQLNET.ENCRYPTION_CLIENT='REQUIRED' SCOPE=
    BOTH;
ALTER SYSTEM SET SQLNET.ENCRYPTION_TYPES_CLIENT='(AES256)'
    SCOPE=BOTH;
```

When encryption techniques are correctly configured, the output observed in the log files will verify successful encryption:

```
SQL> ALTER SYSTEM SET SQLNET.ENCRYPTION_SERVER='REQUIRED' SCOPE=BOTH;
System altered.

SQL> ALTER SYSTEM SET SQLNET.ENCRYPTION_TYPES_SERVER='(AES256)' SCOPE=BOTH;
System altered.
```

Effective data encryption strategies help mitigate risks of data breaches and ensure compliance with various regulatory requirements. Understanding and implementing these features in Oracle Database will significantly enhance the security posture of your database environment.

9.6 Network Security

Network security within Oracle Database is an essential component for protecting sensitive data as it travels between clients and servers over potentially vulnerable networks. Adequately securing the network ensures that data remains confidential, untampered, and accessible only to authorized parties.

Securing Connections with Oracle Net

Oracle Net, the network layer in Oracle Database, provides the connectivity services between a client application and an Oracle Database. Securing Oracle Net involves multiple configurations, including encrypting data and ensuring the integrity of communications. The Oracle Net layer can use either Secure Sockets Layer (SSL) or Transport Layer Security (TLS) for these purposes.

```
# Example of SQLNET.ORA configuration for SSL

WALLET_LOCATION =
  (SOURCE =
    (METHOD = FILE)
    (METHOD_DATA =
      (DIRECTORY = /etc/oracle/ssl_wallet)
    )
  )

SSL_VERSION = 1.0
SSL_CIPHER_SUITES = (SSL_RSA_WITH_AES_256_CBC_SHA)
```

This configuration specifies the location of the SSL wallet and the desired SSL/TLS version and cipher suites. The SSL_WALLET needs to be appropriately configured with the correct certificates.

Configuring Firewalls and Network Segmentation

Firewalls are fundamental to managing and restricting network traffic between the database and external networks. Network segmentation involves dividing a network into multiple segments or subnets, each act-ing as a barrier to limit traffic between them, thereby isolating security incidents.

Implementing proper firewall rules ensures only necessary traffic reaches the database servers. Below is a high-level example of firewall rules:

```
# Example Firewall Rules for Oracle Database

# Allow inbound traffic on SQL*Net port
-A INPUT -p tcp --dport 1521 -j ACCEPT

# Allow Oracle Enterprise Manager traffic
-A INPUT -p tcp --dport 1158 -j ACCEPT

# Deny all other inbound traffic by default
-A INPUT -j DROP
```

These rules permit only necessary traffic specific to Oracle operations and drop all other inbound traffic, enhancing security.

Network Encryption and Integrity

Network encryption protects data during transmission, while network integrity checks ensure the data has not been tampered with. Oracle Advanced Security provides Transparent Data Encryption (TDE) and Data Integrity through checksums. TDE encrypts data before it is written to storage and decrypts it when read from storage, ensuring that data-at-rest, as well as in transit, is secure.

To enable network encryption and integrity, modify the sqlnet.ora configuration file as follows:

```
# Encryption parameters for client and server

SQLNET.ENCRYPTION_CLIENT = REQUIRED
SQLNET.ENCRYPTION_TYPES_CLIENT = (AES256)

SQLNET.ENCRYPTION_SERVER = REQUIRED
SQLNET.ENCRYPTION_TYPES_SERVER = (AES256)

# Integrity parameter settings

SQLNET.CRYPTO_CHECKSUM_CLIENT = REQUIRED
SQLNET.CRYPTO_CHECKSUM_TYPES_CLIENT = (SHA256)

SQLNET.CRYPTO_CHECKSUM_SERVER = REQUIRED
SQLNET.CRYPTO_CHECKSUM_TYPES_SERVER = (SHA256)
```

These configurations enforce encryption and integrity checks using AES256 for encryption and SHA256 for integrity.

VPN and Dedicated Network Links

Utilizing Virtual Private Networks (VPN) and dedicated network links provide an additional layer of security by creating secure tunnels through which data can travel. VPNs encrypt all data transmitted over the public internet, ensuring that even if data packets are intercepted, they remain unreadable. In contrast, dedicated network links physically separate the network infrastructure used by the Oracle Database from the public internet, thereby reducing exposure to potential threats.

Configuring and maintaining a VPN or setting up dedicated network links involve coordination with network and security teams, ensuring alignment with organizational policies and compliance requirements.

Securing Oracle Data Guard Networks

Oracle Data Guard ensures high availability by creating standby databases that can take over in case of primary database failures. Securing the communication between the primary and standby databases is crucial, as these links carry sensitive and sometimes entire database backups.

To configure security for Data Guard, ensure that tnsnames.ora and related configurations are encrypted:

```
# TNSNAMES.ORA configuration for Data Guard with secure transport

Primary_DB =
  (DESCRIPTION =
    (ADDRESS =
      (PROTOCOL = TCP)(HOST = primary_host.com)(PORT = 1521)
    )
    (CONNECT_DATA =
      (SERVICE_NAME = primary_service)
    )
  )

Standby_DB =
  (DESCRIPTION =
    (ADDRESS =
      (PROTOCOL = TCP)(HOST = standby_host.com)(PORT = 1521)
    )
    (CONNECT_DATA =
      (SERVICE_NAME = standby_service)
    )
    (SECURITY =
      (SSL_SERVER_CERT_DN = "CN=StandbyHost, OU=Database, O=
          MyCompany, L=Location, ST=State, C=Country")
    )
  )
```

The SECURITY parameter ensures that the standby database only accepts communications from a host presenting a valid SSL certificate, enhancing the security of the replication.

Intrusion Detection and Prevention Systems (IDPS)

Deploying IDPS helps to monitor and analyze network traffic for malicious activities and policy violations. These systems can detect potential threats in real-time and block or alarm administrators of suspicious activities. An effective IDPS setup involves regular updating and tuning of its detection rules to reflect the latest threat patterns.

Capturing logs of network activity and analyzing these logs periodically gives insight into potential security incidents. Integration with Oracle's Audit Vault and Database Firewall can provide comprehensive coverage by monitoring SQL traffic and issuing real-time alerts.

By implementing these strategies, Oracle Database administrators can ensure robust network security, thereby safeguarding the database from unauthorized access and potential threats. Each aspect involves precise configurations and collaborative efforts with network administrators, aligning with the broader organizational security policies.

9.7 Managing User Profiles and Password Policies

User profiles in Oracle Database serve as a mechanism for enforcing a variety of user-specific limitations and attributes, impacting elements such as resource consumption and password management. This functionality is instrumental in maintaining database security and ensuring compliance with organizational policies.

A user profile can include restrictions on session durations, limits on CPU usage, constraints on logical reads, and rules for password management. Profiles are assigned to users at the time of user creation or subsequently, modifying the user's behavior according to the profile parameters.

Creating User Profiles

Begin by creating a profile with the desired attributes. Here is the syntax to create a profile:

```
CREATE PROFILE profile_name
LIMIT
   SESSIONS_PER_USER integer,
   CPU_PER_SESSION integer,
   CPU_PER_CALL integer,
   CONNECT_TIME integer,
   IDLE_TIME integer,
   LOGICAL_READS_PER_SESSION integer,
   LOGICAL_READS_PER_CALL integer,
   COMPOSITE_LIMIT integer,
```

```
PRIVATE_SGA integer,
FAILED_LOGIN_ATTEMPTS integer,
PASSWORD_LIFE_TIME integer,
PASSWORD_REUSE_TIME integer,
PASSWORD_REUSE_MAX integer,
PASSWORD_VERIFY_FUNCTION function_name,
PASSWORD_LOCK_TIME integer,
PASSWORD_GRACE_TIME integer;
```

Each parameter in the profile creates specific limitations:

- SESSIONS_PER_USER: Limits the number of concurrent sessions for a user.
- CPU_PER_SESSION and CPU_PER_CALL: Restrict CPU usage per session or per call.
- CONNECT_TIME: Sets the maximum time a user session can remain connected.
- IDLE_TIME: Specifies the maximum idle time allowed for a user session.
- LOGICAL_READS_PER_SESSION and LOGICAL_READS_PER_CALL: Set limits on logical I/O operations for a session or call.
- COMPOSITE_LIMIT: Imposes an overall resource consumption limit.
- PRIVATE_SGA: Determines the amount of private space a session can allocate in the shared global area.
- FAILED_LOGIN_ATTEMPTS: Specifies the number of allowed failed login attempts before the account is locked.
- PASSWORD_LIFE_TIME: Sets the lifespan of a password before a change is mandated.
- PASSWORD_REUSE_TIME and PASSWORD_REUSE_MAX: Governs the reuse policy of old passwords.
- PASSWORD_VERIFY_FUNCTION: Calls a PL/SQL function that contains logic to enforce password complexity rules.
- PASSWORD_LOCK_TIME: Defines the duration for which an account remains locked after reaching the maximum allowed failed login attempts.

- PASSWORD_GRACE_TIME: Provides a grace period during which users receive warnings about password expiration but can still log in.

Assigning Profiles to Users

To associate a profile with a user, the ALTER USER command is used:

```
ALTER USER username PROFILE profile_name;
```

This command modifies the specified user's profile to the designated one, thereby enforcing the relevant restrictions immediately.

Modifying Profiles

Alterations to existing profiles are made using the ALTER PROFILE command. For example, to modify the idle time constraint:

```
ALTER PROFILE profile_name LIMIT IDLE_TIME new_value;
```

Dropping Profiles

If a profile is no longer required, it can be dropped. Note that dropping a profile impacts users assigned to it, reassigning the default profile:

```
DROP PROFILE profile_name CASCADE;
```

The CASCADE option ensures the profile is dropped even if it is assigned to users, reassigning them to the default profile.

Managing Password Policies

Strong password policies are essential for protecting user accounts from unauthorized access. Oracle Database allows setting password policies within profiles, using parameters such as FAILED_LOGIN_ATTEMPTS, PASSWORD_LIFE_TIME, PASSWORD_REUSE_TIME, PASSWORD_REUSE_MAX, and custom password verify functions.

The function VERIFY_FUNCTION enables specifying custom rules. Here is an example of such a function:

```
CREATE OR REPLACE FUNCTION custom_verify_function (
  username VARCHAR2,
  password VARCHAR2,
  old_password VARCHAR2
) RETURN BOOLEAN IS
BEGIN
  IF LENGTH(password) < 8 THEN
    raise_application_error(-20001, 'Password length must be at least 8 characters.');
  END IF;
```

```
  IF password NOT LIKE '%[A-Z]%' THEN
    raise_application_error(-20002, 'Password must include at least one uppercase
        letter.');
  END IF;

  IF password NOT LIKE '%[0-9]%' THEN
    raise_application_error(-20003, 'Password must include at least one number.');
  END IF;

  RETURN TRUE;
END;
```

Assign the custom_verify_function within a profile to enforce these rules:

```
CREATE PROFILE secure_profile
LIMIT
    FAILED_LOGIN_ATTEMPTS 5
    PASSWORD_LIFE_TIME 30
    PASSWORD_REUSE_TIME 365
    PASSWORD_REUSE_MAX 10
    PASSWORD_VERIFY_FUNCTION custom_verify_function
    PASSWORD_LOCK_TIME 1
    PASSWORD_GRACE_TIME 10;
```

Password policies in Oracle databases, when configured correctly, enhance security by deterring unauthorized access through robust authentication measures.

Ensuring that profiles and password policies are consistently reviewed and updated according to evolving security standards and organizational requirements is crucial to maintaining a secure database environment, serving as the linchpin in the overarching strategy of Oracle Database security management.

9.8 Auditing and Compliance

Auditing in Oracle Database is a critical aspect that ensures all database activities are tracked and recorded. This section delves into the mechanisms, features, and strategies for implementing robust auditing practices within Oracle Database to maintain compliance with various regulations and organizational policies.

Oracle Database provides various auditing capabilities that enable tracking access and changes to data, configurations, and overall database activity. These capabilities include traditional auditing, unified auditing, and fine-grained auditing (FGA). Each approach serves different needs depending on the level of detail required and the specific compliance requirements.

Traditional Auditing

Traditional auditing is the legacy method in Oracle Database for tracking user activities. It encompasses statement, privilege, object, and network auditing. Configuring traditional auditing involves using the AUDIT SQL command along with parameters that specify what needs to be audited.

Configuration example:

```
AUDIT SELECT ON employees BY SESSION;
AUDIT INSERT, UPDATE, DELETE ON sensitive_table BY ACCESS;
```

The above commands configure auditing for SELECT operations on the employees table by session and auditing for INSERT, UPDATE, and DELETE operations on sensitive_table by access. Audit records are stored in SYS.AUD$ table, or if the AUDIT_TRAIL initialization parameter is set to DB, EXTENDED, XML, or XML,EXTENDED, they can be written to database tables, operating system files, or XML files.

Unified Auditing

Unified Auditing, introduced in Oracle Database 12c, consolidates all auditing activities into a single repository. It simplifies the management and increases the performance of database auditing. Unified Auditing can be enabled either in the Standard Audit Trail or the Unified Audit Trail mode.

Unified Auditing is instantiated using audit policies, which can be tailored to specific needs:

Creating a unified audit policy:

```
CREATE AUDIT POLICY admin_policy
  ACTIONS ALL ON sensitive_table;
```

Enabling the policy:

```
AUDIT POLICY admin_policy;
```

The audit records are stored in the UNIFIED_AUDIT_TRAIL view, providing a comprehensive dataset for compliance monitoring.

Fine-Grained Auditing (FGA)

Fine-Grained Auditing (FGA) offers more granularity by allowing auditing based on conditions defined by SQL predicates. FGA is highly suited for environments requiring detailed tracking based on data content or context.

Configuring FGA:

```
BEGIN
  DBMS_FGA.add_policy(
    object_schema => 'hr',
    object_name => 'employees',
    policy_name => 'fga_policy',
    audit_condition => 'salary > 10000',
    audit_column => 'salary'
  );
END;
/
```

In this example, the policy fga_policy is configured to audit access to the salary column of the employees table where the salary is greater than 10,000. The audit trail for FGA policies is located in the DBA_-AUDIT_POLICIES and DBA_AUDIT_TRAIL views.

Configuring Audit Trails and Policies

Audit trails need to be carefully managed to ensure the integrity, security, and performance of the Oracle Database. Administrative tasks include regularly monitoring the audit trail, purging old records, and securing audit data from unauthorized access.

Purging example:

```
BEGIN
  DBMS_AUDIT_MGMT.clean_audit_trail(
    audit_trail_type => DBMS_AUDIT_MGMT.AUDIT_TRAIL_AUD_STD,
    use_last_arch_timestamp => TRUE
  );
END;
/
```

The DBMS_AUDIT_MGMT package assists in purging audit data to maintain database performance and ensure compliance with data retention policies.

Securing audit data involves limiting access to audit trails by using secure roles and privileges. Typically, only DBA or security administrators have the requisite access to manage routine audit operations.

Automating Audit Administration

Automation of audit-related activities through job scheduling can ease management tasks and provide uninterrupted compliance. Scheduling jobs can be achieved using Oracle Scheduler.

Example of scheduling a weekly audit cleanup:

```
BEGIN
```

```
  DBMS_SCHEDULER.create_job (
    job_name => 'weekly_audit_cleanup',
    job_type => 'PLSQL_BLOCK',
    job_action => 'BEGIN DBMS_AUDIT_MGMT.clean_audit_trail(
          audit_trail_type => DBMS_AUDIT_MGMT.AUDIT_TRAIL_UNIFIED,
          use_last_arch_timestamp => TRUE); END;',
    start_date => SYSTIMESTAMP,
    repeat_interval => 'FREQ=WEEKLY; BYDAY=SAT; BYHOUR=2; BYMINUTE
          =0; BYSECOND=0',
    enabled => TRUE
  );
END;
/
```

This job ensures the cleanup of audit trails every Saturday at 2:00 AM, helping in maintaining database performance.

Compliance Considerations

Organizations must adhere to regulatory requirements such as GDPR, HIPAA, SOX, and others. These regulations mandate specific auditing and logging practices to protect sensitive data and provide accountability. Ensuring compliance involves:

- Defining audit policies that meet regulatory requirements.
- Implementing regular reviews of audit logs.
- Establishing and verifying the integrity of audit trails.
- Utilizing encryption for audit trail protection.

Auditing and compliance in Oracle Database are indispensable for secure, accountable, and regulatory-compliant database operations. Implementing various types of audits and effectively managing audit trails ensures comprehensive monitoring and security of database activities.

9.9 Virtual Private Database (VPD)

The Virtual Private Database (VPD) feature in Oracle Database is an advanced security mechanism that enables the definition of security policies to control the visibility and accessibility of data at a granular level. This is achieved through creating dynamic security predicates, which are appended to SQL statements, thereby restricting data access based on specific conditions such as the user's identity or execution context.

The VPD allows for the implementation of row-level security, ensuring that users can only access data that they are explicitly authorized to view or manipulate. This is instrumental in scenarios where different users need to interact with the same set of data but with varying levels of access permissions.

VPD leverages fine-grained access controls by attaching security policies directly to database objects such as tables, views, or synonyms. These policies invoke functions that generate dynamic predicates, appended to SQL queries, filtering data automatically based on the security context of the operation.

To illustrate the implementation of VPD, consider the following steps:

- Define a policy function that returns a predicate condition.
- Associate this policy function with a database object using the DBMS_RLS package.
- Apply the policy to control access according to specific requirements.

Step 1: Defining a Policy Function

A policy function is a PL/SQL function that constructs and returns a predicate used to filter rows. The function can incorporate logic to check various factors, such as the current user's identity, session variables, or other contextual information.

Consider the following example function:

```
CREATE OR REPLACE FUNCTION hr.emp_policy (schema_name IN VARCHAR2,
    table_name IN VARCHAR2)
RETURN VARCHAR2 AS
BEGIN
  RETURN 'department_id = SYS_CONTEXT("USERENV", "SESSION_USER")'
      ;
END;
/
```

This function returns a predicate that filters rows based on the current user's department_id. The SYS_CONTEXT function retrieves the current session user, ensuring that users can only see records corresponding to their department.

Step 2: Creating the Security Policy

The DBMS_RLS package is employed to create and manage the VPD policies. The DBMS_RLS.ADD_POLICY procedure is used to attach the policy function to a table.

```
BEGIN
  DBMS_RLS.ADD_POLICY(
    object_schema => 'HR',
    object_name => 'EMPLOYEES',
    policy_name => 'EMP_POLICY',
    function_schema => 'HR',
    policy_function => 'emp_policy',
    statement_types => 'SELECT, INSERT, UPDATE, DELETE'
  );
END;
/
```

In this configuration, the emp_policy function is applied to the EMPLOYEES table for all SQL statement types (SELECT, INSERT, UPDATE, DELETE).

Step 3: Accessing Data with VPD Applied

With the policy in place, any query or data manipulation operation performed on the EMPLOYEES table will automatically include the predicate from the emp_policy function.

For example, when a user queries the EMPLOYEES table:

```
SELECT * FROM employees;
```

The database will transparently modify the query to:

```
SELECT * FROM employees WHERE department_id = SYS_CONTEXT('USERENV
', 'SESSION_USER');
```

This ensures that the retrieved rows are filtered according to the specified policy, providing row-level security.

Additional Considerations

Several key aspects require attention when implementing VPD:

- **Performance:** VPD introduces additional processing overhead due to the evaluation of policy functions and dynamic predicates. It is crucial to optimize policy functions to minimize performance impact.
- **Policy Types:** VPD supports three types of policies: static, dynamic, and shared contexts. Selection of policy type depends on the data access patterns and security requirements.
- **Auditing:** Policies can be audited to track and log policy evaluations and predicate applications, aiding in compliance and forensic investigations.

- **Error Handling:** Proper error handling within policy functions should be implemented to ensure data access issues do not disrupt application functionality.

The intricate nature of VPD demands a thorough understanding of the organization's security requirements and a meticulous implementation strategy to enforce robust data security efficiently.

9.10 Row-Level Security

Row-Level Security (RLS) in Oracle Database is a sophisticated feature that provides fine-grained access control at the level of individual rows in a table. This is achieved through the creation and management of policies that determine which rows a user can access, modify, or delete based on predefined criteria. RLS is particularly useful in multi-tenant applications where different users or groups need access to different subsets of data within the same table.

The primary mechanism for implementing row-level security in Oracle Database is the Virtual Private Database (VPD) feature. VPD uses policy functions to dynamically add predicates to SQL statements, thereby restricting the rows returned or affected by the query based on the user's context.

Steps to Implement Row-Level Security

- **Create Policy Function**: The policy function generates a dynamic predicate, which is a WHERE clause condition appended to SQL statements. This function is invoked whenever a query on the table is executed.

```
CREATE OR REPLACE FUNCTION secure_dept (
    schema_name IN VARCHAR2,
    table_name IN VARCHAR2
) RETURN VARCHAR2 AS
BEGIN
    -- Example predicate condition based on the department column
    RETURN 'department_id = USERENV(''SESSION_USER'')';
END secure_dept;
/
```

- **Apply Security Policy**: The DBMS_RLS.ADD_POLICY procedure is used to attach the policy to the table. This procedure specifies the table, the policy function, and the types of statements

(SELECT, INSERT, UPDATE, DELETE) the policy should apply to.

```
BEGIN
    DBMS_RLS.ADD_POLICY(
        object_schema => 'HR',
        object_name => 'EMPLOYEES',
        policy_name => 'emp_dept_policy',
        function_schema => 'HR',
        policy_function => 'secure_dept',
        statement_types => 'SELECT, INSERT, UPDATE, DELETE',
        update_check => TRUE
    );
END;
/
```

By adding this policy, any SQL operation on the EMPLOYEES table will automatically include the predicate defined in the secure_dept function.

Policy Enforcement and Predicates

Oracle automatically enforces the policies by appending the predicate returned by the policy function to SQL statements. For instance, if a user executes the following query:

```
SELECT * FROM EMPLOYEES;
```

The resulting query executed by Oracle would effectively be:

```
SELECT * FROM EMPLOYEES WHERE department_id = USERENV("
    SESSION_USER");
```

As a result, the data returned by the query is filtered based on the user's department.

Managing Existing Policies

To manage existing security policies, various procedures in the DBMS_RLS package are available:

- **REMOVE_POLICY**: To remove a policy from a table.

```
BEGIN
    DBMS_RLS.REMOVE_POLICY(
        object_schema => 'HR',
        object_name => 'EMPLOYEES',
        policy_name => 'emp_dept_policy'
    );
END;
/
```

- **ENABLE_POLICY**: To enable a previously disabled policy.

```
BEGIN
    DBMS_RLS.ENABLE_POLICY(
        object_schema => 'HR',
        object_name => 'EMPLOYEES',
        policy_name => 'emp_dept_policy',
        enable => TRUE
    );
END;
/
```

- **DISABLE_POLICY**: To temporarily disable a policy.

```
BEGIN
    DBMS_RLS.DISABLE_POLICY(
        object_schema => 'HR',
        object_name => 'EMPLOYEES',
        policy_name => 'emp_dept_policy',
        enable => FALSE
    );
END;
/
```

Performance Considerations

While RLS provides enhanced security, it is essential to monitor and assess the performance impact, as the enforcement of policies can introduce overhead. Optimizing the policy functions and minimizing the complexity of predicates can mitigate potential performance issues.

Debugging and Testing Policies

Debugging and testing the policies can be achieved using the DBMS_RLS.EXPN_POLICY procedure, which explains the predicates applied by the policy on a session.

```
BEGIN
    DBMS_RLS.EXPN_POLICY(
        object_schema => 'HR',
        object_name => 'EMPLOYEES',
        policy_name => 'emp_dept_policy'
    );
END;
/
```

This aids in understanding the exact behavior and effectiveness of the policy, ensuring it functions as intended.

Oracle's Row-Level Security mechanism is a robust method for implementing fine-grained access control, providing an additional layer of security and ensuring that users can only access data pertinent to their roles and responsibilities.

9.11 Handling Security Incidents

Security incidents in Oracle Database environments can have critical implications. Prompt and effective handling is essential to minimize damage and ensure data integrity. This section will discuss procedures and best practices for responding to security incidents, including identifying incidents, initial response actions, forensic analysis, mitigating vulnerabilities, and post-incident activities.

Identifying Security Incidents: Recognizing a security breach at the earliest stage is pivotal. Incidents can be identified through various indicators such as system alerts, unusual database activity, failed login attempts, unauthorized data access, and changes in database performance. Efficient monitoring tools and logs, such as Oracle's Unified Auditing and Database Firewalls, must be continually analyzed to detect anomalies.

```
-- Enabling Unified Auditing
ALTER SYSTEM SET audit_trail = DB, EXTENDED SCOPE = SPFILE;

-- Restart the database to apply changes
SHUTDOWN IMMEDIATE;
STARTUP;
```

Unified Auditing ensures comprehensive logging, aiding in the identification of security incidents. Additionally, setting up alerts for specific events significantly improves incident detection.

Initial Response Actions: Upon identifying a potential security incident, immediate steps must be taken to contain the threat. The following actions are recommended:

- Isolate the affected system to prevent further damage.
- Change administrator passwords and revoke access from potentially compromised accounts.
- Preserve evidence for forensic analysis by taking snapshots and backups.
- Notify the security response team and relevant stakeholders.

A sample SQL command to revoke privileges from a user could be:

```
-- Revoking all privileges from a compromised user
REVOKE ALL PRIVILEGES FROM compromised_user;
DROP USER compromised_user CASCADE;
```

Forensic Analysis: Conducting a thorough forensic analysis helps understand the breach's extent and origin. Steps include:

- Reviewing database audit logs and transaction histories.
- Employing forensic tools to analyze system and network logs.
- Identifying the vulnerability exploited and the data compromised.

Automated tools such as Oracle Audit Vault and Database Firewall can assist in collecting and analyzing audit data. The use of redaction policies might be crucial in this step.

```
-- Setting up a data redaction policy for sensitive columns
BEGIN
   DBMS_REDACT.ADD_POLICY(
      object_schema => 'hr',
      object_name => 'employees',
      column_name => 'ssn',
      policy_name => 'redact_ssn_policy',
      function_type => DBMS_REDACT.FULL
   );
END;
/
```

Ensuring that no additional data exposure continues is vital during and after the forensic process.

Mitigating Vulnerabilities: Once the cause of the incident is identified, steps must be taken to mitigate the exploited vulnerabilities:

- Apply necessary patches and updates to the Oracle Database.
- Implement stronger access controls and reconfigure security settings.
- Conduct a security audit to identify any additional weak points.

Example of updating Oracle Database:

```
# Assuming OPatch is set up correctly
cd $ORACLE_HOME/OPatch
opatch apply /u01/patch/29850759
```

Post-Incident Activities: After successfully mitigating the incident, it is essential to perform activities to prevent future incidents:

- Update security policies based on lessons learned during the incident.

- Conduct user training sessions to enhance awareness of security practices.
- Regularly review and strengthen incident response plans.

Establishing a continuous improvement cycle where each incident enhances the security posture of the database is crucial. Documenting the incident and response actions aids in refining future strategies and ensuring compliance with regulatory requirements.

```
-- Record keeping for training
INSERT INTO compliance_logs (event_type, description, timestamp)
VALUES ('User Training', 'Security training for user awareness', SYSTIMESTAMP);
```

By adhering to these procedures and remaining vigilant, organizations can effectively handle and mitigate security incidents, maintaining the integrity and security of their Oracle Database environments.

9.12 Best Practices for Database Security

Database security is a multifaceted domain encompassing the protection of data, access control, authentication, authorization, and ensuring compliance with legal mandates. Implementing best practices is crucial to mitigate vulnerabilities and safeguard sensitive information. This section provides an in-depth exploration of the recommended practices for ensuring robust security in Oracle Databases.

One of the fundamental aspects of database security is the principle of least privilege. This principle dictates that users should be granted the minimum level of access necessary to perform their job functions. To achieve this, carefully assess the roles and privileges assigned to each user. Use role-based access control (RBAC) to streamline and manage access permissions efficiently. Create distinct roles tailored to job responsibilities and assign these roles to users rather than granting privileges directly.

Another essential best practice is the use of strong authentication mechanisms. Employ multi-factor authentication (MFA) to add an additional layer of security. Oracle Database offers several authentication methods, including password-based authentication, Kerberos, and PKI-based authentication. Implement strong password policies, requiring complex passwords that combine upper and lower case letters, numbers, and special characters. Enforce regular password changes and account lockout mechanisms to thwart brute-force attacks.

Encryption of data at rest and in transit is an indispensable practice. Oracle Advanced Security provides Transparent Data Encryption (TDE) for protecting stored data. Use TDE to encrypt database files at the storage level, ensuring that sensitive data is unreadable without proper decryption keys. For data in transit, implement Oracle's native network encryption or use SSL/TLS to secure communications between clients and the database server.

Regular auditing and monitoring are critical for detecting and responding to suspicious activities. Configure Oracle Database Auditing to track and record user activities. Use both standard and fine-grained auditing to capture relevant events and actions. The following is an example of configuring fine-grained auditing:

```
BEGIN
  DBMS_FGA.add_policy(
    object_schema => 'HR',
    object_name => 'EMPLOYEES',
    policy_name => 'SALARY_AUDIT',
    audit_column => 'SALARY',
    enable => TRUE
  );
END;
/
```

Ensure that audit logs are securely stored and regularly reviewed. Use Oracle Audit Vault and Database Firewall for comprehensive auditing and real-time monitoring.

Implementing robust user profile and password policies helps enhance security. Define user profiles that enforce limits on resource usage, such as CPU time and the number of sessions per user. The following SQL statement creates a user profile with specific password policies:

```
CREATE PROFILE secure_profile LIMIT
  FAILED_LOGIN_ATTEMPTS 5
  PASSWORD_LIFE_TIME 90
  PASSWORD_REUSE_TIME 365
  PASSWORD_REUSE_MAX 5
  PASSWORD_LOCK_TIME 1
  PASSWORD_GRACE_TIME 7
  PASSWORD_VERIFY_FUNCTION VERIFY_FUNCTION_11G;
```

Assign this profile to users to ensure that they adhere to the defined password and resource policies.

Network security is another significant aspect of database security. Restrict database access to trusted IP addresses using Oracle Net Services parameters. Configure the sqlnet.ora file with appropriate settings to limit network access, such as:

```
SQLNET.ALLOWED_LOGON_VERSION_SERVER = 12
SQLNET.ENCRYPTION_SERVER = REQUIRED
SQLNET.CRYPTO_CHECKSUM_SERVER = REQUIRED
TCP.VALIDNODE_CHECKING = YES
TCP.INVITED_NODES = (192.168.0.100, 192.168.0.101)
```

Use firewalls and network segmentation to isolate the database server from untrusted networks. Apply patches and updates promptly to address vulnerabilities and keep the database software secure.

Virtual Private Database (VPD) and Data Redaction are advanced techniques for enforcing fine-grained access control and masking sensitive data. Use VPD to create security policies that add dynamic predicates to SQL statements. Here is an example of creating a VPD policy:

```
BEGIN
  DBMS_RLS.add_policy(
    object_schema => 'HR',
    object_name => 'EMPLOYEES',
    policy_name => 'HR_POLICY',
    function_schema => 'HR',
    policy_function => 'hr_security_function'
  );
END;
/
```

Data Redaction can mask data in query results, ensuring that sensitive information is not exposed to unauthorized users. Set up data redaction policies using the DBMS_REDACT package.

Lastly, develop and maintain a comprehensive security incident response plan. This plan should outline procedures for identifying, analyzing, and mitigating security breaches. Regularly train your team on security best practices and conduct drills to ensure preparedness in the event of a security incident.

By observing these best practices, you can significantly enhance the security posture of your Oracle Database, protecting sensitive data and ensuring compliance with regulatory requirements.

Chapter 10

Data Modeling and Design

This chapter explores the principles and practices of data modeling and design. It includes discussions on conceptual, logical, and physical data models, and the process of entity-relationship (ER) modeling. Topics such as normalization, denormalization, table design, indexing, and data integrity are covered. The chapter also addresses performance considerations, the use of Oracle SQL Developer Data Modeler, generating DDL scripts, and best practices in data modeling.

10.1 Introduction to Data Modeling

Data modeling is a vital step in the design of a database system. It involves creating a visual representation of the data and the relationships between different data elements. Data modeling provides a coherent framework that can guide the database design process, ensuring that the final database structure is efficient, scalable, and well-organized.

Definition and Importance: Data modeling is defined as the process of creating a data model for the data to be stored in a database. This data model is a conceptual representation of the data structures, including the data objects, the associations between different data objects, and the rules governing these associations. It serves multiple purposes, such as:

- Providing a clear and precise view of the database requirements.

- Facilitating communication between stakeholders (e.g., developers, analysts, end-users).
- Assisting in identifying data redundancy, inconsistency, and other potential issues.
- Helping in enforcing data integrity and business rules.
- Serving as a blueprint for designing the physical database structure.

Types of Data Models: Data modeling typically involves three types of models, namely: conceptual, logical, and physical. Each type has a specific scope and level of detail:

- *Conceptual Data Models*: These provide a high-level view of the business requirements and the broad structure of the database. It focuses on the entities and the relationships among them, without bothering about the actual implementation details. Entity-Relationship (ER) Diagrams are commonly used in conceptual data modeling.
- *Logical Data Models*: These bridge the gap between the conceptual models and the physical implementation. They delve deeper into the structure of the database, specifying the data types, constraints, keys (primary and foreign), and the relationships in more detail. Logical models are platform-independent and aim to represent the business requirements more closely.
- *Physical Data Models*: These are highly detailed and describe how the database is actually implemented in the database management system (DBMS). It includes tables, columns, indexes, partitions, and other physical storage structures. This model is specific to the chosen DBMS and often addresses performance considerations and physical storage requirements.

Role of Entity-Relationship (ER) Modeling: ER modeling is a technique used in the creation of conceptual and logical data models. It involves identifying entities, which are objects or things of interest, and their relationships. An entity is defined by a set of attributes that describe its properties. For example, in a school database, "Student" and "Course" could be entities, while "Enrollment" would be a relationship between students and courses.

- *Entities*: Represent real-world objects or concepts. Each entity has a unique key attribute that identifies instances of the entity.
- *Relationships*: Describe how entities interact with each other. They can be one-to-one, one-to-many, or many-to-many, based on the nature of the interaction.
- *Attributes*: Properties or characteristics of entities. For instance, a "Student" entity might have attributes like student ID, name, date of birth, etc.

ER diagrams provide a graphical approach to data modeling, making it easier to understand and communicate the database structure to various stakeholders.

Normalization in Data Modeling: One of the primary goals of data modeling is to optimize the database design to eliminate redundancy and ensure data integrity through a process known as normalization. Normalization breaks down larger data sets into smaller, manageable tables, which can be easily maintained and queried. Key normal forms include:

- *First Normal Form (1NF)*: Ensures that each column contains atomic, indivisible values, and each record is unique.
- *Second Normal Form (2NF)*: Builds on 1NF by removing subsets of data that apply to multiple rows and placing them into separate tables; ensures that all columns depend on the primary key.
- *Third Normal Form (3NF)*: Further refines 2NF by removing columns that are transitively dependent on the primary key.

```
// Sample table that is not normalized
CREATE TABLE StudentsCourses (
    studentID INT,
    studentName VARCHAR(100),
    courseCode VARCHAR(10),
    courseName VARCHAR(100),
    instructorName VARCHAR(100),
    PRIMARY KEY (studentID)
);

// Normalized tables in 3NF
CREATE TABLE Students (
    studentID INT PRIMARY KEY,
    studentName VARCHAR(100)
);

CREATE TABLE Courses (
```

```
    courseCode VARCHAR(10) PRIMARY KEY,
    courseName VARCHAR(100),
    instructorName VARCHAR(100)
);

CREATE TABLE Enrollment (
    studentID INT,
    courseCode VARCHAR(10),
    PRIMARY KEY (studentID, courseCode),
    FOREIGN KEY (studentID) REFERENCES Students(studentID),
    FOREIGN KEY (courseCode) REFERENCES Courses(courseCode)
);
```

The normalized structure ensures that data is logically stored, minimizing redundancy and ensuring data integrity.

By understanding and applying data modeling principles, database designers can craft efficient, scalable, and robust database systems. Such systems facilitate improved data management, quicker retrieval times, and enhanced integrity across the data lifecycle.

10.2 Conceptual, Logical, and Physical Data Models

Data modeling is a critical component in the database design process. It involves creating representations of the data structures required by a system and their relationships. These representations are captured at different levels of abstraction: conceptual, logical, and physical. Understanding these distinctions allows for more effective planning, communication, and implementation of database systems.

Conceptual Data Model represents the highest level of abstraction. It focuses on identifying the entities, their attributes, and the relationships between entities, without considering how these entities and relationships will be implemented physically. The primary goal of the conceptual data model is to provide a comprehensive and easily understandable representation of the overall system structure. This model is typically used for communication between stakeholders, including business users, analysts, and designers.

The conceptual model often uses the Entity-Relationship (ER) diagram for representation. Each entity within the diagram corresponds to a real-world object or concept that is relevant to the business, and relationships depict the associations between these entities. For example:

```
CREATE TABLE Customer (
```

```
    CustomerID int NOT NULL,
    Name varchar(255) NOT NULL,
    Email varchar(255),
    PRIMARY KEY (CustomerID)
);

CREATE TABLE Order (
    OrderID int NOT NULL,
    OrderDate date NOT NULL,
    CustomerID int,
    PRIMARY KEY (OrderID),
    FOREIGN KEY (CustomerID) REFERENCES Customer(CustomerID)
);
```

In this example, Customer and Order are entities, with attributes such as Name, Email, and OrderDate. The relationship between Customer and Order is indicated by the foreign key constraint. Specifically, it implies that each order is associated with a customer.

Logical Data Model takes the abstract structures defined in the conceptual model and translates them into a more detailed form, considering the business rules and data types. This model serves to define the logical structure of the database, independent of the physical considerations. Key activities in developing a logical data model include:

- Defining primary and foreign keys.
- Specifying data types and constraints.
- Normalizing data to eliminate redundancy and ensure data integrity.

Logical models often use tables to represent entities and columns representing attributes. Continuing the previous example:

```
CREATE TABLE Customer (
    CustomerID int NOT NULL PRIMARY KEY,
    Name varchar(255) NOT NULL,
    Email varchar(255) UNIQUE
);

CREATE TABLE Order (
    OrderID int NOT NULL PRIMARY KEY,
    OrderDate date NOT NULL,
    CustomerID int,
    FOREIGN KEY (CustomerID) REFERENCES Customer(CustomerID)
);
```

The logical model introduces data types and constraints, such as setting CustomerID as the primary key and ensuring that Email maintains unique values.

Physical Data Model provides the implementation details necessary to create the actual database. This model considers the performance, storage, and hardware specifications of the database system. Key considerations include indexing strategies, partitioning schemes, and physical storage allocations.

The physical model defines tables, indexes, constraints, and storage parameters. For instance:

```
CREATE TABLE Customer (
    CustomerID int NOT NULL PRIMARY KEY,
    Name varchar(255) NOT NULL,
    Email varchar(255) UNIQUE
) STORAGE (INITIAL 50K);

CREATE INDEX idx_customer_email ON Customer (Email);

CREATE TABLE Order (
    OrderID int NOT NULL PRIMARY KEY,
    OrderDate date NOT NULL,
    CustomerID int,
    FOREIGN KEY (CustomerID) REFERENCES Customer(CustomerID)
) PARTITION BY RANGE (OrderDate) (
    PARTITION p1 VALUES LESS THAN (TO_DATE('2022-01-01','YYYY-MM-DD')
        ),
    PARTITION p2 VALUES LESS THAN (TO_DATE('2023-01-01','YYYY-MM-DD')
        )
);
```

In this example, the physical model specifies storage parameters for the Customer table and establishes an index on the Email attribute. Additionally, the Order table is partitioned based on the OrderDate to enhance performance and manageability.

The interplay between these data models aids in a systematic development approach. The conceptual model provides a high-level overview, the logical model refines this with detailed planning, and the physical model finalizes the implementation and optimization strategies. Each model informs and constrains the other, ensuring a robust, scalable, and business-aligned database structure.

10.3 Entity-Relationship (ER) Modeling

ER modeling represents a pivotal technique for database design, aiding in the conceptual framework necessary before delving into logical and physical database layers. This model serves as a blueprint for data, giving structure to the information flow within an organization. It focuses on the identification and relationships between data entities, ensuring comprehensive and precise data representation.

The core constructs of the ER model include entities, attributes, and relationships. An **entity** is any object of significance about which data needs to be stored. For example, in a university database, entities might include "Student," "Course," and "Instructor." Each entity has **attributes**, which represent the data elements related to the entity. For example, a "Student" entity might have attributes such as "StudentID," "Name," and "BirthDate."

Entities are interconnected through **relationships**, whereby connections signify dependencies or interactions between two or more entities. In the university example, a "Student" might enroll in a "Course" taught by an "Instructor."

Cardinality and **participation constraints** are essential principles governing how entities relate. Cardinality indicates the numerical relationship between instances of entities, which can be one-to-one (1:1), one-to-many (1:N), or many-to-many (M:N). Participation constraints, which are either total or partial, dictate whether all instances of an entity participate in a relationship.

- **One-to-One (1:1) Relationship**: Each instance in an entity relates to a single instance in another entity and vice versa. For example, in some systems, each student might have one unique student ID card.
- **One-to-Many (1:N) Relationship**: One instance in an entity can relate to multiple instances in another. A single instructor may teach multiple courses.
- **Many-to-Many (M:N) Relationship**: Instances in one entity can relate to multiple instances in another and vice versa. Students can enroll in multiple courses, and each course can have multiple students.

```
-- Example ER Diagram in SQL
Student (
    StudentID INT PRIMARY KEY,
    Name VARCHAR(100),
    BirthDate DATE
);

Course (
    CourseID INT PRIMARY KEY,
    CourseName VARCHAR(100),
    InstructorID INT,
    FOREIGN KEY (InstructorID) REFERENCES Instructor(InstructorID)
```

```
);

Instructor (
    InstructorID INT PRIMARY KEY,
    InstructorName VARCHAR(100)
);

Enrollment (
    StudentID INT,
    CourseID INT,
    Grade CHAR(1),
    PRIMARY KEY (StudentID, CourseID),
    FOREIGN KEY (StudentID) REFERENCES Student(StudentID),
    FOREIGN KEY (CourseID) REFERENCES Course(CourseID)
);
```

Above, the ‘Enrollment‘ table acts as an associative entity resolving the many-to-many relationship between ‘Student‘ and ‘Course‘.

When designing ER models, adherence to naming conventions and clear, decipherable diagram representations remains crucial. Entities should have singular, descriptive names and attribute names should be intuitive and meaningful. Relationships should be depicted in a way that clearly identifies their cardinality and constraints.

For logical ER diagrams, attributes are typically categorized as key attributes, simple attributes, composite attributes, multi-valued attributes, and derived attributes.

- **Key Attributes**: Uniquely identify an entity instance. For example, ‘StudentID‘ uniquely identifies a "Student."
- **Simple Attributes**: Indivisible atomic values, such as ‘Name‘.
- **Composite Attributes**: Can be divided into simpler sub-parts. For instance, a composite attribute ‘Address‘ might include ‘Street‘, ‘City‘, and ‘ZipCode‘.
- **Multi-valued Attributes**: Can hold multiple values. An example is ‘PhoneNumbers‘ for the "Student" entity.
- **Derived Attributes**: Values calculable from other attributes. For instance, ‘Age‘ might be derived from ‘BirthDate‘.

Weak entities are another important concept; they cannot be uniquely identified by their attributes alone and typically rely on a **strong entity** for identification. For instance, consider ‘Dependent‘ as a weak entity related to ‘Employee‘ as shown:

```
-- Example of Strong and Weak Entity Relationship
Employee (
    EmpID INT PRIMARY KEY,
    Name VARCHAR(100)
);

Dependent (
    DependentID INT,
    DependentName VARCHAR(100),
    EmpID INT,
    PRIMARY KEY (EmpID, DependentID),
    FOREIGN KEY (EmpID) REFERENCES Employee(EmpID)
);
```

Through the ER design process, both diagrammatic and descriptive techniques have proven invaluable, ensuring that the entire database design is robust, non-redundant, and effective in meeting organizational needs. Diagrammatic representation using tools like Oracle SQL Developer Data Modeler facilitates visualization and validation of the ER model before proceeding to the logical relational schema and subsequent physical implementation.

10.4 Normalization and Denormalization

Normalization is a database design technique that reduces data redundancy and improves data integrity by organizing columns and tables of a relational database. The primary goals of normalization are to separate data into logical units to minimize redundancy and dependencies. The process involves dividing a database into two or more tables and defining relationships between the tables.

The levels of normalization are referred to as normal forms (NF). The most commonly used normal forms are the first (1NF), second (2NF), third (3NF), and Boyce-Codd Normal Form (BCNF). Each successive normal form requires that the database adheres to additional rules to increase its normalization.

First Normal Form (1NF): A table is in 1NF if it only contains atomic (indivisible) values; that is, each column value must be a single value, not a set of values or composite values. Additionally, each column must contain values of a single type.

Second Normal Form (2NF): A table is in 2NF if it is in 1NF and all non-key attributes are fully functionally dependent on the primary key. In other words, there should be no partial dependency; no non-prime attribute depends on a part of any candidate key.

Third Normal Form (3NF): A table is in 3NF if it is in 2NF and all its attributes are functionally dependent only on the primary key. There should be no transitive dependency for non-prime attributes on the primary key.

Boyce-Codd Normal Form (BCNF): A table is in BCNF if it is in 3NF and for every one of its dependencies $(X \to Y)$, X is a superkey. BCNF is a stronger version of the 3NF.

Consider the following example that illustrates the progression through the normal forms:

```
CREATE TABLE Students (
    StudentID INT,
    StudentName VARCHAR(50),
    Courses VARCHAR(255)
);

INSERT INTO Students (StudentID, StudentName, Courses) VALUES (1, 'John Doe', '
    Math,Science,English');
INSERT INTO Students (StudentID, StudentName, Courses) VALUES (2, 'Jane Doe', '
    Math,History');
```

The table is not in 1NF because the Courses column contains multiple values. To transform this into 1NF, create a separate row for each course:

```
CREATE TABLE Students (
    StudentID INT,
    StudentName VARCHAR(50),
    Course VARCHAR(50)
);

INSERT INTO Students (StudentID, StudentName, Course) VALUES (1, 'John Doe', '
    Math');
INSERT INTO Students (StudentID, StudentName, Course) VALUES (1, 'John Doe', '
    Science');
INSERT INTO Students (StudentID, StudentName, Course) VALUES (1, 'John Doe', '
    English');
INSERT INTO Students (StudentID, StudentName, Course) VALUES (2, 'Jane Doe', '
    Math');
INSERT INTO Students (StudentID, StudentName, Course) VALUES (2, 'Jane Doe', '
    History');
```

Next, to move to 2NF, ensure that all non-key attributes are fully dependent on the primary key. Suppose the database needs to record the CourseName as well:

```
CREATE TABLE Students (
    StudentID INT,
    StudentName VARCHAR(50)
);
```

```
CREATE TABLE Courses (
    CourseID INT,
    CourseName VARCHAR(50)
);

CREATE TABLE StudentCourses (
    StudentID INT,
    CourseID INT
);

INSERT INTO Students (StudentID, StudentName) VALUES (1, 'John Doe');
INSERT INTO Students (StudentID, StudentName) VALUES (2, 'Jane Doe');

INSERT INTO Courses (CourseID, CourseName) VALUES (1, 'Math');
INSERT INTO Courses (CourseID, CourseName) VALUES (2, 'Science');
INSERT INTO Courses (CourseID, CourseName) VALUES (3, 'English');
INSERT INTO Courses (CourseID, CourseName) VALUES (4, 'History');

INSERT INTO StudentCourses (StudentID, CourseID) VALUES (1, 1);
INSERT INTO StudentCourses (StudentID, CourseID) VALUES (1, 2);
INSERT INTO StudentCourses (StudentID, CourseID) VALUES (1, 3);
INSERT INTO StudentCourses (StudentID, CourseID) VALUES (2, 1);
INSERT INTO StudentCourses (StudentID, CourseID) VALUES (2, 4);
```

To achieve 3NF, ensure no transitive dependencies exist. If, for instance, the Courses table records Instructor information:

```
CREATE TABLE Instructors (
    InstructorID INT,
    InstructorName VARCHAR(50)
);

CREATE TABLE Courses (
    CourseID INT,
    CourseName VARCHAR(50),
    InstructorID INT
);

INSERT INTO Instructors (InstructorID, InstructorName) VALUES (1, 'Dr. Smith');
INSERT INTO Instructors (InstructorID, InstructorName) VALUES (2, 'Dr. Brown');

INSERT INTO Courses (CourseID, CourseName, InstructorID) VALUES (1, 'Math', 1);
INSERT INTO Courses (CourseID, CourseName, InstructorID) VALUES (2, 'Science',
    2);
INSERT INTO Courses (CourseID, CourseName, InstructorID) VALUES (3, 'English',
    1);
INSERT INTO Courses (CourseID, CourseName, InstructorID) VALUES (4, 'History',
    2);
```

Denormalization, the reverse process of normalization, involves combining tables to improve read performance. This is often necessary in data warehousing where queries are optimized for read, not write, performance.

When designing a database, both normalization and denormalization should be considered to balance performance and data integrity. It is crucial to assess data usage patterns before deciding to denormalize. Common denormalization techniques include duplicating data across tables, creating summarized table structures for quick access, and employing database features such as materialized views.

A typical denormalization scenario for faster retrieval might involve combining the Students and StudentCourses tables back into a single table where the redundancy is tolerated for improved query performance.

```
CREATE TABLE StudentCourseDetails (
    StudentID INT,
    StudentName VARCHAR(50),
    CourseID INT,
    CourseName VARCHAR(50)
);

INSERT INTO StudentCourseDetails (StudentID, StudentName, CourseID,
      CourseName) VALUES (1, 'John Doe', 1, 'Math');
INSERT INTO StudentCourseDetails (StudentID, StudentName, CourseID,
      CourseName) VALUES (1, 'John Doe', 2, 'Science');
INSERT INTO StudentCourseDetails (StudentID, StudentName, CourseID,
      CourseName) VALUES (1, 'John Doe', 3, 'English');
INSERT INTO StudentCourseDetails (StudentID, StudentName, CourseID,
      CourseName) VALUES (2, 'Jane Doe', 1, 'Math');
INSERT INTO StudentCourseDetails (StudentID, StudentName, CourseID,
      CourseName) VALUES (2, 'Jane Doe', 4, 'History');
```

The decision to normalize or denormalize depends on specific application requirements, especially those related to query patterns, performance bottlenecks, and maintainability concerns. Each approach has trade-offs that must be carefully weighed.

10.5 Designing Tables and Relationships

Designing tables and relationships is a fundamental aspect of data modeling and involves creating the structures that will store data in a database management system. This section delves into the detailed process of table design, focusing on table structure, column definitions, data types, primary and foreign keys, and establishing relationships between tables.

The design of tables starts with identifying the entities and attributes that need to be represented. In an entity-relationship model, entities become tables, and attributes become columns within those tables. Creating an efficient and normalized table structure ensures that the database remains organized, easy to maintain, and scalable.

To create a table, we use the SQL CREATE TABLE statement. Consider the following example of defining a simple Customers table:

```
CREATE TABLE Customers (
    CustomerID INT PRIMARY KEY,
    FirstName VARCHAR(50),
    LastName VARCHAR(50),
    Email VARCHAR(100),
    PhoneNumber VARCHAR(15)
);
```

In this example, the Customers table is defined with five columns: CustomerID, FirstName, LastName, Email, and PhoneNumber. The CustomerID column is designated as the primary key using the PRIMARY KEY constraint, ensuring that each customer has a unique identifier.

Column Definitions and Data Types

Choosing appropriate data types for columns is crucial. Data types define the nature of data that can be stored in a column, and selecting the right data type optimally impacts storage space and performance. Common data types include:

- INT for integer values
- VARCHAR for variable-length character strings
- DATE for date values
- FLOAT for floating-point numbers
- BOOLEAN for true/false values

Below is an example of a Products table with various data types:

```
CREATE TABLE Products (
    ProductID INT PRIMARY KEY,
    ProductName VARCHAR(100),
    Price FLOAT,
    DateAdded DATE,
    InStock BOOLEAN
);
```

ProductID is an integer that serves as the table's primary key. ProductName is a string with a maximum length of 100 characters. Price is a floating-point number, DateAdded is a date type, and InStock is a boolean.

Primary and Foreign Keys

Primary keys uniquely identify each row in a table and are defined using the PRIMARY KEY constraint. It is a best practice to use an auto-incrementing integer, ensuring uniqueness without manual input errors.

Foreign keys establish relationships between tables. They provide referential integrity by linking a column in one table to the primary key of another table. Example:

```
CREATE TABLE Orders (
    OrderID INT PRIMARY KEY,
    OrderDate DATE,
    CustomerID INT,
    FOREIGN KEY (CustomerID) REFERENCES Customers(CustomerID)
);
```

In the Orders table, CustomerID is a foreign key that references the CustomerID column in the Customers table, ensuring that any value in CustomerID must exist in the Customers table.

Defining Relationships

The relationships between tables are defined through foreign keys. There are three types of relationships in relational databases:

- **One-to-One**: A row in table A is linked to a single row in table B.
- **One-to-Many**: A row in table A is linked to multiple rows in table B.
- **Many-to-Many**: Rows in table A can be linked to multiple rows in table B and vice versa, usually requiring a junction table.

One-to-One Relationship Example

A one-to-one relationship can be represented with a foreign key and a unique constraint:

```
CREATE TABLE Employees (
    EmployeeID INT PRIMARY KEY,
    FirstName VARCHAR(50),
    LastName VARCHAR(50)
);

CREATE TABLE EmployeeDetails (
    EmployeeID INT PRIMARY KEY,
    Address VARCHAR(200),
    SocialSecurityNumber VARCHAR(20),
    FOREIGN KEY (EmployeeID) REFERENCES Employees(EmployeeID)
);
```

Each employee has a unique EmployeeID, and the EmployeeDetails table uses this id as both its primary key and a foreign key, linking each row uniquely without allowing duplicate entries.

One-to-Many Relationship Example

In a one-to-many relationship, one record in the parent table can relate to many records in the child table.

```
CREATE TABLE Departments (
    DepartmentID INT PRIMARY KEY,
    DepartmentName VARCHAR(100)
);

CREATE TABLE Employees (
    EmployeeID INT PRIMARY KEY,
    FirstName VARCHAR(50),
    LastName VARCHAR(50),
    DepartmentID INT,
    FOREIGN KEY (DepartmentID) REFERENCES Departments(DepartmentID)
);
```

Here, the DepartmentID in the Employees table is a foreign key referring to DepartmentID in the Departments table. Each department can have multiple employees.

Many-to-Many Relationship Example

Many-to-many relationships require a junction table to manage associations. For instance, if each student can enroll in multiple courses and each course can have multiple students:

```
CREATE TABLE Students (
    StudentID INT PRIMARY KEY,
    StudentName VARCHAR(100)
);

CREATE TABLE Courses (
    CourseID INT PRIMARY KEY,
    CourseName VARCHAR(100)
);

CREATE TABLE Enrollments (
    StudentID INT,
    CourseID INT,
    PRIMARY KEY (StudentID, CourseID),
    FOREIGN KEY (StudentID) REFERENCES Students(StudentID),
    FOREIGN KEY (CourseID) REFERENCES Courses(CourseID)
);
```

The Enrollments table serves as a junction table with a composite primary key consisting of StudentID and CourseID, referencing the primary keys in the Students and Courses tables.

Table and relationship design in multi-table environments requires careful planning to ensure data integrity, efficient retrieval, and updating of data. It is essential to understand and properly implement primary and foreign keys, select suitable data types, and design relationships to optimize the database's overall structure and performance.

10.6 Indexes and Constraints

Indexes and constraints are critical components in database design, ensuring efficient data retrieval and maintaining data integrity. An index enhances the speed of data retrieval operations by providing quick access paths to the data, while constraints enforce rules that ensure data consistency and accuracy. This section delves into the types, creation, and usage of indexes and constraints, and their implications on database performance and integrity.

Indexes

Indexes are database objects that significantly improve the performance of query operations. They allow the database system to find the required rows more quickly than by scanning the entire table. In Oracle, several types of indexes can be created:

- **B-tree Index:** This is the default and most commonly used index type. It is suitable for columns with a wide range of values.
- **Bitmap Index:** Best used for columns with a limited number of distinct values. It is more storage-efficient for such columns and efficient for complex queries and joins involving large datasets.
- **Unique Index:** Ensures that no two rows have the same value in the indexed columns. It is automatically created when you define a unique constraint or a primary key constraint on a table.
- **Composite Index:** An index on multiple columns. It is beneficial when queries use multiple columns in the WHERE clause.
- **Function-based Index:** This type of index is created based on expressions or functions applied on the table columns. It is useful for queries that involve functions in the WHERE clause.

To create an index in Oracle, use the CREATE INDEX statement. Here is an example of creating a B-tree index on the EMP table for the LAST_NAME column:

```
CREATE INDEX idx_emp_lastname
ON EMP (LAST_NAME);
```

For a composite index on DEPT_ID and EMP_STATUS columns:

```
CREATE INDEX idx_emp_dept_status
ON EMP (DEPT_ID, EMP_STATUS);
```

Constraints

Constraints enforce rules at the table level to maintain data integrity and accuracy. Oracle supports several types of constraints:

- **Primary Key (PK):** Uniquely identifies each row in a table. A table can have only one primary key, which consists of one or more columns. A primary key constraint implicitly creates a unique index on the column(s).
- **Unique (UQ):** Ensures all values in a column or a set of columns are distinct. Unlike the primary key, a table can have multiple unique constraints.
- **Foreign Key (FK):** Establishes a relationship between a column or a set of columns in one table and the primary key or unique key in another table. It ensures referential integrity.
- **Check (CK):** Ensures values in a column satisfy a specific condition. It can refer to one or more columns in the same table.
- **Not Null (NN):** Ensures a column cannot have a NULL value.

Creating primary key constraint:

```
ALTER TABLE EMP
ADD CONSTRAINT pk_emp
PRIMARY KEY (EMP_ID);
```

Creating unique constraint:

```
ALTER TABLE EMP
ADD CONSTRAINT uq_emp_email
UNIQUE (EMAIL);
```

Creating foreign key constraint:

```
ALTER TABLE EMP
ADD CONSTRAINT fk_emp_dept
FOREIGN KEY (DEPT_ID)
REFERENCES DEPT (DEPT_ID);
```

Creating check constraint:

```
ALTER TABLE EMP
ADD CONSTRAINT ck_emp_salary
CHECK (SALARY > 0);
```

Performance Considerations

Indexes and constraints significantly influence database performance. While indexes speed up query execution, they also require storage and maintenance, especially on tables with frequent insertions, updates, and deletions. Oracle uses the cost-based optimizer (CBO) to decide the most efficient way to execute a query, and the presence of indexes can affect these decisions.

Constraints, while maintaining data integrity, might add overhead during data modification operations. Each constraint violation check incurs a performance cost, which might affect large-scale data operations. However, their role in maintaining the consistency and validity of the data far outweighs the overhead in most scenarios.

To balance performance and integrity, carefully consider which columns require indexing and constraint enforcement. Use indexes primarily on columns frequently used in query conditions (WHERE clauses and joins). Avoid over-indexing as this can negate the performance benefits due to excessive index maintenance overhead.

Using the right constraints ensures data meets all business rules without compromising performance excessively. For columns that must always contain values, the NOT NULL constraint ensures that no nulls are allowed, enhancing query performance as the optimizer can assume that there are no null values present.

Through understanding indexes and constraints, you can design databases that are both efficient and maintained for integrity. The appropriate use of these components is instrumental in achieving optimal database performance and reliable data storage.

10.7 Modeling for Performance

Data modeling aims not only at creating an accurate representation of the data but also at ensuring that the database operates efficiently under various workloads. Performance modeling encompasses designing the database schema to optimize query response times, efficient storage utilization, and minimal maintenance overhead. This section delves into several techniques and considerations that impact the performance of database models created using Oracle Database.

Primary considerations in performance modeling include indexing strategies, partitioning, materialized views, and denormalization for read-intensive databases. Properly implemented, these techniques contribute significantly to achieving optimal performance.

Indexing is a crucial technique in performance optimization. Indexes can dramatically reduce the amount of data scanned during query execution by allowing the database to retrieve data directly using the index structure.

```
CREATE INDEX idx_employee_name ON employee (last_name, first_name);
```

In the above command, an index idx_employee_name is created on the last_name and first_name columns of the employee table. This composite index is particularly beneficial when queries commonly filter results based on both last_name and first_name.

However, over-indexing can also degrade performance by increasing the overhead for DML (Data Manipulation Language) operations such as inserts, updates, and deletes. Therefore, careful analysis of query patterns and access statistics is required to identify the most beneficial indexes.

Partitioning is another vital strategy to improve performance and manageability of large databases. Partitioning divides large tables and indexes into smaller, more manageable pieces, yet allows SQL queries to sometimes access multiple partitions simultaneously. This improves query performance by reducing the amount of data scanned as only relevant partitions are processed.

```
CREATE TABLE sales (
    sale_id NUMBER,
    sale_date DATE,
    amount NUMBER
)
PARTITION BY RANGE (sale_date) (
    PARTITION sales_q1 VALUES LESS THAN (TO_DATE('01-APR-2023', 'DD-
        MON-YYYY')),
    PARTITION sales_q2 VALUES LESS THAN (TO_DATE('01-JUL-2023', 'DD-
        MON-YYYY')),
    PARTITION sales_q3 VALUES LESS THAN (TO_DATE('01-OCT-2023', 'DD-
        MON-YYYY')),
    PARTITION sales_q4 VALUES LESS THAN (TO_DATE('01-JAN-2024', 'DD-
        MON-YYYY'))
);
```

The above example shows a table sales partitioned by the range of sale_date. Each partition holds the data for one quarter, significantly improving the querying speed for date-specific searches.

Materialized views store the results of complex queries and can be periodically refreshed. They reduce the computation needed for repetitive heavy queries, enhancing performance.

```
CREATE MATERIALIZED VIEW mv_sales_summary
REFRESH FAST ON COMMIT
AS
SELECT sale_date, SUM(amount) AS total_sales
FROM sales
GROUP BY sale_date;
```

In this context, the materialized view mv_sales_summary precomputes and stores the daily total sales, speeding up any future queries that require these computations.

Denormalization might be adopted to optimize read-heavy environments. While normalization aims at reducing data redundancy to improve integrity, denormalization intentionally brings in redundancy to minimize complex joins, thus reducing read times.

Consider a denormalized table that includes often-joined information:

```
CREATE TABLE order_summary (
    order_id NUMBER,
    customer_name VARCHAR2(50),
    order_date DATE,
    product_description VARCHAR2(200),
    quantity NUMBER,
    total_amount NUMBER
);
```

This order_summary table merges data from orders, customers, and products to reduce the need for expensive join operations and provide faster read access.

This section emphasizes how strategic modeling decisions, such as judicious indexing, effective partitioning, the use of materialized views, and controlled denormalization, lead to significant performance improvements. These decisions should always be informed by detailed query analysis and performance testing to match the specific requirements and usage patterns of the database system under design.

10.8 Designing for Data Integrity

Designing for data integrity is a critical aspect of database modeling, ensuring that the data remains accurate, consistent, and reliable throughout its lifecycle. Data integrity can be categorized into several types: entity integrity, referential integrity, domain integrity, and user-defined integrity. Each of these types encompasses specific rules and constraints that must be implemented and enforced within the database environment.

Entity integrity ensures that each row in a table is uniquely identifiable, typically by using a primary key. This key constraint mandates that every table must have a column, or a set of columns, designated as the primary key, which uniquely identifies each row in the table. The primary key must contain unique values and should not allow null values. The SQL statement to define a primary key constraint during table creation is shown below:

```
CREATE TABLE employees (
    employee_id NUMBER PRIMARY KEY,
    first_name VARCHAR2(50),
    last_name VARCHAR2(50)
);
```

Referential integrity ensures that relationships between tables remain consistent. This is enforced using foreign key constraints, which require that a value in one table must correspond to a value in another table, or be null. A foreign key establishes and enforces a link between the data in two tables, typically between a primary key in one table and a foreign key in another. The syntax for creating a foreign key is as follows:

```
CREATE TABLE departments (
    department_id NUMBER PRIMARY KEY,
    department_name VARCHAR2(100)
);

CREATE TABLE employees (
    employee_id NUMBER PRIMARY KEY,
    first_name VARCHAR2(50),
    last_name VARCHAR2(50),
    department_id NUMBER,
    CONSTRAINT fk_department
        FOREIGN KEY (department_id)
        REFERENCES departments (department_id)
);
```

Domain integrity pertains to the validity of the data according to predefined rules, confining data to a specific set of values. This is implemented through data types, constraints, and default values. For instance, defining a column to only allow numbers within a specific range, as shown below:

```
CREATE TABLE products (
    product_id NUMBER PRIMARY KEY,
    product_name VARCHAR2(200),
    price NUMBER CHECK (price >= 0)
);
```

User-defined integrity involves the creation of additional business rules that cannot be classified under entity, referential, or domain integrity. These rules can often be implemented using triggers, procedures, and custom constraints.

Triggers are special types of stored procedures that are executed automatically in response to certain events on a particular table or view. Triggers help enforce complex business rules that cannot be enforced using only constraints. For example, a trigger to enforce that an employee's salary must be greater than a specific threshold:

```
CREATE OR REPLACE TRIGGER trg_check_salary
BEFORE INSERT OR UPDATE ON employees
FOR EACH ROW
DECLARE
    min_salary NUMBER := 2000;
BEGIN
    IF :NEW.salary < min_salary THEN
        RAISE_APPLICATION_ERROR(-20001, 'Salary must be at least ' ||
              min_salary);
    END IF;
END;
```

Data integrity is also maintained via transactions. A transaction is a sequence of one or more SQL operations treated as a single unit. Transactions must have the properties encapsulated by the ACID acronym: Atomicity, Consistency, Isolation, and Durability. These properties ensure that transactions are processed reliably. For instance, a transaction that transfers money between bank accounts must ensure that the entire process is completed successfully; if any part of the transaction fails, the entire transaction should be rolled back to maintain data integrity.

```
BEGIN
    -- Start of transaction
    UPDATE accounts
    SET balance = balance - 100
    WHERE account_id = 1;

    UPDATE accounts
    SET balance = balance + 100
    WHERE account_id = 2;
```

```
    -- Commit the transaction
    COMMIT;
EXCEPTION
    WHEN OTHERS THEN
        -- Roll back the transaction in case of error
        ROLLBACK;
        RAISE;
END;
```

Effective database design practices include regular audits and data validation routines to ensure ongoing data integrity. Constraints, triggers, and transactions form a robust architecture that guards against data anomalies, ensuring that the database remains a trustworthy and reliable source of information.

10.9 Using Oracle SQL Developer Data Modeler

Oracle SQL Developer Data Modeler is an advanced modeling tool that facilitates the creation, viewing, and management of database designs. It supports logical, relational, and physical modeling of data, and integrates seamlessly with Oracle databases. This section explores the functionality and features of Oracle SQL Developer Data Modeler by detailing its usage, including installation, interface overview, and practical application in data modeling.

Installation and Setup

To begin using Oracle SQL Developer Data Modeler, download the software from the official Oracle website and follow the provided installation instructions. The software is available for various operating systems including Windows, macOS, and Linux. Ensure that you have the necessary system requirements before proceeding with the installation.

Interface Overview

Upon launching Oracle SQL Developer Data Modeler, the main interface is presented, which comprises several components designed for efficient navigation and modeling. Key components include:

- **Menu Bar**: Provides access to various functionality including file operations, view options, and tools.
- **Toolbars**: Offer quick access to commonly used functions.

- **Diagram Area**: The primary workspace where data models are visually constructed and edited.
- **Browser Panel**: Lists open models and provides navigational capabilities to various objects within a model.
- **Properties Panel**: Displays and permits editing of properties for selected objects.

Creating a New Data Model

To create a new data model, follow these steps:

```
1. Select "File" from the menu bar.
2. Choose "New" > "Logical Data Model" or "Relational Data Model" based on the
   requirements.
3. Define the scope and purpose of the data model, and any initial settings.
```

Logical and Relational Modeling

Two primary types of data modeling supported by Oracle SQL Developer Data Modeler are logical and relational modeling. Logical modeling is concerned with high-level design, focusing on entities, attributes, and their relationships without regard to the eventual database structure. Relational modeling translates these entities and relationships into tables, columns, and foreign keys.

Entity Creation

Entities represent the core components of logical models. To create an entity:

```
1. Right-click within the diagram area.
2. Select "New Entity."
3. Provide a name and optionally define attributes (fields) for the entity.
4. Specify any additional properties or constraints as required.
```

Attributes and Keys

Attributes are fundamental to entity definitions. Each attribute should be uniquely named within an entity and assigned a data type. Define a primary key to ensure entity uniqueness. To add attributes and define keys:

```
1. Select the entity and open the "Properties" panel.
2. Navigate to the "Attributes" tab.
3. Add the desired attributes and specify their data types.
4. Designate one or more attributes as the primary key.
```

Relationships

Relationships are established between entities to reflect business rules and data dependencies. To create a relationship:

```
1. Use the "Relationship" tool from the toolbar.
2. Click on the parent entity and then on the child entity.
3. Define the type of relationship (one-to-one, one-to-many, many-to-many).
4. Specify any other relevant properties such as cardinality and optionality.
```

The relationship details can be edited in the properties panel to fine-tune its characteristics.

Transforming Logical Models to Relational Models

The transformation process from logical to relational models is supported by several automated and manual steps to ensure accuracy and consistency. To transform:

```
1. Open the logical model.
2. Select "Engineer to Relational Model" from the "Tools" menu.
3. Follow the wizard to map entities to tables and attributes to columns.
4. Review and adjust mappings as necessary.
5. Finalize the relational model for further development.
```

Generating DDL Scripts

Once the relational model is complete, generate Data Definition Language (DDL) scripts to create the database schema. To generate DDL scripts:

```
1. Select the "Relational Model."
2. Navigate to "File" > "Export" > "DDL File."
3. Choose the desired options for script generation including schema elements to
   include.
4. Save the generated script for execution in an Oracle database environment.
```

Using Reverse Engineering

Oracle SQL Developer Data Modeler also supports reverse engineering, which allows the import of an existing database schema into a data model. This is useful for analysis and modification of existing databases. To reverse engineer a schema:

```
1. Select "File" > "Import" > "Data Dictionary."
2. Connect to the desired Oracle database instance.
3. Choose the schemas and objects to be imported.
4. Follow the wizard to import the selected schema into a model.
```

Best Practices

When using Oracle SQL Developer Data Modeler, following best practices ensures efficient and accurate modeling:

- Regularly save and version control your data models to maintain a history of changes.
- Utilize naming conventions and standard practices to ensure clarity and consistency.
- Validate the model frequently using built-in validation tools to catch and correct errors early.
- Document any design decisions and assumptions within the model for future reference.

Practical application of Oracle SQL Developer Data Modeler in a real-world scenario can significantly streamline the database design process. The intuitive interface, combined with extensive features, facilitates the development and management of robust data models which can be readily implemented in an Oracle database environment. The tool's ability to synchronize changes, generate accurate DDL scripts, and maintain data integrity proves invaluable in comprehensive data modeling and design practices.

10.10 Generating DDL Scripts from Data Models

Generating Data Definition Language (DDL) scripts from data models is a crucial step in transforming abstract data representations into live databases. This section delineates the process of converting conceptual, logical, or physical data models into DDL scripts using Oracle SQL Developer Data Modeler.

A DDL script contains SQL commands used to create, alter, and manage database objects such as tables, indexes, constraints, and other objects within the Oracle Database Management System. The Oracle SQL Developer Data Modeler automates this conversion, ensuring accuracy and compliance with the model design.

Creating a Database Design with Oracle SQL Developer Data Modeler Before generating DDL scripts, one must first create a database design within Oracle SQL Developer Data Modeler. Follow these steps:

- Launch Oracle SQL Developer Data Modeler and create a new design.

- Define entities and attributes, specifying data types and other properties.
- Establish relationships between entities, ensuring referential integrity.
- Apply constraints such as primary keys, foreign keys, and unique constraints.

Export to DDL Once the design is complete, we can proceed to generate the DDL scripts:

- Navigate to *File → Export → DDL File...*.
- In the *Export* dialog box, specify the objects to be included in the DDL script (e.g., tables, constraints, indexes).
- Select the *specify file* option to define the output file name and location for the generated script.
- Customize options such as *include schema name*, *drop statement before create*, and other preferences.

Sample DDL Script The generated DDL script will contain the SQL commands reflecting the data model. Below is an example of a DDL script for a simple schema with two tables, Department and Employee:

```
CREATE TABLE Department (
    DepartmentID NUMBER PRIMARY KEY,
    DepartmentName VARCHAR2(100) NOT NULL
);

CREATE TABLE Employee (
    EmployeeID NUMBER PRIMARY KEY,
    FirstName VARCHAR2(50) NOT NULL,
    LastName VARCHAR2(50) NOT NULL,
    DepartmentID NUMBER,
    CONSTRAINT fk_department
        FOREIGN KEY (DepartmentID)
        REFERENCES Department(DepartmentID)
);
```

In this script, the CREATE TABLE statements define the structure of the Department and Employee tables. The Department table has two columns: DepartmentID and DepartmentName. The Employee table includes columns for the employee's ID, first name, last name, and a foreign key column that references the Department table.

Executing the DDL script in the Oracle SQL*Plus client or another SQL execution environment will create the structure defined in the data model.

Refining the DDL Script Oracle SQL Developer Data Modeler provides advanced features to refine the generated DDL scripts:

- Customize naming conventions for tables, columns, and constraints.
- Include comments and annotations for documentation purposes.
- Specify tablespace allocation and storage parameters.
- Define triggers and additional integrity constraints.

These refinements ensure that the DDL scripts align with organizational standards and performance requirements.

Validation and Testing Before deploying the DDL script to a production environment, validate and test the script:

- Run the script in a development or staging environment.
- Verify the creation of database objects as per the data model.
- Test data insertion, updates, and deletion to ensure referential integrity constraints are enforced.
- Review and optimize performance by analyzing execution plans and indexing strategies.

The process of generating DDL scripts from data models provides a robust and error-free means to implement the database structure as envisioned during the design phase. It ensures consistency and adherence to the defined data requirements, laying the foundation for a reliable and efficient database system.

10.11 Case Studies in Data Modeling

To consolidate our understanding of data modeling and design, we will examine several case studies that illustrate practical applications of the concepts discussed in previous sections. These case studies cover different industries and scenarios, providing a broad perspective on how to approach data modeling in various contexts. The aim is to provide concrete examples that demonstrate the principles of entity-relationship (ER) modeling, normalization, table design, indexing, and data integrity.

Case Study 1: Online Retail Store

Consider an online retail store that sells products to customers through its website. The primary entities involved are **Customer**, **Order**, **Product**, **Category**, and **Payment**.

- **Customer**: Represents individuals who purchase products from the store. Attributes include CustomerID, Name, Email, PhoneNumber, Address, and DateRegistered.
- **Order**: Represents purchase transactions made by customers. Attributes include OrderID, OrderDate, CustomerID, TotalAmount, ShippingAddress, and OrderStatus.
- **Product**: Represents the items available for sale. Attributes include ProductID, Name, Description, Price, QuantityInStock, CategoryID, and ImageURL.
- **Category**: Represents the classification of products. Attributes include CategoryID, Name, and Description.
- **Payment**: Represents the payment details for each order. Attributes include PaymentID, OrderID, PaymentDate, Amount, PaymentMethod, and TransactionID.

The ER diagram for the online retail store is constructed by identifying relationships among these entities:

- **Customer-Order**: A one-to-many relationship where a customer can place multiple orders but each order is associated with a single customer.
- **Order-Product**: A many-to-many relationship because an order can contain multiple products and a product can be part of multiple orders. This relationship is typically modeled using a junction table called **OrderDetails** with attributes OrderID, ProductID, Quantity, and Subtotal.
- **Product-Category**: A many-to-one relationship where each product belongs to one category but a category can include multiple products.

- **Order-Payment**: A one-to-one relationship where each order is associated with a single payment.

Below is the SQL code to create the corresponding tables and establish relationships:

```
CREATE TABLE Customer (
    CustomerID INT PRIMARY KEY,
    Name VARCHAR(100),
    Email VARCHAR(100) UNIQUE,
    PhoneNumber VARCHAR(15),
    Address VARCHAR(255),
    DateRegistered DATE
);

CREATE TABLE Category (
    CategoryID INT PRIMARY KEY,
    Name VARCHAR(100),
    Description VARCHAR(255)
);

CREATE TABLE Product (
    ProductID INT PRIMARY KEY,
    Name VARCHAR(100),
    Description TEXT,
    Price DECIMAL(10, 2),
    QuantityInStock INT,
    CategoryID INT,
    ImageURL VARCHAR(255),
    FOREIGN KEY (CategoryID) REFERENCES Category(CategoryID)
);

CREATE TABLE Order (
    OrderID INT PRIMARY KEY,
    OrderDate DATE,
    CustomerID INT,
    TotalAmount DECIMAL(10, 2),
    ShippingAddress VARCHAR(255),
    OrderStatus VARCHAR(50),
    FOREIGN KEY (CustomerID) REFERENCES Customer(CustomerID)
);

CREATE TABLE Payment (
    PaymentID INT PRIMARY KEY,
    OrderID INT,
    PaymentDate DATE,
    Amount DECIMAL(10, 2),
    PaymentMethod VARCHAR(50),
    TransactionID VARCHAR(50),
    FOREIGN KEY (OrderID) REFERENCES Order(OrderID)
);

CREATE TABLE OrderDetails (
    OrderID INT,
    ProductID INT,
    Quantity INT,
    Subtotal DECIMAL(10, 2),
    PRIMARY KEY (OrderID, ProductID),
    FOREIGN KEY (OrderID) REFERENCES Order(OrderID),
    FOREIGN KEY (ProductID) REFERENCES Product(ProductID)
);
```

Through this case study, we apply normalization principles to avoid redundancy and ensure data integrity by defining primary keys, foreign keys, and unique constraints. Indexes can be added to frequently queried columns to enhance performance.

Case Study 2: University Student Enrollment System

A university requires a data model to manage students, courses, and enrollments. The primary entities are **Student**, **Course**, and **Enrollment**.

- **Student**: Represents students enrolled in the university. Attributes include StudentID, FirstName, LastName, Email, PhoneNumber, DateOfBirth, and DateEnrolled.
- **Course**: Represents courses offered by the university. Attributes include CourseID, CourseName, Department, Credits, and InstructorName.
- **Enrollment**: Represents the enrollment of students in courses. Attributes include EnrollmentID, StudentID, CourseID, EnrollmentDate, and Grade.

The relationships include:

- **Student-Enrollment**: A one-to-many relationship where a student can enroll in multiple courses.
- **Course-Enrollment**: A many-to-many relationship because a course can have multiple students enrolled, and each student can enroll in multiple courses. This relationship is realized through the Enrollment entity.

The SQL code for this data model is as follows:

```
CREATE TABLE Student (
    StudentID INT PRIMARY KEY,
    FirstName VARCHAR(50),
    LastName VARCHAR(50),
    Email VARCHAR(100) UNIQUE,
    PhoneNumber VARCHAR(15),
    DateOfBirth DATE,
    DateEnrolled DATE
);

CREATE TABLE Course (
```

```
    CourseID INT PRIMARY KEY,
    CourseName VARCHAR(100),
    Department VARCHAR(100),
    Credits INT,
    InstructorName VARCHAR(100)
);

CREATE TABLE Enrollment (
    EnrollmentID INT PRIMARY KEY,
    StudentID INT,
    CourseID INT,
    EnrollmentDate DATE,
    Grade CHAR(2),
    FOREIGN KEY (StudentID) REFERENCES Student(StudentID),
    FOREIGN KEY (CourseID) REFERENCES Course(CourseID)
);
```

Indexes should be established on Email, CourseName, and other frequently queried columns to improve query performance.

Case Study 3: Hospital Management System

A hospital system requires a data model to manage patients, doctors, appointments, and treatments. The primary entities are **Patient**, **Doctor**, **Appointment**, and **Treatment**.

- **Patient**: Represents patients receiving treatment. Attributes include PatientID, FirstName, LastName, DateOfBirth, Address, and PhoneNumber.
- **Doctor**: Represents doctors who provide treatment. Attributes include DoctorID, FirstName, LastName, Specialization, PhoneNumber, and Email.
- **Appointment**: Represents appointments scheduled between patients and doctors. Attributes include AppointmentID, PatientID, DoctorID, AppointmentDate, AppointmentTime, and Purpose.
- **Treatment**: Represents treatments administered to patients. Attributes include TreatmentID, PatientID, DoctorID, TreatmentDate, TreatmentDescription, and Prescription.

The relationships include:

- **Patient-Appointment**: A one-to-many relationship, where a patient can have multiple appointments.
- **Doctor-Appointment**: A one-to-many relationship, where a doctor can have multiple appointments.

- **Patient-Treatment**: A one-to-many relationship, where a patient can have multiple treatments.
- **Doctor-Treatment**: A one-to-many relationship, where a doctor can administer multiple treatments.

The SQL code for this data model is as follows:

```
CREATE TABLE Patient (
    PatientID INT PRIMARY KEY,
    FirstName VARCHAR(50),
    LastName VARCHAR(50),
    DateOfBirth DATE,
    Address VARCHAR(255),
    PhoneNumber VARCHAR(15)
);

CREATE TABLE Doctor (
    DoctorID INT PRIMARY KEY,
    FirstName VARCHAR(50),
    LastName VARCHAR(50),
    Specialization VARCHAR(100),
    PhoneNumber VARCHAR(15),
    Email VARCHAR(100) UNIQUE
);

CREATE TABLE Appointment (
    AppointmentID INT PRIMARY KEY,
    PatientID INT,
    DoctorID INT,
    AppointmentDate DATE,
    AppointmentTime TIME,
    Purpose VARCHAR(255),
    FOREIGN KEY (PatientID) REFERENCES Patient(PatientID),
    FOREIGN KEY (DoctorID) REFERENCES Doctor(DoctorID)
);

CREATE TABLE Treatment (
    TreatmentID INT PRIMARY KEY,
    PatientID INT,
    DoctorID INT,
    TreatmentDate DATE,
    TreatmentDescription TEXT,
    Prescription TEXT,
    FOREIGN KEY (PatientID) REFERENCES Patient(PatientID),
    FOREIGN KEY (DoctorID) REFERENCES Doctor(DoctorID)
);
```

By examining the relationships and applying normalization, this data model ensures data integrity and reduces redundancy. Indexes can be added to columns commonly used in queries, such as LastName, Specialization, and AppointmentDate.

These case studies illustrate the practical application of data modeling principles in different scenarios, emphasizing the importance of correctly identifying relationships, ensuring data integrity, and optimizing database performance.

10.12 Best Practices in Data Modeling and Design

Best practices in data modeling and design ensure database systems are robust, scalable, and efficient. By adhering to established guidelines and strategies, database designers can enhance the performance, maintainability, and accuracy of data systems deployed in an enterprise environment. This section outlines key best practices that should be followed during the data modeling and design phases.

Data modeling and design start with understanding the business requirements and translating them into a data model that aligns with the objectives of the organization. Establishing a clear communication channel with stakeholders is crucial to gather accurate and comprehensive requirements. It is essential to frequently validate these requirements to align the data model with evolving business needs.

Documentation of the data model is a critical component. A well-maintained repository of entity-relationship diagrams (ERD), data dictionaries, and metadata contributes to the clarity and understanding of the data model among team members and future maintainers. Consistent documentation practices aid in tracking changes, understanding data lineage, and ensuring the completeness of the data model.

Normalization is a fundamental principle in data modeling aimed at reducing redundancy and improving data integrity. Applying normalization rules, such as organizing the database in normal forms (1NF, 2NF, 3NF, etc.), helps eliminate anomalies and ensures consistent data updates. However, it is vital to balance normalization with performance requirements. Over-normalization can lead to excessive joins, impacting query performance. De-normalization may be selectively applied to optimize read-heavy operations where appropriate.

Indexes play a significant role in improving the speed of data retrieval. Designing indexes involves carefully choosing indexed columns based on query patterns and workload characteristics. Composite indexes, covering indexes, and partitioned indexes are advanced indexing techniques to consider. Nevertheless, excessive indexing can incur a performance overhead on data modification operations as indexes need to be updated. Regularly monitoring index usage and performance is recommended to maintain an optimal balance.

Data integrity constraints such as primary keys, foreign keys, unique constraints, and check constraints enforce rules at the database level, ensuring that only valid and consistent data is stored. Creating comprehensive integrity constraints reduces the risk of data anomalies and supports reliable data storage. Constraints should be defined as part of the model and not deferred to application logic to avoid potential inconsistencies.

Performance considerations are integral to the success of a data model. This includes designing with an understanding of how data will be accessed and manipulated. Techniques such as partitioning, clustering, and proper use of joins and subqueries can vastly improve database performance. Avoiding non-scalable design choices, such as extensive use of triggers and overly complex queries, helps maintain the system's responsiveness as data volumes grow.

Using tools like Oracle SQL Developer Data Modeler facilitates the creation, maintenance, and visualization of data models. Leveraging such tools not only provides a graphical representation of the database schema but also assists in generating physical DDL scripts, reverse engineering existing databases, and performing impact analysis for modifications.

Design review and iterative improvement are key in the lifecycle of data models. Conducting regular design reviews with peers and stakeholders reveals potential issues early and encourages collaborative problem-solving. An iterative approach allows for continuous refinement of the model, incorporating feedback and addressing shortcomings identified through practical use.

Adopting industry standards and conventions in naming and coding promotes consistency and predictability within the database schema. Conventions should be established for table names, column names, and other database objects, ensuring they are descriptive and standardized.

Application of security principles from the outset of the data modeling process is paramount. Defining access controls, encryption for sensitive data, and adherence to compliance requirements protect the database from unauthorized access and breaches. Security considerations should be embedded into the design rather than added as an afterthought.

Effective collaboration between database administrators (DBAs), designers, and developers fosters a shared understanding and alignment of goals. Cross-functional collaboration ensures that different perspectives are incorporated, leading to a more comprehensive and robust data model.

Best practices in data modeling and design also include planning for future scalability. Designing the database with growth in mind avoids the necessity for frequent re-architecting. This involves anticipating increases in data volume, concurrent user load, and changes in business requirements.

Adhering to these best practices establishes a sound foundation for any database system, facilitating efficient, reliable, and maintainable data-driven applications. These principles are not isolated steps but interconnected actions that collectively contribute to creating robust data models fit for long-term success.

Made in the USA
Monee, IL
14 September 2026

62974512R00187